#  TRAINLAND

# TRAINLAND

## HOW RAILWAYS MADE NEW ZEALAND

Neill Atkinson

RANDOM HOUSE
NEW ZEALAND

**Abbreviations used in image captions**
ANZ   Archives New Zealand Te Rua Mahara o Te Kawanatanga, Wellington Office
ATL   Alexander Turnbull Library, National Library of New Zealand Te Puna Matauranga, Wellington
NZRLS   New Zealand Railway and Locomotive Society
NZRM   *New Zealand Railways Magazine*

A catalogue record for this book is available from the National Library of New Zealand

A RANDOM HOUSE BOOK
published by
Random House New Zealand
18 Poland Road, Glenfield, Auckland, New Zealand
www.randomhouse.co.nz

First published 2007

© 2007 Crown copyright

ISBN 978 1 86941 905 9

This book is copyright. Except for the purposes of fair reviewing no part of this publication may be reproduced or transmitted in any form or by any means, electronic or mechanical, including photocopying, recording or any information storage and retrieval system, without permission in writing from the publisher.

Cover and text design: Sharon Grace, Grace Design
Front cover illustration: Archives New Zealand, AAVK, W3493, C106
Back cover illustrations: (left to right):
    Alexander Turnbull Library, Non-ATL0015/ANZ, AAOK, W3241, 78
    Alexander Turnbull Library, Eph-E-Rail-1940s-01
    Alexander Turnbull Library, NON-ATL-00155/ANZ, AAOK, W3241, 1
    Alexander Turnbull Library, NON-ATL-0020/ANZ, AAOK, W3241, 85
Front flap illustration: Alexander Turnbull Library, Eph-B-Rail-1930s-01

Printed in China

# Contents

| | | |
|---|---|---|
| | Acknowledgements | 7 |
| | Introduction | 8 |
| 1 | The Railmaking State | 18 |
| 2 | Business and Pleasure | 58 |
| 3 | Exploring New Zealand | 96 |
| 4 | Citizens of Trainland | 136 |
| 5 | The Long Train Journey | 188 |
| | Notes | 227 |
| | Select Bibliography | 239 |
| | Index | 245 |

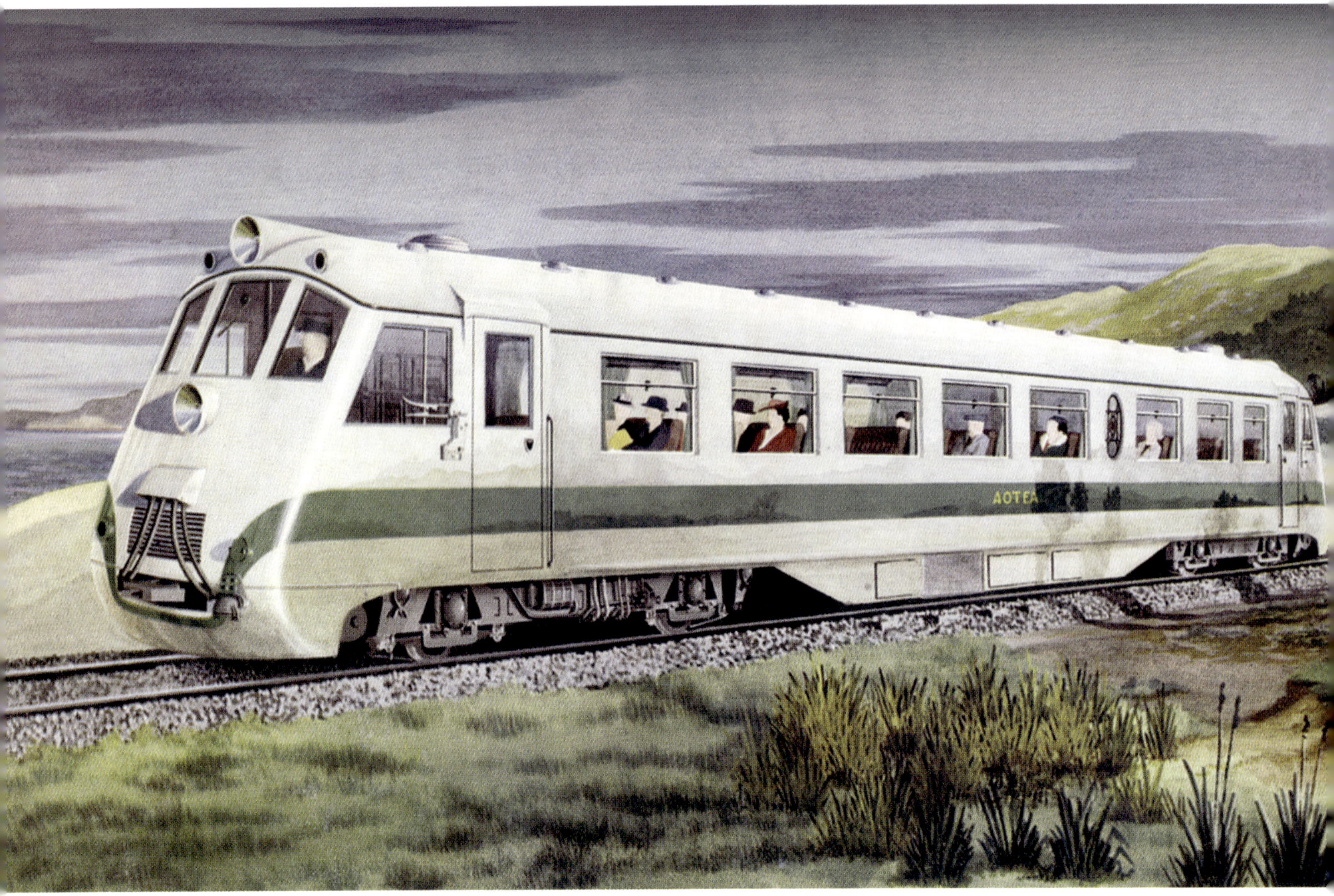
AOTEA

# Acknowledgements

Many people and institutions have assisted in the research, writing and production of this book. I am particularly grateful to Euan McQueen for lending me source material and photographs, reading drafts and making valuable suggestions; and to John Horner and Hamish Thompson, who generously shared their own research into railways art and advertising respectively.

Thanks also to the Christchurch Art Gallery, the Estate of Rita Angus, Miriam Gibson, Pamela Gordon and the Janet Frame Literary Trust, Paul Hamer, Helen Henderson, Helensville & District Historical Society, Peter McGavin, Alex McGowan, Diane McKegg, Gavin McLean, *New Zealand Herald*, the New Zealand Railway and Locomotive Society (especially Mark Cole and Alan Spencer), Ontrack, *Otago Daily Times*, Allan Paterson, Jack Perkins, Jackson Perry, Ian Spicer, Graham Stewart/Grantham House Publishing, Toll New Zealand/Tranz Scenic and D.L.A. Turner for supplying images and/or granting permission to reproduce material.

As always, I must thank the staffs of Archives New Zealand (Wellington and Christchurch) and the National and Alexander Turnbull Libraries, in particular Barbara Brownlie at ATL Ephemera and Thomasin Sleigh at ANZ; and my colleagues at the Ministry for Culture and Heritage, especially Bronwyn Dalley, Gavin McLean and Redmer Yska for their useful comments on drafts, Claire Taggart for help ordering images, Kynan Gentry, David Green, Fran McGowan and Jamie Mackay.

I would also like to thank the team at Random House, especially Jenny Hellen, who enthusiastically supported the project from an early stage, and Susan Brierley for her careful editing. Finally, thanks to my family and friends, especially Lauren Perry, who found many of the literary references and listened patiently to numerous railway stories.

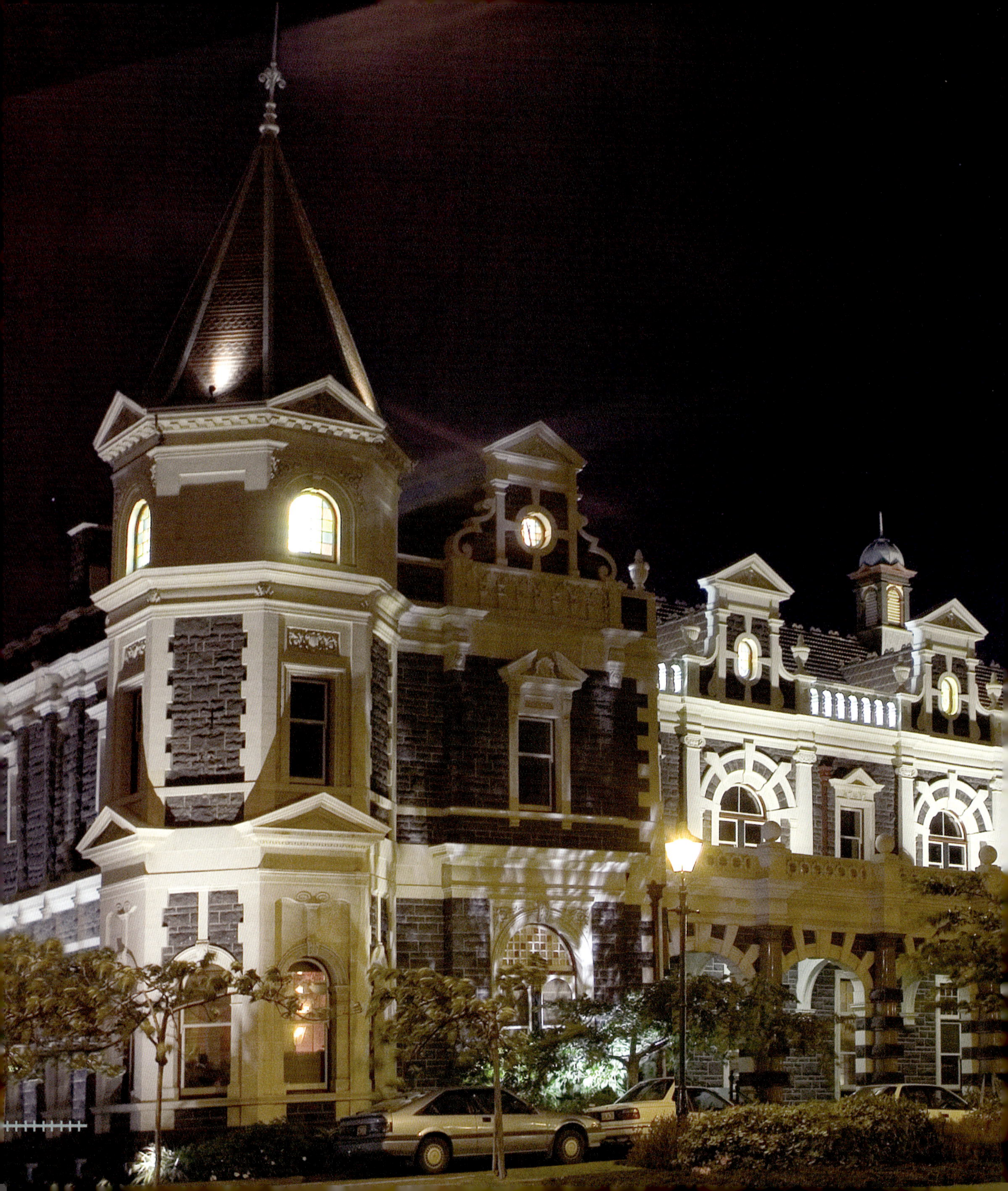

# Introduction

D. L. A. Turne

# Trainland

In September 2006 the Overlander train between Auckland and Wellington was threatened with closure by its owners, Toll New Zealand. Although patronage had been dwindling for decades, the imminent demise of the last regular passenger service on the North Island's main trunk — just two years short of the line's centenary — provoked a flood of nostalgia for New Zealand's vanishing rail heritage. After a flurry of petitions, publicity and last-chance patronage, the service was saved — for the moment, at least.

A month later, 10,000 people enjoyed a weekend of rail-related festivities to celebrate the one-hundredth birthday of Dunedin railway station, one of New Zealand's best-known buildings. Just a few weeks earlier, a leading international travel-guide publisher, DK Eyewitness Travel, had named the spectacular building 'one of the 200 must-see places in the world', alongside Rome's Colosseum and India's Taj Mahal.[1] These events, together with the runaway success of the Television New Zealand series *Off the Rails* (first screened in 2005), clearly show that railways still hold a place in the public imagination.

Rail may not be quite the 'new black', but its charms have never faded for many New Zealanders. Certainly, few would dispute its role in this country's development. In the century after its first appearance in 1830s England, the steam-powered railway changed the world forever — and New Zealand was no exception. Britain's farthest-flung South Pacific colony was a child of the railway age, an epic era when the steam locomotive was the snorting spearhead of modernity. As a recent American survey has argued, 'we call "modern" everything that happened in any other culture after it had built its first railroad'.[2] The steam railway was the first of the complex, large-scale technological systems that would dominate the industrial-capitalist age, helping to kickstart more than 170 years of ceaseless,

PREVIOUS PAGE:

*Dunedin's spectacular railway station is a testament to the power and prestige of rail transport in the early twentieth century. The station was designed in Flemish Renaissance style by Railways Department architect George Troup and completed in 1906.*

D.L.A. Turner

*A rail enthusiasts' train, headed by restored locomotives J$^A$ 1271 and A$^B$ 663, curves around Katiki Beach, south of Moeraki, on its way to Dunedin railway station's centenary celebrations in October 2006.*

*Otago Daily Times*

ever-accelerating change. The very concept of acceleration is inextricably linked to the railway, the first form of land transport able to surpass the speed of a galloping horse — even if some early New Zealand trains struggled to get much above walking pace.

The railway was above all a 'timely' invention. Together with the electric telegraph and the steamship, it facilitated the 'eradication of space by time' and radically altered the way people understood their world. It led to the adoption of 'standard time' across regions and nations, and entrenched the modern concept of 'industrial time', as opposed to traditional notions based on the time needed to complete a task or job.[3] Whether or not the trains actually ran on time, the railway world was fundamentally shaped by its timetables, station clocks, signals

# Trainland

and lights, tablet systems and Centralised Traffic Control — essential elements in the pursuit of safety and efficiency.

The huge workforce needed to operate and maintain this great 'machine ensemble' was similarly enmeshed in a web of bureaucratic control, symbolised by its meticulous timekeeping and military-style hierarchies, discipline and uniforms. Long before Henry Ford and his automobile factories, the great railway workshops of Britain and the United States (and later New Zealand) pioneered the technical specialisation, division of labour and management control usually associated with 'Fordism'.[4] This was a world of order, clarity and reason, its carefully oiled parts working as one, making the railway the ultimate metaphor for the industrial age.

*Railway workers at Kingston station pose for a Christmas photograph in 1900. The earnest expressions and facial hair are typical of the era; the style (or absence) of uniforms, hats and ties hints at the hierarchical, almost militaristic organisation of the rail workforce.*

ANZ, AAVK, W3493, E5761

# Introduction

This book explores the relationship between railways, society and culture. Rather than being a rivet-counting record of locomotives and engineering feats, it focuses on ordinary New Zealanders' experiences of rail.[5] Viewed from this angle, railway history offers a lens on society, revealing much about attitudes to class, race, gender, food and drink, mobility and recreation. Rail has also had a longstanding public service role, especially in countries like New Zealand where the system was almost exclusively constructed and (until recent decades) operated by the state. This made New Zealand Railways (NZR) a key tool of state-led economic development, and rail policy fair game for politicians, parties, voters, local interests and lobby groups of all stripes. Some branch lines were built to exploit political rather than economic opportunities, and in the 1890s Richard Seddon's Liberal regime turned rail patronage into an art form. Under the Labour government of the late 1930s, NZR advertisements trumpeted 'The People's Railways for the People's Profits'.[6] But even conservative governments like the 1920s Reform administration ranked rail's developmental and public service roles above profit and performance.

The following chapters explore different facets of the 'people's railway'. The book's structure also reflects three broad phases of our railway history. The first of these, outlined in Chapter 1, is the 'heroic' pioneering era. Beginning with the tentative provincial and private experiments of the 1860s, it gathered momentum when the 'railmaking state' took centre stage in the 1870s. In these years iron and steel rails welded cities and towns to their hinterlands, connected farms, forests and mines to markets and ports, and widened New Zealanders' physical and cultural horizons. By establishing reliable overland communication between the original coastal 'islands' of European settlement and 'opening up' previously inaccessible inland districts, railways promoted centralisation and standardisation, and helped forge a straggle of disparate provinces into a modern nation. Settlers lauded the steam locomotive as a civilising force — 'the breaker down of barbarism' in the propaganda of the day — and scrambled for a piece of the railway action.[7] But rail-led progress came at a price, especially for the Maori communities and 'Great Bush' of the central North Island. Although major gaps remained in the national network until the 1940s, the 'heroic' railmaking era peaked with the completion of the North Island main trunk line in 1908.

The second phase essentially covers the first half of the twentieth century, a period often celebrated as the heyday or golden age of rail. In these years the railway was New Zealand's premier form of land-based passenger and freight transport, especially over longer distances. For a new generation of 'mobile' citizens, this once-startling novelty was now a familiar part of daily life. By the early 1920s annual passenger

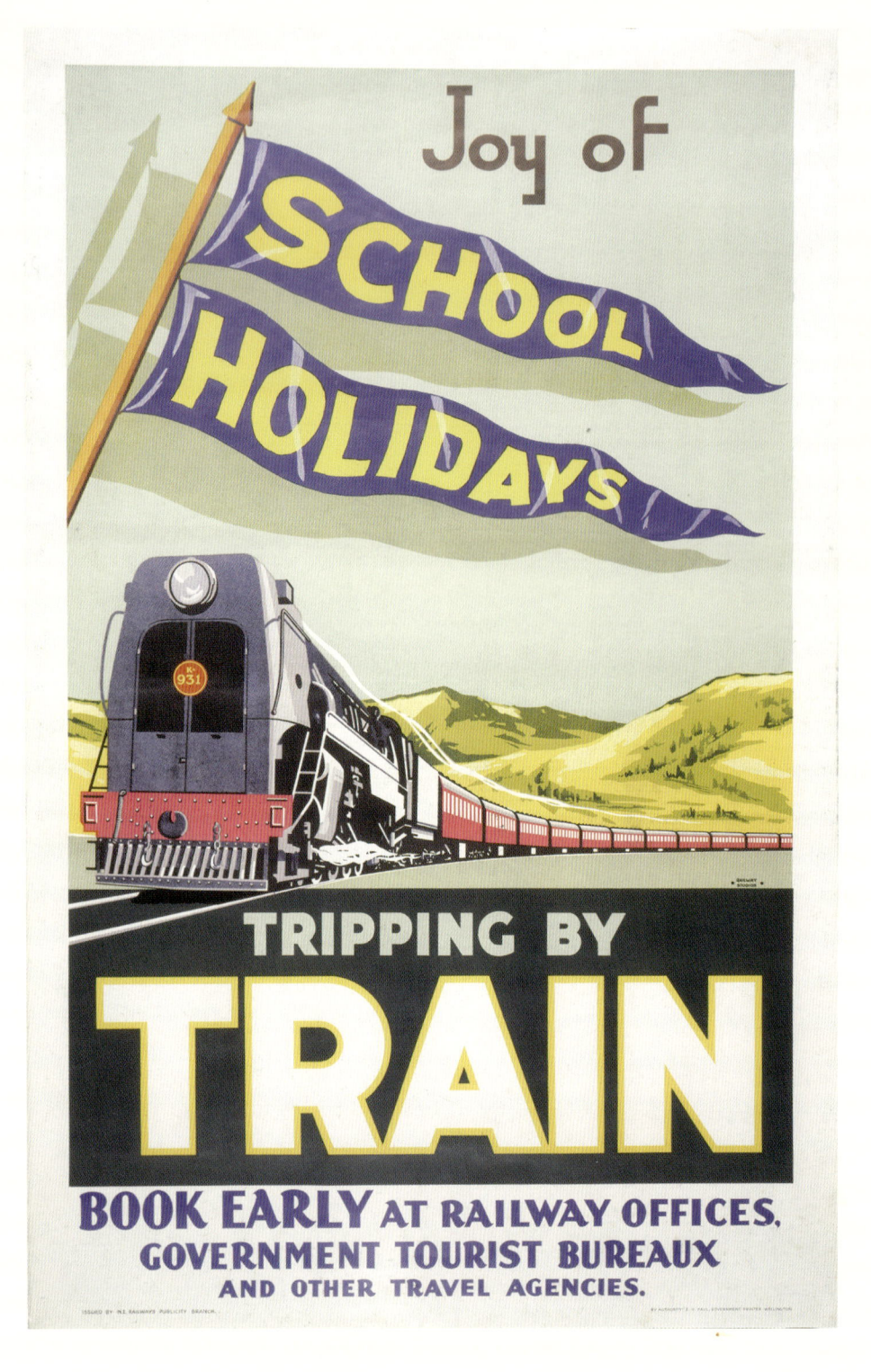

'Tripping by Train': from the 1920s the Railways Studios and Publicity Branch produced hundreds of eye-catching posters, pamphlets and maps, including this late-1940s advertisement starring a streamlined K$^A$ locomotive. Early NZR tourist posters have recently fetched as much as $8,000 at auction.

ATL, Eph-E-RAIL-1940s-01

## Introduction

journeys had climbed to 28 million, a staggering achievement for a nation of a little over a million people.

The popularity of this people's railway was no accident. Since the late nineteenth century the state had used its expanding rail network to promote not just the development of agriculture, industry, forestry and mining, but to further policies in areas as diverse as education, town planning and recreation. Trains ferried school children to the classroom, suburban workers to factories and offices, sportspeople to competitions, and thousands of picnickers and punters to beaches, parks and racetracks. Rail travel accelerated the formation of regional and national organisations, the distribution of newspapers and magazines, and touring by local and international cultural performers. The railway station — whether grand urban monument or modest country shed — became a central community hub, a place of welcomes and farewells, joy and sorrow. So too, especially after the First World War, did the ubiquitous Railway Refreshment Rooms, with their uniformed 'girls' offering rows of pies, sandwiches, cakes and steaming tea in the legendarily thick NZR cups.

By the mid 1920s, however, competition from the new forms of road transport was already beginning to bite. After a boom in the early twenties, passenger numbers began to slide, bottoming out at 18 million during the Great Depression of the early thirties. Spurred on by Minister Gordon Coates' modernisation drive, the Railways Department responded by establishing its own coach and bus services and Publicity Branch, launching a popular monthly magazine, and becoming the country's leading

*'The Industry that Made New Zealand': this 1938 advert from the New Zealand Railways Magazine emphasises NZR's public ownership and developmental mission.*

NZRM, May 1938

tourism promoter. As reduced working hours, higher pay and smaller families created new leisure opportunities for working people, NZR provided tens of thousands of ordinary New Zealanders with affordable, convenient access to beach, lake, alpine and spa resorts. Tourism, publicity and innovations like railcars and suburban electric units sparked a late-thirties revival in passenger traffic, as the first Labour government sought to reinvigorate the people's railway. The Second World War boosted passenger numbers to all-time record levels, but also signalled the beginning of the end of rail's golden weather.

In the 1950s railways entered a third age. Just as the national network reached its greatest-ever route length — 3535 miles (5689 kilometres) in 1953 — rail transport (especially passenger travel) began to falter in the face of increasingly

*The threatened closure of the Overlander service in late 2006 — subsequently averted — provoked a mixture of nostalgia, protest and apprehension, especially in affected central North Island communities like National Park.*

Tranz Scenic

## Introduction

intense road and air competition. The private automobile offered a flexibility, convenience and social status that trains could not match, while trucks and buses multiplied in number, size and performance; aeroplanes, especially the new jets, linked major centres in a fraction of the time taken by rail. In the half-century from 1944, a period in which the country's population doubled, annual rail passenger journeys slumped from 38 million to barely ten million, before beginning a modest commuter-led recovery over the last decade. As politicians and rail operators wrestled with the issues of deregulation, rationalisation and privatisation, many long-distance passenger services, branch lines, rail jobs, stations and other facilities disappeared.

> **As the furore over the Overlander has shown, New Zealand's 'long train journey' is far from over.**

To be sure, rail has remained an essential freight carrier — and, in contrast to the passenger-dominated British and European networks, this country's has always been primarily a freight railway. But despite moving record freight tonnages in recent years, the modern rail system no longer touches the lives of most New Zealanders.

The transformation of the railway scene over the last half-century has produced a surge of nostalgia for a lost golden age, a flourishing of rail history writing and earnest attempts to salvage and protect this country's vanishing railway heritage. In a rapidly changing world, the people's railway — and especially the much-loved steam locomotive — has come to symbolise an idealised past of intimate communities and simple certainties. Despite its perceived decline since the 1950s, the railway retains its ability to fascinate and inspire. As the furore over the Overlander has shown, New Zealand's 'long train journey' is far from over.

CHAPTER 1

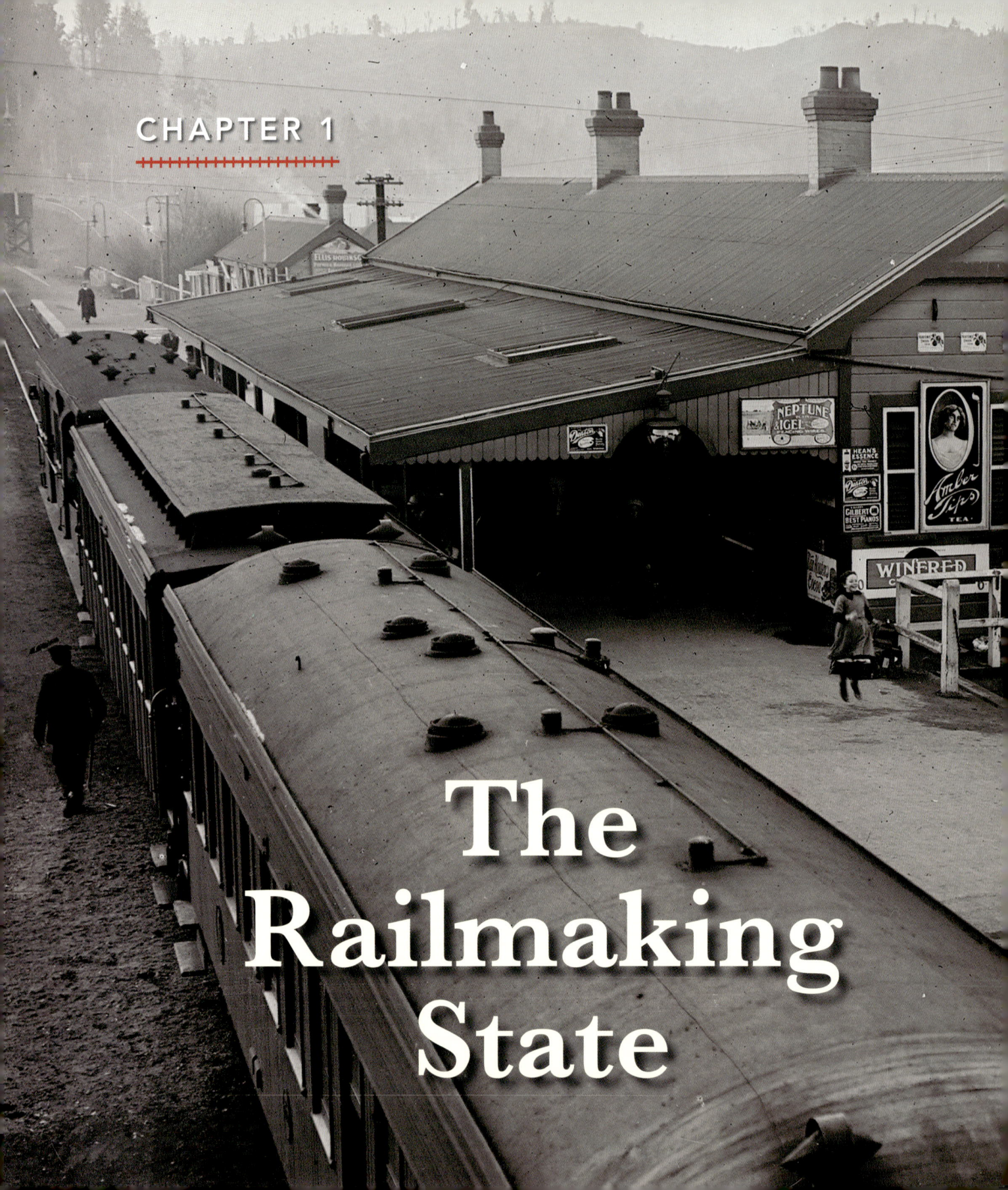

# The Railmaking State

REFRESHMENT
TAIHAPE
REFRESHMENTS
DRAPERY STORE.
COLLINSON & CUNNINGHAME Ltd
PALMERSTON N.
REFRESHMENT
MILNE & JOLLIE
BAKERS
CONFECTIONERS
TAIHAPE
TEA ROOMS
REFRESHMENT
MILLIONS OF PEOPLE Are Making Money, WE MAKE HOMES HAPPY.
PURSER & SON
THE AUTHORITATIVE
House Furnishers, WANGANUI.

## Trainland

> New Zealand is a peculiar country. You cannot get over its geographical configuration. You cannot bring together the two ends nearer than they are. There will always be a certain amount of isolation in different parts until the iron horse runs through the two islands.
>
> — *Julius Vogel*[1]

The European settlement of New Zealand belonged to the railway age. By the time the Treaty of Waitangi was signed in 1840 Durham's Stockton and Darlington Railway had been open for fifteen years, and a decade had passed since George and Robert Stephenson's *Rocket* had thundered between Liverpool and Manchester and changed the world. Britain already boasted 1775 miles (2857 kilometres) of track, and railways were operating in France, the German states, the Netherlands, the Austrian and Russian empires, the United States, Canada, even Cuba. By 1854 India and Australia had joined the club. In New Zealand, the early settlers who dreamed of building a 'Better Britain' in the South Seas knew all about this most British of inventions, the wonder of the industrial age. They left behind a homeland in the iron grip of 'railwaymania'; many would have begun their 12,000-mile voyage to New Zealand with a train journey to their port of departure.

When they fetched up on New Zealand's muddy shores no trains were waiting to whisk them into town. Instead, they encountered a raw maritime frontier: a string of coastal enclaves connected by sailing ships, small steamers and waka, or by rough tracks hacked through dense bush and across dangerous river fords. The parlous state of colonial communications is illustrated by Canterbury politician Henry Sewell's 1854 trip to Auckland to sit in New Zealand's first Parliament. A reluctant sailor, he dreaded the 'terrible' prospect of a sea voyage to a city 'about as distant from Canterbury as England from Lisbon — a much severer work than going to America per Steamboat from England'. The new steamer *Nelson*,

PREVIOUS PAGE:

*Like many inland towns, Taihape on the North Island main trunk line was a child of the railmaking state. In this 1910s photograph, a girl skips along the platform towards the station's well-known refreshment rooms.*

ATL, FG Radcliffe Collection, G-6010-1/2

*Maritime frontier: like most colonial settlements in the pre-railway era, mid-nineteenth-century Auckland was dominated by seaborne trade and communications.*

ATL, lithograph by Patrick Joseph Hogan, 1852, A-109-044

the first on the New Zealand coast, at least promised a quicker, safer passage than the tiny schooners and ketches that dominated coastal routes.

After a frustrating five-day wait for the ship to reach Lyttelton, Sewell set sail on 11 May and reached Wellington in nineteen hours — a quick trip at the time, though 'of course the people were all sick' in the churning seas. Stopovers in Nelson and New Plymouth to pick up more politicians combined with strong headwinds, fog and a minor stranding stretched the total journey out to twelve days. Eventually, on the morning of 23 May, the *Nelson* crossed the Manukau bar and dropped anchor off Onehunga. As the tide was out, the passengers had to wade from the boats across mudflats and stones. After lugging their trunks along the beach, the MPs endured a jolting six-mile coach ride into the city, reaching their digs well after dark. Still, they were the lucky ones: the Otago members who sailed on the government brig took two months to reach Auckland.[2]

The composition of that first Parliament illustrated the fragmentary geographic reach of European settlement fourteen years after the signing of the Treaty. Almost

## Trainland

all of Sewell's colleagues lived in or close to Auckland, Wellington, New Plymouth, Wanganui, Nelson, Christchurch or Dunedin. A vast swathe of the lower North Island, stretching from Lake Taupo south to the Patea River, Tararua Range and Cape Turnagain, was not even included in an electorate because no Europeans lived there. The interior of the island was a Maori world and would remain so for decades — until it was prised open by railways. With towering mountains and dark forests at their backs, most colonists were preoccupied with 'pothole politics' and local squabbles. Everyone wanted to improve their own district's infrastructure while avoiding paying for anyone else's. From the outset, transport, politics and parochialism went hand in hand.

## Nation-building

Over the following half-century railways would help knit these isolated coastal enclaves into a modern, unified nation. First and foremost, rail was an engine of colonisation. In contrast to the older, densely populated societies of Europe, where trains essentially provided new, faster connections between existing communities, New Zealand railmaking followed the American model of opening up supposedly uninhabited wildernesses. In many regions, the first roads were built at the same time as the railway (often specifically to provide access to sites of rail construction) and pioneer towns and homesteads sprouted in the rails' wake. Improved communications led to the adoption of standard time across the colony in 1868, and helped central government outmuscle its provincial rivals in the 1870s. The ongoing public works programme, the management of working railways and the development of railway workshops as major industrial plants would also help entrench the state as a pre-eminent force in the national economy.

The railmaking project helped shape modern New Zealand in other ways. Despite the emphasis on opening up new lands, rail development ultimately helped cement the dominance of New Zealand's four main cities. Rural branch and secondary lines locked hinterlands into their nearest centres and export ports, stimulating urban economic activity and employment as much as rural settlement. In the pioneering phase, emerging country towns fostered their own service industries, merchants and local newspapers. But quick and reliable transport links soon enabled larger city-based firms to exploit economies of scale, notably in the clothing, footwear, brewing and toolmaking trades. Metropolitan newspapers also benefited from swift delivery into rural towns, often forcing local rivals to fold. Later, Hamilton and Palmerston North emerged as major centres in their own right, largely because their location on the main trunk gave them an advantage over older rivals like Wanganui, which the trunk bypassed, and Nelson, which had no interprovincial rail links at all. Regions poorly served by rail, notably the Far North, Urewera–East Coast, Nelson–Buller and Fiordland, remain among New Zealand's most isolated and least developed.

Railways also helped make the twentieth century the North Island's century. Although Canterbury and Otago set the railmaking pace in the 1870s, the north slowly caught and passed its southern rivals. Auckland's Waikato line fuelled that city's boom in the late 1870s and early eighties, and by the 1890s Wellington's rail links with Manawatu, Wairarapa and Hawke's Bay had confirmed its status as a central transport hub. The completion of the North Island main trunk in 1908 and later rail development in Northland and the Bay of Plenty, which together opened up vast new districts to settlement and exploitation, set the seal on northern supremacy. The North Island's Pakeha population exceeded the South Island's for the first time in 1901 and never looked back; between 1890 and 1940 the

*A hardy crowd gathers in a sodden, scarred landscape to celebrate the opening of Toko station in Taranaki, probably in 1902. This simple image conveys both the significance of the railway for isolated communities and the deforestation and environmental change that often followed in its wake.*

ATL, James McAllister Collection, G-9815-1/1

populations of Auckland and Wellington increased eightfold, far outstripping their southern rivals.

Rail's role in the making of modern New Zealand was vital and wide-ranging, but it should not be overstated or viewed in isolation. While the 'romance of rail' and state ownership ensured a high public profile, other forms of transport continued to survive and flourish. Rail's closest relative, the horse-drawn and electric tramway systems of the main centres, stimulated the spread of suburbia in the early twentieth century, while thousands of people continued to cycle or walk to work. In the pre-automobile age, many rural dwellers relied on horses, carts and stagecoaches to get them and their freight where no railways reached, or to provide feeder services from railheads and stations along the track. The coastal shipping industry, historically the preserve of private enterprise, continued to prosper until well after the Second World War. Although some ports fell victim to rail competition, others boomed as railways stimulated trade with newly opened hinterlands, and port towns from Helensville to Bluff ran 'boat trains' timed to connect with shipping arrivals and departures. The

*Railways and shipping have long enjoyed a close relationship, with 'boat trains' connecting cities and harbours, and many larger ports boasting 'Railway' wharves. First linked to Auckland by rail in 1881, Helensville on the Kaipara River — seen here in the 1930s — was an important timber (and passenger) port, while the nearby Parakai hot springs also attracted rail excursionists from the city.*

Helensville Pioneer Museum

## The Railmaking State

symbiotic relationship between rail and shipping is clearly demonstrated by the number of early railways linking cities, farms, forests and mines to their nearest ports — a pattern that survives today at Mount Maunganui, Lyttelton, Port Chalmers and elsewhere.

Nor should the romance of rail, the rear-view mirror of nostalgia or the undoubtedly impressive achievements of 'heroic' railmakers blind us to the costs of railway development. So-called progress is never free. Among the victims were those communities that lost the race for rail and were condemned to obscurity, and the Maori landlords and 'Great Bush' of the central North Island. As in the United States, Australia and elsewhere, indigenous communities were largely invisible to colonists and engineers, except where they posed an obstacle to railmaking.

The railways boom that began in the 1870s accelerated the alienation of Maori land generally by opening new districts to Pakeha settlement, strengthening the power of the state and fuelling immigration, as well as directly through the compulsory acquisition of land under the Public Works and Railways Acts. As the prophet Te Kooti warned in 1883, 'the whistling God of the Pakeha' — a 'ngarara' (monster) 'belching flames, and smoke' — would help break the Maori grip on the central North Island, leaving only 'traces of broken branches in [its] pathway'.[3]

At the same time, rail accelerated the destruction of New Zealand's natural environment. In Manawatu, Taranaki, southern Hawke's Bay, Southland and elsewhere, it facilitated massive deforestation and the wholesale replacement of one ecosystem, native bush and swamp, with a new, largely imported one — English grass. Sporadic Maori resistance, occasional pleas for environmental preservation and other dissenting voices were swept aside by the trumpet blast of progress and the local strain of railwaymania.

## Pilgrim's Progress

In the 1850s, all that lay in the future. The complex ensemble of locomotives, rolling stock, rails and sleepers, cuttings, tunnels, bridges, stations and engineers required capital and labour far beyond the capabilities

## Trainland

of an infant colony with a tiny, scattered population and no major urban centres. Within a decade, however, impatient provincial and private pioneers would lay the country's first tracks and fire up its first locomotives.

The most influential of these early experiments took place in Henry Sewell's home province of Canterbury on 1 December 1863, when a little British locomotive named *Pilgrim* puffed along a four-mile track from Christchurch to Ferrymead, a makeshift port on the Heathcote River. This was not New Zealand's first 'railway': the Dun Mountain mine in Nelson had opened a 13-mile line a year earlier, but it was powered by horses and gravity alone. Nor was *Pilgrim* the colony's first steam locomotive, as the Ballarat-built *Lady Barkly* had snorted up and down Invercargill's jetty on 8 August 1863. The Ferrymead line was, however, the colony's first locomotive-powered public railway, and like its Nelson and Southland contemporaries, it followed the pioneering patterns of Europe and North America, where most early railways similarly served ports and mines.

But Ferrymead was only a stopgap. The Canterbury Provincial Council had since the early 1850s dreamed of driving a rail tunnel through the Port Hills to link Christchurch with the deep-water port at Lyttelton. When an exploratory commission was set up in 1854, Sewell was typically pessimistic: 'I am fretted at a mad project which is on foot for a railway and tunnel to cost they say [up to] £200,000.' The idea, he thought, was 'mere moonstruck madness', and would 'end in nothing'.[4] In fact, spurred on by provincial Superintendent William Moorhouse, work on New Zealand's first 'think big' project began in 1861. After six difficult years of digging, the Lyttelton tunnel — then one of the longest in the world — was officially opened on 9 December 1867. As well as unlocking the rich agricultural potential of the Canterbury plains, it rendered the four-year-old Ferrymead line redundant and prompted the country's first railway closure. By the end of the decade Canterbury had laid 30 miles of broad 5 foot 3 inch ('Irish') gauge track from Lyttelton to the Selwyn River. But further progress was hamstrung by a lack of capital, the challenges of bridging braided rivers to north and south, and the

*This view of* Pilgrim's *historic first journey in December 1863, painted by the renowned rail artist W.W. Stewart, captures something of the excitement and novelty of early rail experiments.*

Grantham House Publishing

quick deterioration of existing track and rolling stock.[5]

Meanwhile, the Southland provincial government, recently separated from Otago, harboured railway ambitions of its own. Desperate to trump their provincial big brother, the Southlanders dreamed of driving a 'Great Northern Railway' into the gold-rich Lakes District, starting with a cheap wooden-railed section across swampland from Invercargill to Makarewa. Sadly, the line's gala opening in October 1864 ended in a slippery, sodden fiasco. It was a sign of things to come: the *Lady Barkly* (and two other engines that followed) crushed and splintered the wooden rails, and in dry weather sparks set them alight. The journalist Charles Rous-Marten recalled how he and fellow passengers were 'politely requested by the guard to leave

## Trainland

the carriage and help to *push* the carriage and engine to the summit of the bank. This we did with colonial cheerfulness, and on returning to our seats the guard promptly collected 2s. 6d. apiece from us as our fares!'[6] A more useful iron track to the port at Bluff (built to the 4 foot 8½ inch 'standard' gauge) was completed in 1867, and by the end of the decade the Makarewa route had also been upgraded. Unfortunately, Southland's rail fever had bankrupted its provincial council.

> '. . . politely requested by the guard to leave the carriage and help to *push* the carriage and engine to the summit of the bank. This we did with colonial cheerfulness, and on returning to our seats the guard promptly collected 2s. 6d. apiece from us as our fares!'

By 1870 rail's conquest of nature and distance was gathering pace across the globe. Britain, France, Germany and other European states had vast nationwide networks; the United States had just completed its staggering transcontinental railroad, boosting its national route mileage to over 30,000 miles; India too had opened a coast-to-coast line from Bombay to Calcutta. New Zealand, meanwhile, had a mere 46 miles (74 kilometres) of track, confined to the flat eastern and southern plains of the South Island.[7] A projected military line from Auckland to Drury had come to nothing, and apart from a private coalmining track at Kawakawa, Northland (opened in 1867 and horse-powered until 1870) the North Island was still a land without trains. Ringed by mountains and thick bush, burdened by war debt and lacking the south's gold or pastoral potential, fretful northern settlers looked to central government to deliver the promise of rail and riches.

## Vogel's Iron Horse

In June 1870, Julius Vogel, the Colonial Treasurer in William Fox's government, unveiled the most ambitious immigration and public works programme in New Zealand's history. Its implementation, he assured Parliament, was essential to reawaken the 'colonizing spirit', conquer isolation and fuse the colony's far-flung settlements into a unified, prosperous nation. The cornerstone of this staggering development drive, funded by overseas borrowing rising to £10 million by 1876, was a promise to build more than a thousand miles of railway in nine years. As Vogel explained, these would be modelled on the 'revenue railways' of the western United States, which were 'constructed in the manner precisely suited to the traffic, and out of the traffic returns

## The Railmaking State

. . . from time to time, improved, in accordance with the traffic demands. The constructors are satisfied with a moderate speed, and . . . satisfied to do without expensive stations.'[8] In contrast to Europe, New Zealand lacked capital and labour, but land was relatively cheap. This combination discouraged expensive earthworks, tunnels and stone bridges in favour of more circuitous routes around obstacles, wooden trestle bridges, tight curves and severe gradients. These factors, together with the desire to build quickly and cheaply, also explained the government's decision to adopt a narrow 3 foot 6 inch (1067 millimetre) gauge as the national standard.

Reaction to Vogel's vision was mixed. One member spluttered that 'he had never heard of a scheme so wild' and 'so impracticable', and parliamentary alarm at the sheer scale of debt forced the Treasurer to lower his initial borrowing target from £6 million to £4 million.[9] The response of the press and public, however, was largely starry-eyed enthusiasm. The *Wellington Independent* hailed it 'the most masterly scheme ever propounded for the advancement of the colony'. 'We are already in imagination travelling by express trains to Waikato and Kaipara,' daydreamed Auckland Government Agent Daniel Pollen, 'and a cloud of seedy looking civil engineers hangs about the Superintendent's office in waiting for the good time coming.'[10] The verdict of historians has been equally glowing, most endorsing the early assessment of the Liberal politician and historian William Pember Reeves, who hailed Vogel as 'one of the short list of statesmen whose work has left a permanent mark on the Dominion' and praised his public works policy as 'virtually the beginning of State Socialism in New Zealand'.[11]

The government's intention was not only to revitalise a stagnant, war-weary colonial economy but to reignite New Zealand's faltering colonisation project — to 're-illume that sacred flame', as Premier Fox grandly proclaimed. To Pakeha eyes, much of the North Island remained a wilderness of bush, native 'wasteland' and simmering rebellion. Recent clashes with the warrior prophets Titokowaru and Te Kooti had shredded settlers' nerves and forced many to flee their isolated homesteads. Instead of war, Vogel hoped that immigrants, roads

*An 1874 engraving of the London-born Dutch-Jewish politician Sir Julius Vogel, the architect of the colonial railmaking state.*

ATL, F-83251-1/2

## Trainland

and railways would spearhead a peaceful Pakeha conquest of the Maori heartland. Profitable employment on public works would hasten the integration of Maori into the European economy, while an influx of settlers into newly opened districts would soon swamp the local Maori population. Two decades later Vogel would state his case even more starkly: 'The Public Works Policy seemed to the Government the sole alternative to a war of extermination with the natives.'[12]

Vogel was not the first colonial politician to promise public works and immigration on the back of borrowed money. Central and provincial government debt had grown eightfold in the 1860s, though only Canterbury and Otago had much to show for it. But where earlier schemes had foundered, the early 1870s offered better prospects. The embers of war in the North Island were all but extinguished. With the British railway network largely complete, English contracting firms like John Brogden and Sons were scouting for new opportunities abroad. When the Franco–Prussian War of 1870 disrupted European development, the distant Pacific became a more attractive option.

At the same time, a spasm of rural unrest in Britain — culminating in the 1872 Revolt of the Field — increased the number of unsettled labourers willing to hazard the long and demanding voyage to the Antipodes. In nine months in 1872–3 Brogdens brought 2172 English immigrants to the colony, including 1298 working-age men (mostly agricultural labourers) contracted to two years' work on railway construction. These numbers would be dwarfed by the massive migrant inflow later that decade but Brogdens' recruitment drive had far-reaching consequences. It spurred the colonial government to offer more liberal assistance to immigrants, and also opened up formal and informal channels of English migration that would flourish that decade and beyond.[13]

Brogdens' 'navvies' (the name derived from the 'navigators' who had dug Britain's eighteenth-century canals) set to work on six contracts at or near Auckland, Wellington, Napier, Picton, Oamaru and Invercargill. Although Vogel promoted these lines as the basis of a future network — partly to ensure broad provincial support — they were all short, isolated sections linking ports with population centres or nearby farmlands. After all, the 'idea of a continuous trunk line from the Bay of Islands to the Bluff was then as remote from the public mind as was the idea of putting men on the moon'.[14]

**RIGHT:** *Railway labourers excavate a cutting through typical New Zealand hill country, probably around the turn of the twentieth century. Their methods and tools — pickaxe, wide-mouth shovel, horse-drawn tip-cart and the gravity-fed timber chute popularly known as a 'Chinaman' — had changed little since the Brogdens era of the 1870s.*

ATL, 51892-1/2

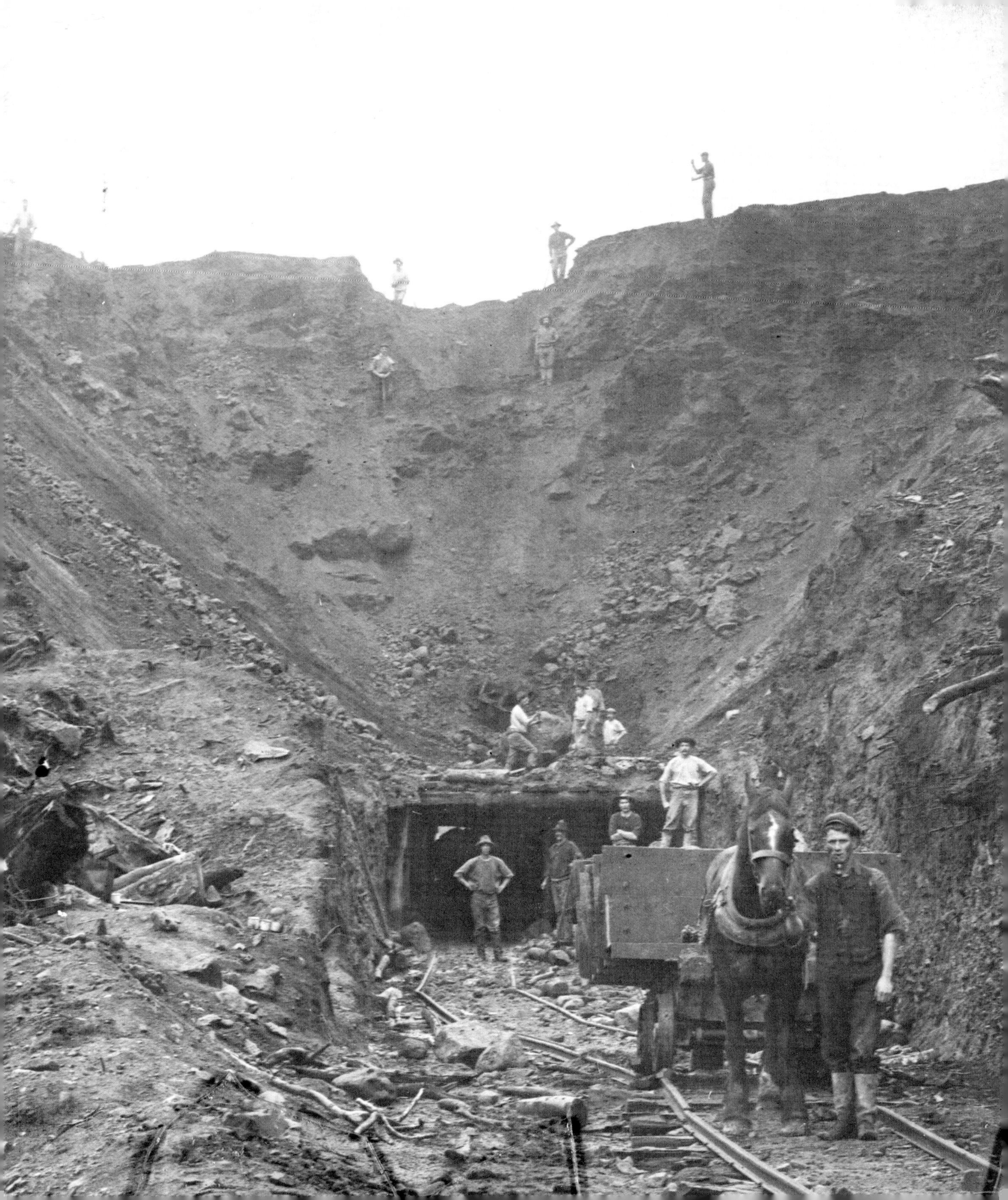

## Trainland

Even this modest programme was soon in disarray. Construction was dogged by delays, disagreements with government officials and disputes with workers over wages and conditions, not least the local custom of an eight-hour working day. Many navvies, dismayed by news that the government was now offering British migrants assisted passages with no work requirements, broke their contracts and drifted off into farming, urban jobs or gold-prospecting. Brodgens took 133 defaulters to court, but most skipped town; some even preferred gaol to railmaking. At the end of 1872 further recruitment was cancelled. By August 1873 only 287 of the almost 1300 navvies the firm had brought to New Zealand were still working on rail contracts.[15]

> **Five years after the launch of Vogel's vision, 316 miles of railway had been completed, three-quarters of it in the more populous and prosperous South Island.**
>
> ++++++++++

By this time Vogel, now Premier, had his own doubts about the pace of progress, rising expectations and escalating debt. Mercenary members were clamouring for railways through their electorates and local Railway Leagues were jostling for a piece of the pie. More borrowing was needed, an estimated £1.5 million for railways alone in 1873. To guarantee further loans, Vogel proposed to reserve six million acres of land along rail routes as a Crown endowment, sure to become a valuable asset at a time of rapidly rising land values. While the Maori landowners of the North Island were not consulted, suspicious South Island provincialists, especially in Canterbury and Otago, denounced the plan as a central government land grab and torpedoed it in the House. Brooding on their defeat, the Premier and centralist allies schemed to sweep the pesky provinces out of the way.[16]

Five years after the launch of Vogel's vision, 316 miles of railway had been completed, three-quarters of it in the more populous and prosperous South Island. The first 3 foot 6 inch line, opened between Dunedin and Port Chalmers in January 1873, was actually built by a private company but was soon absorbed into the government system; another between Blenheim and Picton, the handiwork of the first shipload of Brogdens' navvies, was finally completed in 1875. For a time the contrary Cantabrians continued to expand their 5 foot 3 inch network, but by the end of 1877 it too had been converted to narrow gauge. Elsewhere in the island, short lines sprouted in Nelson, Westland and Otago, while in 1878 an important branch was completed between Invercargill and Kingston in the developing Lakes District.

# The Railmaking State

By that time, New Zealand's first 'main trunk' was taking shape between Christchurch, Dunedin and Invercargill. Canterbury's 'Southern Railway' reached Ashburton in 1874 and Timaru two years later, by which time the Invercargill line stretched as far as Gore. The Christchurch–Dunedin line was completed in 1878, slashing travel time between the South Island's largest cities to under eleven hours (although in 1880, as more stops were added, the trip was lengthened to twelve hours 40 minutes), and the last gap between Balclutha and Clinton was closed at the beginning of 1879. On 21 January a special train, headed by a rakish American Rogers K-class locomotive, left Christchurch on the first 390-mile journey to Invercargill, broken only by an overnight stop in Dunedin. Progress on Canterbury's northern line was slower, but by 1880 rails stretched as far as Waipara. The poet Ursula Bethell, then a young girl, thrilled to the 'incomparable sounds' of the 'North Train' as it sped 'Over the wooden bridge, rumble-bumpy', high above the Ashley River.[17]

*Toffs and toasts: in September 1878 Dunedin's mayor hosted a lavish banquet to celebrate the opening of the city's rail link with Christchurch.*

ATL, Eph-A-RAIL-1878-01

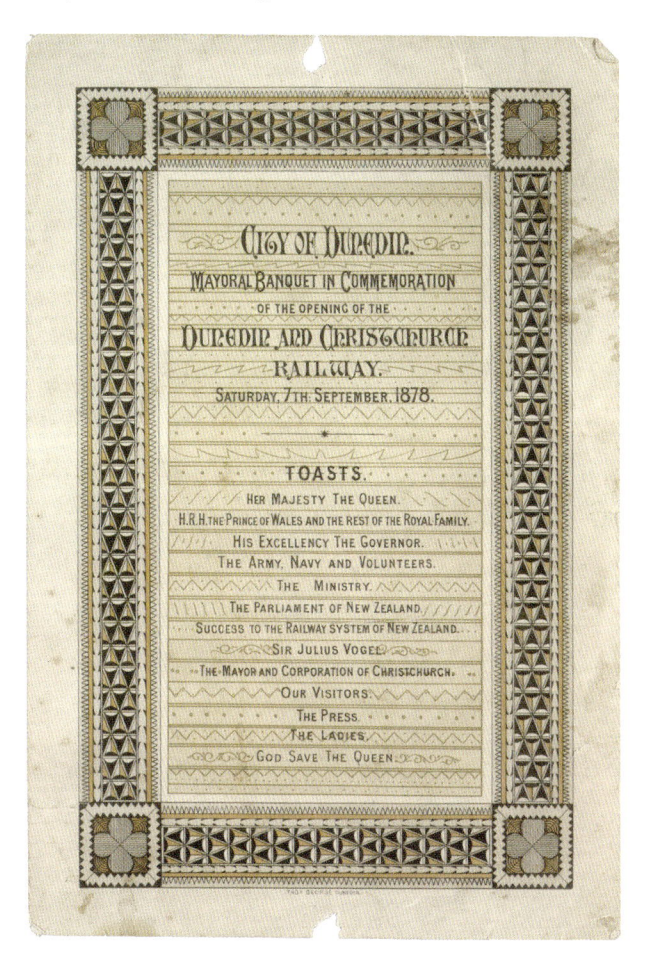

## Sods and Spikes

As in Europe and America, the progress of new lines was marked by 'first sod' and 'last spike' ceremonies, often accompanied by lavish banquets, champagne toasts, speeches, flags and bunting, brass bands, cavalry parades and cannonades. Pakeha settlers welcomed each sod and spike as a glorious milestone in the progress of their town or region, promising a surge in land values and a prosperous future. Sometimes, the festivities took on an almost religious reverence: 'As soon as the ceremony was over a rush was made to the newly turned sod, and handfuls were taken away by the interested crowd as a memento of such historic proceedings.'[18]

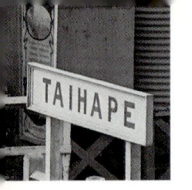

Not all events ran smoothly: celebrations marking the arrival of the first Christchurch train into Timaru in February 1876 descended into a slanging match between central, provincial and local government officials which ended with one guest being hauled away by police. The 1879 festivities in Invercargill — where a holiday was declared and the streets bedecked with banners, bunting and Chinese lanterns — were clouded by a terrible injury to South Island Railway Commissioner William Conyers. Leaning too eagerly from the locomotive cab near Gore, he struck his head on a trackside water tank and tumbled off the train, 'bleeding profusely from a cut on the temple'. Unlike that most famous opening-day victim, Sir William Huskisson, who was struck down by the Stephensons' *Rocket* on the Liverpool and Manchester Railway in 1830, Conyers survived, but he would never return to work.[19]

In the North Island, main trunks were still the stuff of dreams. Auckland's first Brogdens-built railway did link two oceans, but the Waitemata and Manukau harbours were only six miles apart. Its official opening on 20 December 1873 was

*Over the hill: the Rimutaka Incline railway linking Wellington with Wairarapa was one of the great engineering feats of the colonial era. The artist Charles Barraud captured the ruggedness of the terrain in this 1880s pencil wash.*

ATL, B-004-008

marked by a 'champagne luncheon' with 'blowing oratory' and a flurry of toasts, although the first regular train from Britomart to Onehunga four days later attracted only fifteen passengers.[20] More significantly, within eighteen months the South Auckland line — following in the footsteps of General Cameron's Imperial troops a decade before — had been pushed south to Mercer, profitably plugging the fertile Waikato basin and its million acres of recently confiscated Maori land into Auckland's economy.

> **Easily the most ambitious project of the 1870s was the Incline railway over the towering Rimutaka Range between Upper Hutt and Wairarapa.**

By that time Wellington too had a railway, skirting the harbour from Pipitea (Thorndon) to Lower Hutt in 1874 before pushing on up the Hutt Valley. In 1875, lines opened between New Plymouth and Waitara, Port Ahuriri and Pakipaki (four miles south of Hastings), and between Riverhead on the upper Waitemata Harbour and Helensville on the Kaipara River. In the latter case, construction was enthusiastically supported by local Ngati Whatua, who gifted land and provided much of the labour. Tribal leaders even travelled on the first train, pulled by the little D-class *Schnapper* in October 1875, but soon complained that the Auckland Provincial Council had reneged on earlier promises. The taking of further land without consultation or compensation left Ngati Whatua with a simmering grievance.[21] Nor would they be the last iwi to be disappointed by hopes of a railmaking partnership with settlers.

Easily the most ambitious project of the 1870s was the Incline railway over the towering Rimutaka Range between Upper Hutt and Wairarapa. Wellington settlers had dreamed of accessing the fertile Wairarapa plains since the early 1850s, and several routes were surveyed in 1871. The steepness of the range's eastern flank, where the line climbed 896 feet (265 metres) in two and a half miles (4 kilometres), required special Fell locomotives which used a set of horizontal inner wheels to grip a raised centre rail. Befitting its unusual character, when the line reached Featherston in October 1878 it enjoyed two opening ceremonies: the first minus its guest of honour, when the Governor, the Marquess of Normanby, was waylaid by a slip near Kaitoke; the second five days later, when he was greeted by the Volunteers' cannonade and a second banquet. For the next 77 years the same little H-class Fell engines would grind up and down the Incline, gripping the centre rail for dear life on the windswept curves and punishing gradients. Meanwhile, the cumbersome marshalling of carriages, locomotives and brake vans at both ends made the journey one of the country's slowest.[22]

# Trainland

## Heavy Metal

Although early locomotives and rolling stock were imported, mostly from Britain, workshops were needed to maintain the fleet and produce fittings and parts. Despite their unassuming name, these 'shops' would evolve into heavy industrial plants capable of building complex machines like locomotives. The first was set up in 1863 by the Canterbury Provincial Government in Christchurch, and by the early 1870s there were workshops at Port Chalmers and Britomart (Auckland). Dunedin's Hillside shop opened in 1875, soon followed by others at Newmarket (Auckland), Petone (Wellington), Addington (Christchurch) and East Town (Wanganui). The number of isolated sections in the early years saw a proliferation of smaller shops in places like New Plymouth, Napier, Nelson, Greymouth, Westport and Invercargill.

The first locally made wagons rolled out in the 1870s, and the emergence of the refrigerated meat industry in the eighties stimulated the manufacture of specialised rolling stock. Later that decade, economic depression spurred domestic locomotive production, initially by private companies like Scott Brothers of Christchurch.

Addington Workshop, *painted in 1930 by the French-New Zealand artist Louise Henderson.*

Collection Christchurch Art Gallery Te Puna o Waiwhetu (courtesy of Diane McKegg)

*Workshop staff enjoy a 'smoko' break in the 1920s.*

ATL, AP Godber Collection, G-1834-1/2-APG

Soon, locomotives were being built at Addington under the leadership of T.F. Rotheram and R.J. Scott, who blended the latest American, British and European features into a series of distinctive and (mostly) successful New Zealand designs. The first 2-6-2 W-class tank engines of 1889 were followed by tender locomotives such as the 4-6-0 U (1894), 4-8-0 B (1899), the celebrated 4-6-2 'Pacific' A (1906) and later designs. Hillside built tank engines from 1897, and from the early twentieth century the Thames firm A. & G. Price was also a significant locomotive manufacturer.

By the turn of the twentieth century the workshops' complex, hierarchical workforce of engineers, foremen, boilermakers, blacksmiths, carpenters, patternmakers, coppersmiths, moulders, fettlers, furnacemen and rivet-boys topped 1700. The country's largest industrial enterprises, they were also sites of struggle between an inherited British 'shop culture' and modern American-style management practices. All of the workshops were overhauled in the 1920s, with new facilities erected at Lower Hutt and Otahuhu, and much-needed improvements elsewhere. After decades of modernisation and rationalisation, in 2007 only two survive: United Group Rail's facility in Woburn, Lower Hutt, and the Hillside Engineering Group, a division of Toll New Zealand, in Dunedin.[23]

## Trainland

As Vogel's railmaking drive knitted distant settlements together, the centralising impulse became irresistible. Responsibility for managing the new railways initially rested with provincial governments, but even in 1870 the *Otago Daily Times* sensed the shift in power: 'The whole system of Provincialism is virtually abolished. Its utter disappearance is a mere question of time.'[24] That time would come soon enough, especially given the bitter taste left by the provinces' rejection of Vogel's 1873 endowment scheme. Abolition was carried in Parliament in October 1875 and came into effect a year later. Although the Vogel ministry had by then lost power, railmaking remained a priority for subsequent governments, where economic circumstances allowed. Following abolition, the construction and operation of public railways came under the umbrella of the Public Works Department (PWD). In 1880 a separate Railways Department was established to operate the New Zealand Railways (NZR), with a single general manager in Wellington replacing the two earlier commissioners (one for each island). Meanwhile, the PWD continued to oversee the construction of new lines, and also decided where they should be built.

By 1880 NZR was operating almost 1200 miles of working railway, more than three-quarters of it in the South Island. Along with the southern main trunk and isolated sections in the North Island, Nelson, Marlborough and Westland, a patchwork of branch lines served farming communities or tapped timber resources in Canterbury, Otago and Southland. In 1879/80 the country's railways carried 830,000 tons of freight; 215,000 horses, cattle, sheep and pigs; and almost three million passengers (not counting holders of season tickets), a creditable effort for a country of half a million people.[25] Although early train travel was neither cheap nor particularly comfortable, it was clearly preferable to the alternatives: the slow, jolting ordeal of a long-distance coach trip or a long, nauseating and potentially perilous small-ship voyage. In most cases trains offered a faster, safer and more reliable service that was less vulnerable to poor weather. Rail's growing popularity in the late nineteenth century was reflected in the closure of some coach services and the struggles of small ports, especially along the east coast of the South Island.

Although much had been achieved in a short time, the rail system was already struggling to keep pace with galloping public expectations. In his 1880 report, outgoing South Island Commissioner William Conyers argued that 'too much has been expected from, and attempted by, the department'. Most of the 'influential members of the community' were 'familiar with the frequent train-service of the Old Country' and clamoured for 'similar facilities' here — ignoring the differences in population, resources and terrain.

By contemporary European or Atlantic American standards, the Vogel railways had a crude, makeshift appearance, characterised by flimsy wooden station buildings, light iron rails, small British-built tank locomotives, and simple, box-like passenger carriages. Although the 3 foot 6 inch gauge was not in itself an obstacle to performance, steep gradients, tight curves, narrow tunnels and lightweight bridges certainly were. The scarcity of trackside fencing made NZR a notorious stock-killer, while rudimentary signalling and braking equipment and the absence of level-crossing barriers endangered road users and rail crews alike. In their defence, Conyers and his Minister, Richard Oliver, resorted to that favourite colonial tactic, the per capita comparison. With one mile of railway for every 406 inhabitants in 1880, New Zealand's early progress was impressive enough compared to the United States (one mile for every 580 people), New South Wales (1108), Britain (1961) and France (2900).[26]

*Much of the locomotive power on New Zealand's late-nineteenth-century railways was provided by small British-built tank engines like the 2-4-0T D class and 0-6-0T F class. D 170, built in Glasgow in 1880, is currently on static display at Helensville.*

Author's collection

## Trainland

The impact of the Vogel boom, however, had been highly uneven. In the North Island, trade between major centres was still dominated by coastal steamers, while a 'mosquito fleet' of schooners and scows bustled between the muddy estuaries and inlets of Northland, Auckland and the Bay of Plenty. In the centre of the island, rugged landscapes and resolute Maori had blunted rail's progress, especially in the bitter aftermath of the 1860s wars, when the Kingitanga tribes withdrew into their rugged Rohe Potae stronghold — known to Pakeha as the King Country. The rail revolution had yet to reshape the North Island, but that was about to change.

## Opening the North

By the end of 1880 the south-going tentacles of a North Island 'main trunk' had reached the frontier town of Te Awamutu in southern Waikato. Here, work halted while the government tried to persuade King Tawhiao to open his sealed aukati (border) along the Puniu River. In the southern half of the island, isolated sections reached from Foxton to Waitotara, Napier to Makotuku and Wellington to Masterton. Between Waikato and Manawatu was a vast upland of broken country, mountains and forests. It would take another 28 years to link these sections into a main trunk railway. Getting there would involve an arduous process of exploration, engineering challenges, commissions and parliamentary committees, negotiation and confrontation with Maori, and backbreaking work with pick, shovel and horse-drawn cart. As the line pushed onwards, the railmaking state and its private ally, the timber industry, would launch a series of assaults on the last obstacles to progressive colonisation: the Maori fastness of the central North Island, and the 'Great Bush' that cloaked much of Taranaki, King Country, Manawatu, Hawke's Bay and Wairarapa.

Initially at least, hopes of progress were dimmed by the Long Depression, which lasted from the late 1870s to the early 1890s. A royal commission on the civil service fingered the Railways Department for its 'useless expenditure' and demanded savage economies. By August 1880, 266 staff had been laid off, speed restrictions had been imposed, and services reduced by 370,000 train-miles a year. At the same time, a Railways Commission admonished the previous decade's railmakers for overreaching: 'We refer to the making of railways in some parts of the colony far in advance of existing settlement, and consequently of an amount of traffic adequate to their support.' New Zealand simply lacked the population and large areas of fertile flat land that had made 'developmental' railways economically viable in North America. As a result of the Commission's report, 50 projects were postponed or abandoned, including the Helensville–Whangarei, Wellington–Foxton,

## The Railmaking State

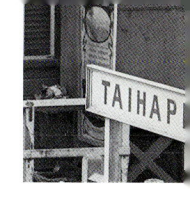

Napier–Gisborne and Otago Central lines. The government was keen to use public works unemployment, however, and by the end of 1880 some 1674 jobless men were labouring on rail projects. Even so, by 1885 only 301 miles had been added to the national network, a far cry from the 1032 miles completed in the previous five years.[27]

Forestry dominated rail freight in the 1870s and early eighties, especially in the North Island. The wooden-railed tramway that looped into the heavily forested Manawatu from the port of Foxton came under government control in 1875 and was relaid in iron; by 1886 it was linked to both New Plymouth and Wellington. As the forests around Palmerston North were harvested, the European population of the Rangitikei–Manawatu district surged from around 3000 in 1871 to more than 26,000 fifteen years later. Hunterville in 1889 was said to be 'like a new goldfield' as rail construction and timber-milling combined to drive development.[28] The next target was the Seventy Mile Bush of southern Hawke's Bay, initially settled by Scandinavian immigrants in the early 1870s. Here, rail-led exploitation was slowed by the Long Depression and the distance to the port at Napier, but in the late 1880s and nineties the region hummed to the miller's axe and saw. As elsewhere, towns grew up around rail camps and mills, and a network of tramways snaked off into the bush.

> **Efficient transport was the key to forest exploitation, and as the more accessible stands were exhausted, millers looked to the progress of the North Island's main trunk to open up vast new reserves.**

In 1885 timber and firewood accounted for 58 per cent of the tonnage carried on the Wanganui–Foxton line, 57 per cent on the Wellington–Masterton route, and 64 per cent between Helensville and Auckland. Elsewhere in Northland and Auckland the large timber trade was largely seaborne, with huge kauri exports flowing out of the Kaipara and Hokianga harbours. Timber and firewood were also important in the south, especially on the short Nelson and Marlborough lines, but also in Canterbury, where local production from the Little River bush and imports through Lyttelton combined to total 37,247 tons in 1885/6.[29] Efficient transport was the key to forest exploitation, and as the more accessible stands were exhausted, millers looked to the progress of the North Island's main trunk to open up vast new reserves.

A North Island main trunk had been mooted since the 1860s. Taranaki and Hawke's Bay settlers hoped it

Trainland

# The Private Way

The gloom of depression and the scathing verdict of the 1880 Railways Commission forced a rethink of the Vogel plan. For John Hall's new conservative government, the answer was private enterprise. Based on United States models, the Railways Construction and Land Act 1881 offered generous land grants to private railmaking companies, notably the Wellington and Manawatu Railway Company (WMR), established by local investors that year. The nation's capital had been slow to benefit from the Vogel boom, with the projected line to Foxton a victim of recent retrenchment. Private contractors now began carving a route through Wellington's difficult north-western hills (following the present-day Johnsonville suburban line) and across Manawatu's flax swamps to link up with the government line at Longburn, south of Palmerston North. On 3 November 1886 over a thousand spectators, including 700 ferried by special train from Wellington, gathered at Otaihanga to watch the Governor, Sir William Jervois, hammer home the last spike (at the third attempt, after two hapless misses).

The opening of the WMR line not only ensured Palmerston North's emergence as a major settlement at the expense of Foxton (and ultimately Wanganui), but also revitalised the capital's flagging fortunes. Plugged into the lower North Island's rail network, and with improved steam-shipping services operating out of its great harbour, Wellington emerged from the gloom of economic stagnation to become *the* central transport hub. For the next two decades, the important Wellington–New Plymouth route — coordinated with steamer services to Onehunga to provide the main link between Auckland and Wellington — operated under a sometimes uneasy public–private partnership, with passengers switching trains at Longburn. Portraying a strong American influence, WMR's powerful Baldwin locomotives, modern carriages and elegant dining cars often put their NZR counterparts to shame. The company enjoyed considerable success until 1908, when the completion of the North Island main trunk prompted a government buy-out.

Other private rail endeavours were less successful. In 1889 the Kaihu Valley Railway

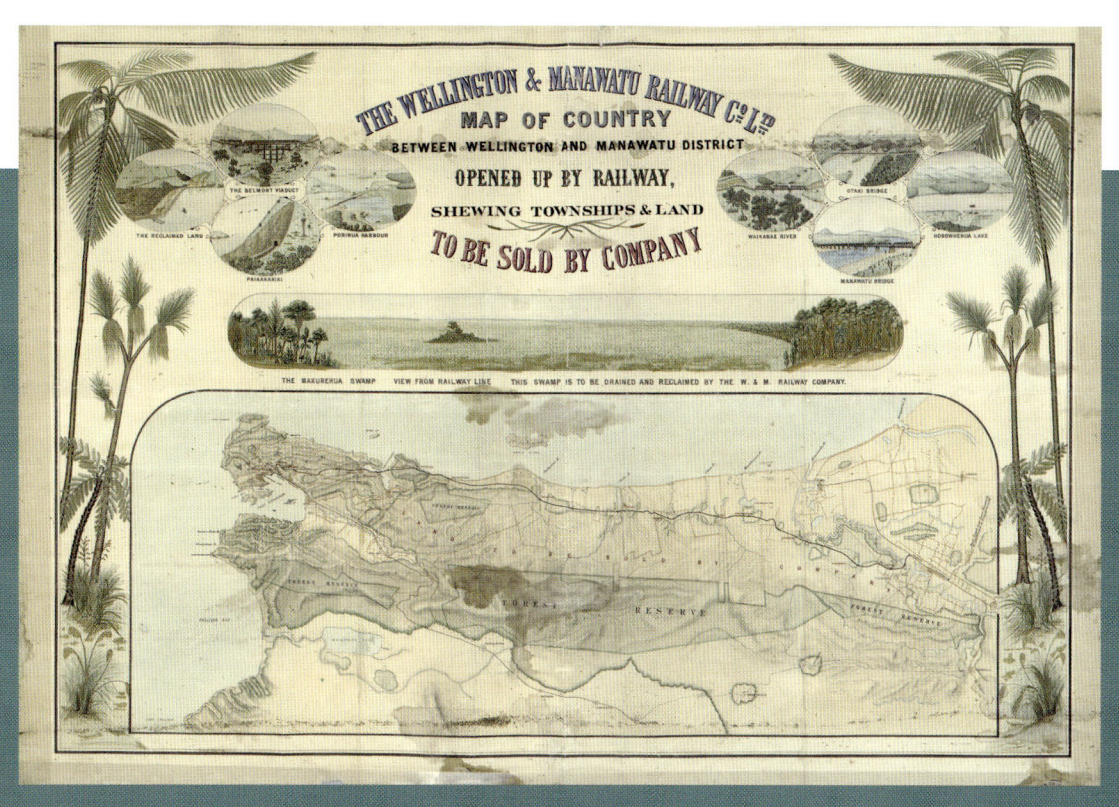

*An 1885 map showing the route of the WMR line and the rich hinterlands it promised to open up for settlement.*

ATL, MapColl-r832.4gme/1885/Acc.2705

Company completed a 16-mile line from Dargaville to tap Northland's kauri resources, but financial troubles soon caused the government to step in (the line came under NZR control from 1893). The biggest flop was the New Zealand Midland Railway Company, floated in London in 1886 with audacious plans to link Canterbury with the West Coast and Nelson. It was a formidable undertaking and progress was slow: by 1894 only 75 miles had been completed at a cost of £1.3 million. The following year the government seized control of the project, sparking a bitter legal wrangle and further delays. The West Coast section reached Otira in 1900, but it was 1914 before its Canterbury counterpart wound its way up to Arthur's Pass. A further nine years were needed to pierce the main divide via the Otira tunnel — at the time the longest in the Southern Hemisphere. Work on the final piece of the jigsaw, connecting Inangahua with Nelson province, continued through the 1920s but was abandoned in 1931, condemning the latter region to isolation from New Zealand's rail network.[30]

# Trainland

## The Railmaking State

*On 15 April 1885 Premier Robert Stout (perched on the end of the plank), Wahanui Huatare (the tall man standing behind the wheelbarrow) and Rewi Maniapoto (far right, in top hat and black jacket) turned the 'first sod' of the central section of the North Island main trunk beside the Puniu River, south of Te Awamutu.*

ATL, DM Beere Collection, G-96208-1/2

might loop west or east through their provinces; others favoured a more direct but as yet undetermined central route. Each option posed considerable engineering difficulties; each would require the cooperation of local Maori and the acquisition of large blocks of their land. Surveys of all three were launched in 1882–3, with engineer John Rochfort mapping the central route north from Marton on the Palmerston North–Wanganui line. It was a journey into unknown and potentially hostile territory. Rochfort's party was forced back at gunpoint three times and held prisoner for three days near Ohakune; another surveyor, Charles Hursthouse, was roughly detained by the prophet Te Mahuki, before being rescued by Ngati Maniapoto leader Wahanui Huatare and Te Kooti (whom the government had recently pardoned as part of negotiations over access to the Rohe Potae).

Despite its enormous political and engineering challenges, in 1884 a parliamentary committee of 'impartial' South Island members endorsed the central course, which was the shortest route and would open up the greatest amount of new land for settlement. The same year, Premier Robert Stout and Native Minister John Ballance sealed a deal with the increasingly influential Wahanui. Ignoring the objections of King Tawhiao and Waikato tribes, Ngati Maniapoto agreed to open the gate to the King Country in return for assurances that alcohol and land speculators would be kept out.[31]

Although Rochfort's surveys would not be completed until 1887, and no decisions had been reached about the exact course of the central section, the government was keen to start work, partly in an attempt to reduce unemployment. On 15 April 1885 Stout, Wahanui and Rewi Maniapoto ceremonially turned the first sod on the south bank of the Puniu River. In front of a triumphal arch bearing the motto 'Te Ika a Maui, Te Rangimarie' ('A day of peace to New Zealand', according to the *Waikato Times*) the tall Wahanui scooped some earth into an 'ornamental' barrow — reportedly 'emblazoned with portraits of North American Indians, in default of Maoris' — which was wheeled off and emptied by the Premier. The sods were whisked away by souvenir hunters.[32]

Within four years the line stretched 34 miles, but PWD retrenchments slowed further progress. Work on the Porootarao tunnel, halfway between Te Kuiti and Taumarunui, was finished in 1891, but it would be another ten years before the rails reached it. In 1892, the year after the Liberal government came to power, the project was reviewed by another parliamentary committee. Rebuffing Taranaki pressure for a western detour, it reaffirmed the central route but demanded more detailed surveying. Little was achieved in the following eight years.

As progress stalled, critics blamed the Liberals. Few politicians were more attuned to the developmental potential of railways — or the political sway of rail promises — than Premier Richard Seddon and his colleagues. Indeed, the Liberals' shameless use of patronage appalled the Governor, Lord Plunket, who called rail construction 'the worst example of this growing evil': 'little bits of lines are made here and there to satisfy Government electorates, whilst unconnected lines of national importance are left unfinished and consequently unproductive.'

In 1894 the Liberals also scrapped their conservative predecessor's experiment

*Barrow boy: the populist Liberal Premier Richard Seddon, seen here celebrating the start of work on the Westport–Inangahua railway in January 1906, seldom missed an opportunity to turn a sod or cut a ribbon for the press photographers. It would take 37 years to complete this line.*

ATL, F-2265-1/2

## The Railmaking State

with an independent board of Railway Commissioners in favour of a return to direct ministerial control. By 1906 political influence over appointments was so deeply ingrained that in a list of test questions school pupils were asked to 'Write a letter to the Member of Parliament for your district, applying for a position on the railways.' For their part, ministers struggled to cope with public demands for a piece of the railway action. As Minister of Railways William Hall-Jones lamented, 'First it's a siding, then a platform, then a goods shed, then a railway porter, then a station master. You'd be surprised how these requests follow each other.'[33]

Nevertheless, the Liberal era (1891–1912) was notable for significant improvements to the rough-and-ready Vogel railways: the widespread replacement of 40-pound iron rails with 52-, 56- or 70-pound steel ones, the construction of larger and more elegant station buildings, and the introduction of more powerful locomotives and comfortable passenger carriages (see Chapter 4). The adoption of modern safety features followed a fatal rear-end collision at Rakaia in 1899. This hastened the fitting of Westinghouse automatic airbrakes to locomotives and rolling stock (long before this was done in Britain), the installation of interlocking points and signals, and the introduction of the electric-tablet system of train control. Even so, double tracks

*Tyer's electric tablet machines at Rakaia, photographed in 1950. Introduced after a fatal collision near this station in 1899, these devices issued a token or 'tablet' that was carried in the locomotive cab, ensuring that only one train at a time could occupy a section of track between tablet stations. The system remained in use on some lines for more than 90 years.*

ANZ, AAVK, W3493, B54

## Trainland

remained rare (New Zealand's first section only appeared in 1905), while the restricted loading gauge and tunnel profile — which together determined the maximum height and width of locomotives and rolling stock — would remain a source of frustration.

The Department's workforce, which rocketed from 4523 in 1891 to 13,523 in 1912, also benefited from the Liberals' state paternalism. After a tense relationship with the Railway Commissioners in the early 1890s, the Amalgamated Society of Railway Servants (established in 1886) regained official recognition in 1894 and soon secured wage increases, reductions in working hours and a week's annual paid leave. Two years later came a comprehensive employee classification system that linked promotion and pay to length of service. The Government Railways Superannuation Fund, the blueprint for later state-sector pension schemes, was launched in 1902. The price of these concessions, however, was the effective isolation of railway workers from the wider labour movement, which contributed to the emergence of a powerful sense of identity among the 'Railway People'.[34]

## The Final Push

In 1900 a final parliamentary committee resolved to plug the central rail gap. By the end of 1903 the rails reached Taumarunui, then little more than a bush clearing but, like many settlements in the rails' wake, soon to grow into a sizeable town. To the south, engineers faced an imposing ascent onto the Waimarino plateau. After much difficulty, the problem was solved by Robert Holmes' remarkable Raurimu Spiral, which included two tunnels, three horseshoe curves and a complete circle. Further south, a series of massive viaducts were needed to bridge deep ravines at Makatote, Hapuawhenua, Mangaweka and Makohine. By 1906 the trunk's workforce had reached almost 2700, and the following year an extra shift was added, work

*This 1929 publicity foldout, designed by E.M. Lovell-Smith, celebrates one of New Zealand's most famous rail engineering features, the Raurimu Spiral.*

ATL, Eph-B-RAIL-1930-01

The Railmaking State

# RAURIMU SPIRAL
## AND NATIONAL PARK
### NEW ZEALAND RAILWAYS

The Line rises from Raurimu Railway Station and Township to National Park Station (on the edge of National Park). In the background, the Volcanic mountains, Tongariro (left), Ngauruhoe (centre) & Ruapehu (right) with the Chateau at its base.

# To "The Spiral" from WELLINGTON

Piopiotea River, tributary of the Retaruke River flowing from plateau crosses, and then accompanies Railway into Raurimu Township.

# Trainland

continuing through the night under the glow of kerosene lamps.

A feature of main trunk construction in these years was the Liberals' encouragement of the 'cooperative system' of labour. This scheme, first introduced in 1892 but of greater significance after 1900, was designed to cut out private contractors. Instead of putting work out to tender, PWD engineers costed sections of track and offered them to gangs of workers. The gang was supervised by a departmental engineer, but chose its own 'headmen' and was responsible for its own work discipline. Despite Liberal rhetoric, in practice the cooperative system was not so much a bold socialist experiment as a limited form of unemployment relief — public works on the cheap. Nor did it help navvies become small farmers, as many had hoped; only a minority benefited from the government's promised land grants along the trunk's route.[35]

The cooperative workers were a cosmopolitan crew: many were of Irish and Australian origin; some had no prior experience at navvying. One visitor to the works discovered 'a jolly tar taking a respite from the sea, a music-hall artist, also men of travel and experience, good training and degree'.[36] Their earnings were reasonable (averaging 8s a day), but local prices for food and provisions were steep, and the work — lumping heavy papa clay, pumice and ash, or hewing solid rhyolite rock, with only picks and shovels, dynamite, wheelbarrows and horse-drawn drays — was hugely demanding. Visiting Raurimu in 1908, G.G. Stewart found the working conditions 'appalling': 'Continuous heavy rain, with occasional hail, sleet and snow, much fog, miry clay, and a tangled bed of wild undergrowth knitting together the forest giants, made a tough job for the workers.'

They also laboured in extreme isolation. According to engineer Peter Keller, who spent five years on the central section, not a single permanent resident — Maori or Pakeha — lived in the 80 miles between Taumarunui and Ohakune (although many

RIGHT: *As main trunk construction edged onwards, dozens of rough timber and calico camps sprouted along the route. A handful grew into permanent settlements but most, like this one at Hapuawhenua, near Ohakune, vanished almost as quickly as they appeared.*

Auckland Weekly News 1908 Christmas supplement, ATL, C-065-006

The Railmaking State

*The young surveyor Peter Keller (left) and his chainman Charlie Williams (centre) at work near Raurimu in 1906.*

ATL, Making NZ Collection, F-699-1/4-MNZ

Maori lived near each of those settlements). The area was so impenetrable that when Keller was transferred from Taihape north to Raurimu in 1905 he caught a train from Marton to New Plymouth, a steamer to Onehunga, then another train south as far as Taumarunui.[37]

The navvies' living conditions were equally harsh, especially in winter. The PWD provided few facilities and took little responsibility for injuries. Keller described how new workers were 'issued with a pick and a long handled shovel, an axe and a tent and fly — a married man the same — if he wanted more he had to buy it. He then had to go and cut poles from the bush and pitch his own camp.' Visitors marvelled at the makeshift nature of these bush shantytowns, which were given names like 'Carson City' and 'Angels Rest'. 'Sacks are a favourite building material. I hardly know what to call some of the erections. They are partly tents, partly cottages, partly slab huts and wholly nondescript, original and miscellaneous.'[38]

A few navvies brought wives and children with them, but the calico camp-towns were overwhelmingly male; the 1906 Census counted 1190 males and just 256 females in the Ruapehu Riding of Waimarino County. In their spare time the men sang ballads, played 'two-up' and drank like fish. Although the King Country was officially 'dry', the 'sly-grog' business boomed; in 1908 even little Horopito had 'ten hop-beer shops all doing a roaring trade'. 'On a Saturday night, following pay-day, drunkenness was at times appalling, and free fights were quite common.'[39] Even so, serious violence was rare. For most navvies, life on the main trunk meant bleak drudgery rather than Wild West mayhem.

By May 1908 only a 15-mile gap remained, between the unfinished Makatote viaduct and Ohakune. The final push was prompted, strangely enough, by the visit to Auckland of the United States Navy's 'Great White Fleet'. With most of Parliament heading north from Wellington, the PWD rushed to complete a temporary, unballasted track between the existing railheads. The first through train, the Parliament Special,

*Prime Minister Sir Joseph Ward and his wife Theresa (left) pose for a photograph at Taumarunui on 8 August 1908, during the historic journey of the Parliament Special. Three months later he returned to the central North Island to drive home the 'last spike' at Manganuioteao.*

ANZ, AAVL, W3493, E4624

left Wellington at 10 pm on 7 August. Hauled in turn by WMR, NZR and PWD locomotives, it completed the 426-mile journey in twenty and a half hours. Three months later, on 6 November, Prime Minister Sir Joseph Ward tapped home a final polished silver spike at Manganuioteao, between Erua and Potaka, in a ceremony 'as impressive as scowling weather, muddy embankments and interfering photographers would permit'.

An *Evening Post* reporter on the PM's train marvelled at the great stands of trees, 'retreating for miles on miles, range after range' between Taumarunui and Ohakune: 'This heart of the King Country possesses possibilities beyond the thought of the maddest optimist.' Ngati Maniapoto may not have shared his gushing enthusiasm. As Te Kooti had prophesied, the 'whistling God of the Pakeha' was a Trojan horse for timber-millers, settlers, sly-groggers, speculators and government land agents. By 1910 the map of central North Island land ownership had been redrawn, with the once great Rohe Potae reduced to a patchwork of Crown, private and Maori land.[40]

Trainland

## Cottage Industry

As its network and workforce expanded in the early twentieth century, the Railways Department took on a new role, as one of the country's largest house-builders and landlords. The department had purchased or erected cottages for stationmasters and other employees since the late 1870s, but by the 1900s it faced a serious accommodation shortage, especially in the North Island. After the First World War it decided to establish a modern sawmill and kitset house factory at Frankton Junction, using rimu and matai from its own central North Island forests. The factory, which eventually employed more than 60 men, utilised the latest American machinery and even had its own plumbing department to produce baths, sinks, pipes and spouting. Designed by George Troup's Architectural Branch, the houses were identical apart from their dimensions — which depended on the employee's occupation and seniority — and variations to their front porches and roofs. Between 1923 and its closure in 1929 the Frankton factory churned out almost 1400 prefabricated houses, as well as precut timber for wagons, signals, office furniture, stockyards, sheds and other buildings. New Zealand's first large-scale government housing initiative, NZR's programme was to exert a major influence on the Labour government's more celebrated state housing scheme of the late 1930s.

Railway houses, hostels and single-men's huts soon dotted the country. NZR was the biggest employer and landlord in many towns, and the rolls of local schools were stuffed with railway kids. Along the North Island main trunk, whole settlements sprang up at Maungaturoto, Frankton,

*A railway house at Ngaio, Wellington.*

Paul Hamer

*As well as family houses, the Railways Department (and PWD) built thousands of portable huts to accommodate single male workers. These two, originally from Matahiwi and Kopua in Hawke's Bay, now sit beside the restored Ormondville railway station.*

Miriam Gibson

Taumarunui, Te Kuiti, Ohakune, Taihape, Marton Junction and at Kaiwharawhara, Ngaio and Petone in Wellington. Reflecting Railways Minister Gordon Coates' 'desire to see every railway settlement a garden suburb', each was to have its own roads, drainage systems and recreation reserves. The largest, Frankton, had 160 houses and its own Troup-designed Railway Institute Hall, packed every Tuesday and Saturday night with workers and partners dancing to the tunes of the Railway Orchestra.

Prefab houses also sprouted in remote locations like Summit and Cross Creek in the Rimutaka Range, and the little settlements along the Stratford–Okahukura and Gisborne–Moutohora lines. On the Midland line, eleven houses and a hostel accommodated 60 workers and their families at Springfield; even tiny Cass had five railway cottages. The Department's housing stock peaked at over 6000 in the 1950s, but the sharp decline in the rail workforce, centralisation of functions and other changes in the 1980s spelled the end of the distinctive railway communities. Thousands of houses were sold to private buyers, shifted or converted to other uses. More recently, local authorities like the Wellington City Council and Ruapehu District Council have moved to protect railway precincts in Ngaio's fashionable Tarikaka Street settlement, 'Railway Row' in Ohakune and the 'Sunshine Settlement' in Taumarunui.[41]

**LEFT:** *Rough as guts: the appalling state of many North Island roads underlined the immense value of the comparatively quick and reliable rail service between Auckland and Wellington. This 1912 photograph was apparently taken during the first road trip between the two cities via Taihape, Taumarunui and Te Kuiti.*

ATL, Making NZ Collection, F-710-1/2-MNZ

**RIGHT:** *This map highlighting the main trunk's historic and scenic delights is from a Daylight Limited brochure issued in 1952–3, a time when the national rail network reached its greatest extent.*

NZRLS

While the main trunk was inching onwards, several other rail projects had been completed. In the east of the North Island, branch lines from Frankton Junction linked Auckland with Rotorua (1894), Thames (1898) and Waihi (1905). The Rotorua line sparked a tourist boom in the 'Hot Lakes District' (see Chapter 3) and for a decade provided Auckland's only express train journey. Further south, in 1897 the Wellington–Wairarapa railway was finally linked to Napier and (via the Manawatu Gorge) Palmerston North, enabling NZR to bypass the WMR route out of Wellington and compete for business — a cause of some friction between the public and private operators. The imminent completion of the main trunk hardened the government's resolve to control the entire North Island network, and in December 1907 the WMR was given the required twelve months' notice of compulsory state purchase. A year later, New Zealand's most successful private railway and all of its locomotives and rolling stock was absorbed into the NZR system.

The opening of the North Island main trunk was one of the pivotal moments in New Zealand history. At a stroke it ended the South Island's 30-year lead in rail development and confirmed the North's growing economic and demographic supremacy. At the outset of the First World War the South Island still led in overall route mileage and freight tonnage carried — by 1655 to 1199 miles, and 3.7 million to 2.3 million tons respectively — but the North Island was already surging ahead in traffic density (7.3 million train-miles to the South's 5.3 million), passenger journeys (5.8 to 5.3 million) and rail revenue (£2.2 to £1.8 million).[42]

Although the completion of the main trunk effectively signalled the end of the 'heroic' railmaking era,

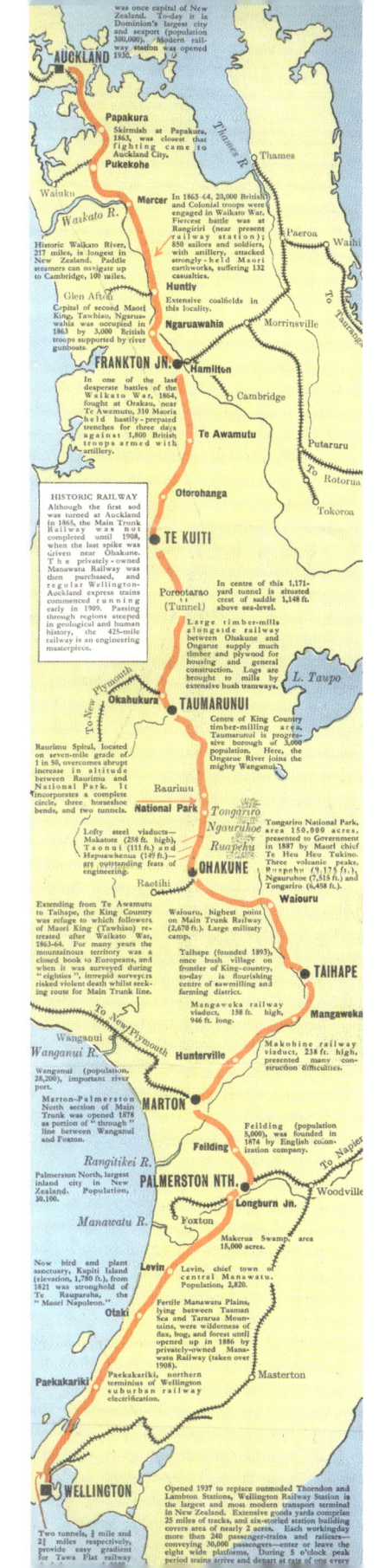

## The Railmaking State

the national network continued to expand throughout rail's golden age. Another burst of construction under the Reform government in the 1920s saw the opening of the long-delayed Midland line between Canterbury and the West Coast (1923) and the linking of Whangarei (1925) and Tauranga (1928) to the main network. In the 1940s, the first Labour government filled in most of the remaining gaps, completing lines from Napier to Gisborne (1942), Westport to Greymouth (1943) and Christchurch to Picton (1945). Even then, the Vogel legacy continued to cast a long shadow. In 1950, NZR's General Manager would respond to criticism of slow journeys by arguing that '"interminable stops" by express trains cannot be readily avoided in a relatively new country such as New Zealand, where the railways still are largely developmental in character'.[43] In fact, the country's 'developmental' railway system was already nearing its greatest-ever route length, the 3535-mile peak of 1953.

In sporadic bursts since 1870, the railmaking state had forged a network of steel and sleeper across plains and swamps, over rivers and gorges, through dense forests and over mountain passes. It was arguably the New Zealand state's greatest achievement, at least in the first century after 1840, and certainly its greatest financial commitment. Between 1870 and 1929 the £52 million devoted to rail construction accounted for 48 per cent of expenditure from central government's Public Works Fund — more than state spending on roads and highways, telegraphs, public buildings, immigration, tourism, defence, lighthouses, harbour works and mining put together.[44] There were other costs too. The railway drove an iron wedge into the Maori heartland of the central North Island, creating a 'permanent way' for European colonisation and hastening the destruction of the natural environment. The chief beneficiaries of the rail revolution were the Pakeha inhabitants of the main centres, the towns that flourished along the rail routes, and the freshly opened hinterlands. Chapter 2 explores how the expanding rail network helped create and sustain these communities, and the ways in which ordinary New Zealanders, as rail users and voters, shaped the character of their people's railway.

CHAPTER 2

# Business and Pleasure

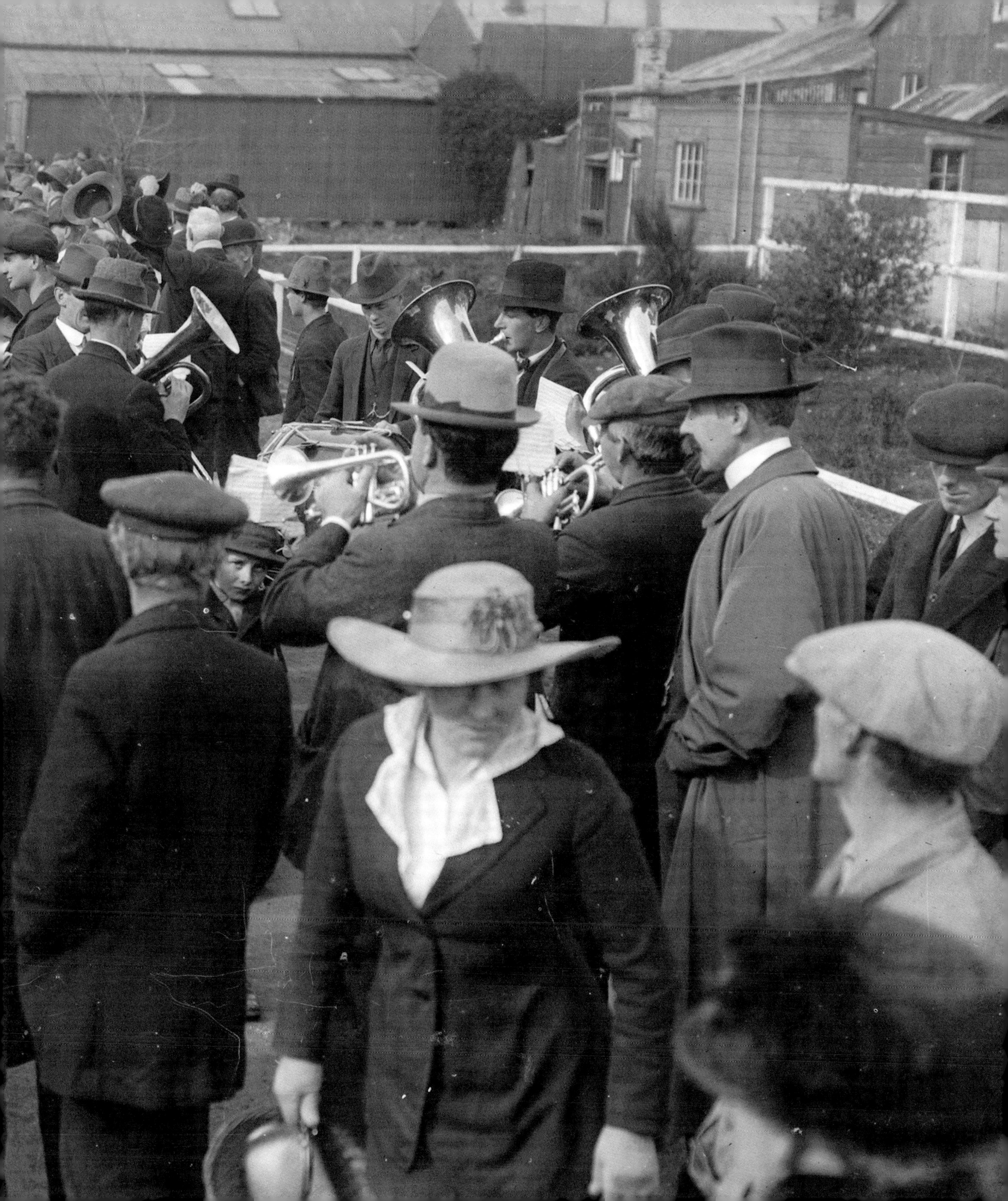

# Trainland

> The train was as much a meeting place as a means of conveyance — a kind of club on wheels. Everyone knew everyone else, and so a trip to town had the excitement of a dozen neighbourly visits in one.
>
> — H.C.D. Somerset, *Littledene*[1]

'The railways in New Zealand have never been regarded, or run, as a profit-making concern,' wrote the Reform Party's Gordon Coates in his first report as Minister of Railways in 1923. If the Department was 'guided solely by considerations of financial return, much greater profits could be earned. But in my view this would not be utilizing the service in the true interests of the Dominion.' Coming from a minister in one of New Zealand's supposedly most conservative governments — a man who campaigned for 'More Business in Government, Less Government in Business' — such socialistic sentiments are striking. Even the nineteen branch lines that had 'failed to earn actual working-expenses, to say nothing of returning interest on capital', were valued for their past contributions: 'They have opened up the country, increased production and consequently the wealth of the Dominion.' Spelling out the benefits granted by NZR to suburban commuters, school pupils, farmers, fruit-growers and manufacturers, Coates lamented that the general public had 'become so accustomed to generous concessions on the railways' that their value was 'not so universally appreciated as it should be'.[2] New Zealanders, it seems, did not know how lucky they were.

In the seven decades since Henry Sewell's 1854 ordeal by sea, New Zealand had changed beyond recognition. Repeating his journey from Canterbury to Auckland still required a sea voyage from Lyttelton to Wellington, now a ten-hour trip on the comfortable SS *Maori*. But the main trunk railway had cut travel between the two North Island centres to under eighteen hours, or fourteen on the new 'Night Limited' from December 1924. If that still seems painfully slow to modern air travellers, the reduction in journey times between the 1850s and the 1920s had been quite as dramatic as it would be over the following seven decades. The railmaking state had helped unlock the central North Island, tag-teamed with the timber industry to

PREVIOUS PAGE: *Adults, children and prams mingle with a blaring brass band as Stratford farewells local troops in 1915.*

ATL, JR Wall Collection, G-017778-1/2

harvest the Great Bush, and connected the country's burgeoning agricultural economy to markets, cities and ports. Apart from a sharp downturn at the end of the First World War passenger numbers had climbed steadily for four decades, increasing tenfold between 1878 and 1921 (more than three times faster than population growth) and doubling in the first decade of the twentieth century.

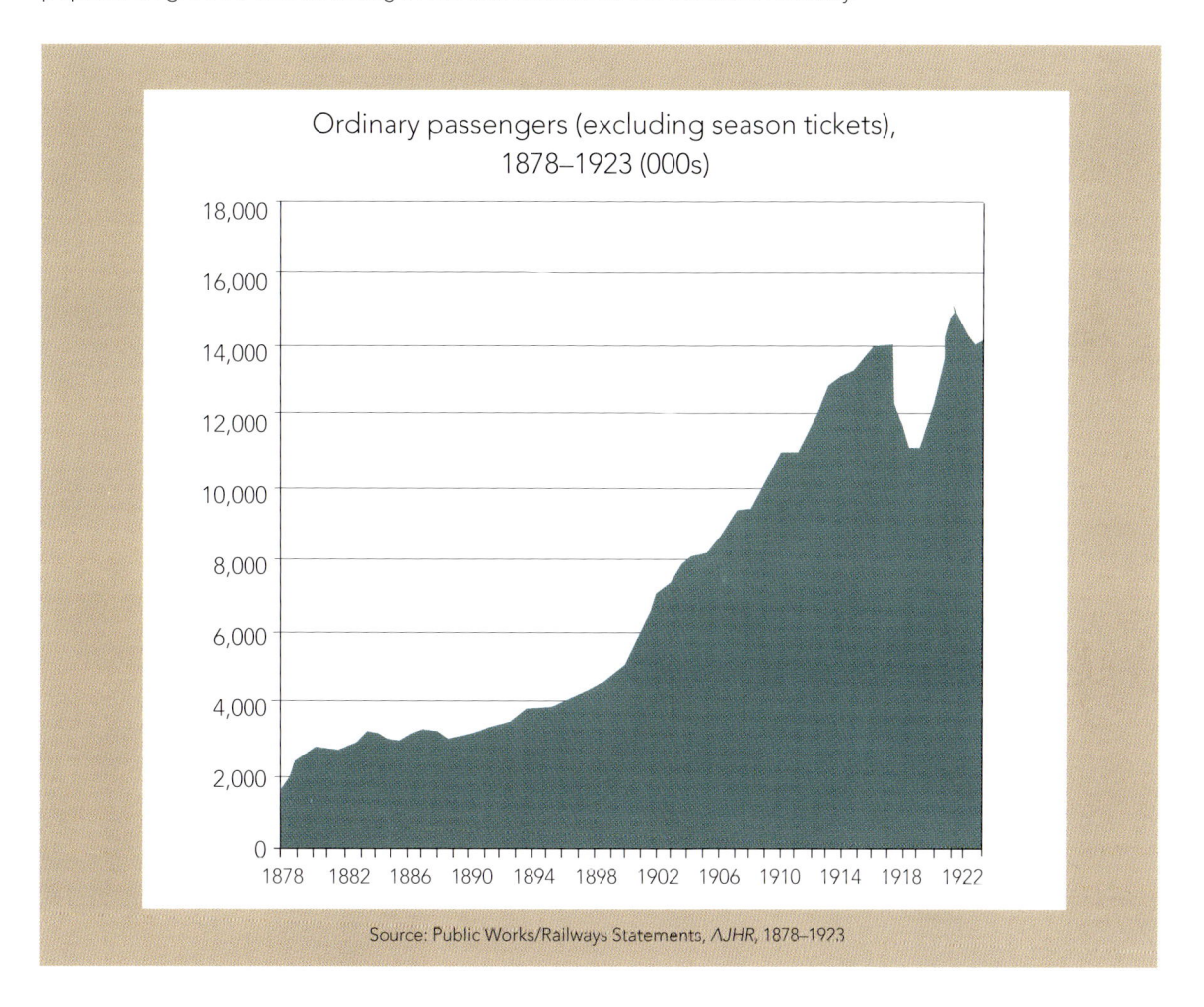

**Ordinary passengers (excluding season tickets), 1878–1923 (000s)**

Source: Public Works/Railways Statements, AJHR, 1878–1923

Not content with merely providing infrastructure, successive governments had run working railways as a kind of public service. From the late 1870s NZR offered a range of freight concessions aimed at fostering and protecting local agriculture, forestry, mining and manufacturing. But rail's influence would reach far beyond economic development, touching on fields as diverse as education, town planning, defence, religion,

## Trainland

tourism, even sports and leisure. In the last decades of the nineteenth century, 'handsome concessions' were extended to students and apprentices, touring entertainers, sports teams and 'pleasure parties', newspaper reporters and newsboys, suburban commuters, delegates of religious bodies and friendly societies, and members of the Volunteer Corps. As well as freight, stock and passengers, railways transported culture and ideas, helping to speed the distribution of newspapers, magazines, books, mail and motion pictures. Together with the faster communication provided by telegraph and telephone, the expanding rail network fostered the development of numerous regional and national organisations by enabling delegates to come together for meetings and annual conferences.

Although a public service ethos infused many private railways overseas, including the 'Big Four' companies of interwar Britain, few matched NZR as a people's railway.[3] As Coates' General Manager, R.W. McVilly, reiterated, the 'management of the Railway Department in New Zealand is … a trustee for the general public'.[4]

## 'Handsome Concessions'

In his 1923 report Coates rattled off a range of rail concessions to local producers, 'in which immediate financial return is sacrificed to secure general advantage to the community':

> For instance, the charges on New-Zealand-grown fresh fruit are obviously below a reasonably remunerative rate. Half a hundredweight of fruit may be carried any distance for 8d. Lime for farm lands is conveyed for distances up to 100 miles free of charge; empty fruit-cases, made from New Zealand timber, under certain conditions are carried free for distances up to 100 miles, and a similar concession applies to timber consigned for the purpose of making fruit-cases. Native brown coal is also carried at an extremely low rate. Native timbers are carried at one-third less than the rate charged for imported timbers . . . Stock, implements, dogs, horses, cattle, produce, &c., consigned to shows, horse-parades, dog-trials, &c., are returned free of charge.[5]

As in any business, concessions were a carrot designed to stimulate trade. Ministerial control, however, made NZR particularly susceptible to political pressure and the constant clamour from local lobbies, farming

*Gordon Coates strikes a seam-bursting pose as he chats to the driver of A$^B$ 825 at Auckland in 1928. Appointed Minister of Railways in 1923, Coates retained the job throughout his term as Prime Minister (1925–8), highlighting both his personal interest and the prominence of the portfolio at that time.*

ATL, NZ Free Lance Collection, F-92658-1/2

interests and other groups. In 1877 it published its tariffs for passengers and bulk cargoes — wool, livestock, grain, coal and other minerals, timber and firewood — as well as an exhaustive roster of rates for goods and parcels of all kinds, from beeswax to billiard tables, glassware to gravestones. Dogs and fowls respectively cost 6d and 1d a head per 25 miles. The standard passenger rates were 3d per mile first class and 2d second class; corpses, at 1s per mile, carried a stiffer rate.[6] Over the following decades, NZR's bill of fare would bulge with special rates and concessions for customers large and small.

Mines and mills were big rail users. Mining companies at Dun Mountain, Kawakawa and elsewhere built some of New Zealand's earliest railways; later, dozens of lines in Northland, Waikato, Taranaki, Southland and especially Westland connected coalmines with ports and industry. For nearly a century NZR was itself one of the country's largest consumers of coal, as well as iron ore, gravel, sand and other minerals. The forestry industry was also a close ally from the beginning, with timber and firewood dominating rail tonnage in the late nineteenth century, especially on North Island lines. As with coal, NZR and the PWD were voracious

Insulated railway wagons designed and built at the Department's Addington workshops provided the crucial link between farm, works and port.

## Business and Pleasure

*From farm and freezing works to wharves and the world: the expanding rail network was a crucial factor in the development of New Zealand's lucrative export trade in refrigerated meat.*

ATL, SC Smith Collection, G-45403-1/2

consumers in their own right, using timber for sleepers, trestle bridges, stations, sheds and workshop buildings, workers' housing, stockyards, signals and telegraph poles, as well as fuel for heating and cooking. In the 1950s and 1960s forestry was to re-emerge as one of rail's most important customers, with new lines to Kinleith and Murupara in the Bay of Plenty countering the postwar trend of branch closures and stimulating the spectacular growth of the port of Mount Maunganui.

For many decades, NZR's most numerous and regular customers were farmers. Railways opened up new areas for settlement and accelerated the conversion of forest and swamp to pastureland. Trains also provided farmers with a quick, reliable means of moving livestock, wool, grain, cream, fruit and vegetables, as well as bringing in grass seed, fertiliser, machinery and other supplies. Canterbury's extensive rail network helped stimulate that region's late-nineteenth-century grain boom, with cereals dominating tonnage on the plains' main trunk and branch lines. In 1890, for example, 20,351 tons of grain was railed out of Rakaia and nearby stations, 18,345 tons from Ashburton, 15,702 tons from Kaiapoi and 5964 tons from Pleasant Point. Some was consumed locally, but 250,000 tons rolled onto the Lyttelton or Timaru wharves for shipment to other cities, Australia or Britain.[7]

By that time an agricultural export industry of far greater significance was emerging: the frozen meat trade. The nearly 5000 mutton, lamb and pork carcasses famously dispatched to London on the sailing ship *Dunedin* in February 1882 were slaughtered at Totara Estate, near Oamaru, and railed to Port Chalmers in iceboxes for freezing on board the ship. By the end of the year freezing works were operating at Petone and at Burnside and Belfast in Christchurch; by the mid 1890s there were twelve in the North Island and nine in the South. Insulated railway wagons designed and built at the Department's Addington workshops provided the crucial link between farm, works and port.

Farmers soon coalesced into a powerful political lobby, especially from the 1880s when Parliament's

*Livestock transport was the lifeblood of many rural branch and secondary lines, at least until trucking restrictions were lifted in the 1960s. This scene was photographed at Omakau, Central Otago, in 1953.*

ANZ, AAVK, W3493, B3778

Country Quota inflated their electoral muscle. As in other areas of society, enhanced transport and communications encouraged the formation of national organisations, most notably the New Zealand Farmers' Union (later Federated Farmers) in 1902 and the farmer-dominated Reform Party in 1909, which in turn pushed for further rail concessions. From the mid 1880s successive governments had targeted an annual railways profit of 3 per cent (often not achieved), with any excess returned to customers in the form of reduced charges. As rail traffic surged in the 1890s, the Liberal government bowed to the farm lobby by offering concession fares to drovers (1894), slashing freight rates for butter and cheese by 45 per cent (1897) and generously subsidising shipments of lime (1898). Grain rates were pared in 1899 and wool charges in 1902. After coming to power in 1912 the new Reform administration sought a higher return from railways, with some success (profit peaked at over 5 per cent in 1916/17 before tumbling to 1 per cent during the postwar slump of 1922).[8] Regardless of performance, profit-making (and reinvestment in maintenance and improvements) continued to play second fiddle to NZR's developmental mission.

As well as moving produce and supplies, railways enabled farmers and their families to travel for business and pleasure. For the community at Oxford in North Canterbury, the railway was the 'chief line of communication' with the outside world until at least the mid 1920s. Crawford Somerset captured the importance of the farmer's regular 'trip to town':

> Christchurch at that time [1923] was essentially a rural centre; to the farmer, coming in for the day, the city was an extension of his farm. The people he recognized in the streets and hotel, were, like himself, 'in from the country'; those he sought out in his usual haunts, at the saleyards, the banks, the shops, the law offices, the stock and station agencies, were deeply concerned with people from the country.[9]

The backbone of the rural passenger system until the 1950s was the humble 'mixed' (passenger-freight) train and the even humbler 'goods with car', an assortment of wagons with one or two carriages tacked on the rear (or in winter sometimes directly behind the locomotive to provide steam heating). In an era before sealed roads and widespread car ownership, mixed trains were an essential form of passenger transport. They offered a cheap alternative to express travel on main routes, and were widely used for short-distance hops on rural branches. If locals couldn't make the 'trip to town' themselves, guards would routinely deliver neighbours' mail or even shop for them.[10]

Travelling on mixed trains could be agonisingly slow, with frequent stops to shunt wagons or wait for other trains to pass. The writer Janet Frame recalled how the 'slow train' took seven hours to travel the 78 miles between Oamaru and Dunedin, stopping at every station and 'waiting for at least half an hour by the gum trees at Waianakarua until the midday Limited rushed by on its way north'. 'As usual there were unloadings, loadings, jolts as the trucks were removed, long periods when the carriage at the end seemed to stand alone in the midst of paddocks of gum trees, tussock, manuka scrub, *matagouri*, swamp, sheep, derelict houses.'[11] But as Somerset noted with regard to the Oxford branch line, the leisurely pace offered welcome opportunities for social interaction:

> The whole journey of 40 miles [to Christchurch], with all the many stops on the way, took a full three hours. But few ever found it tedious. The train was as much a meeting place as a means of conveyance — a kind of club on wheels. Everyone knew everyone else, and so a trip to town had the excitement of a dozen neighbourly visits in one. The silence of people who work in the isolation of farming was broken in talk and one arrived in town briefed and relaxed with the latest gossip. As one farmer remarked in recalling times past, 'the train was a good place for an occasional loaf and a yarn'.[12]

# Trainland

*Show time: this 1927 poster (one of a series used for different agricultural shows) offers special return excursion fares for visitors to Palmerston North's A&P Show from as far afield as Hamilton and Invercargill.*

ATL, NON-ATL-0015 / ANZ, AAOK, W3241, 78

Trains also ferried farmers and their families to Agricultural and Pastoral (A&P) Shows. Although the first A&P Associations had been founded in the 1840s, local groups multiplied along with the rail network in the late nineteenth century. They held their first national conference in 1892, and by 1908 there were 64 associations in the North Island and 41 in the South, each running popular annual shows. Mixing commerce and competition with 'all the fun of the fair', A&P Shows offered parades and pageants, dances, sports events, sideshows and circuses.

For many years, trains provided the only quick and reliable means of moving large consignments of livestock, produce, machinery and other exhibits to and from shows. In 1884 NZR offered to return unsold stock, implements, sheepdogs and poultry to their station of origin free of charge; from 1891 it even refunded half the charge for the forwarding trip. It also reduced rates for the travelling 'side-showmen' and circus troupes that entertained show patrons, and laid on special trains to bring buyers and browsers from near

## Business and Pleasure

and far. In response to further A&P Association lobbying, in 1899 judges of exhibits were granted cheap tickets and in 1900 the period of time in which exhibitors and attendants could travel on special show fares was extended. By 1908 special trains were bringing 2000 Aucklanders to the annual Helensville A&P Show, while even in the late 1920s the painter Toss Woollaston remembered 'large-hatted, flowery-print-dressed women' pouring 'in gay and laughing hundreds' from a Stratford show special. By that time, however, the growing availability of cars and trucks in rural areas had already begun to eat away at show traffic.[13]

Other popular rural pastimes like ploughing and sheepdog competitions similarly relied on trains for the delivery of competitors, spectators and heavy equipment. Free-return concessions were granted to farmers attending 'prize ploughing matches' in 1900 and in the late 1920s were extended to include tractor-drawn ploughs. The first recorded sheepdog trials were held in South Canterbury in 1889 and at Porangahau, Hawke's Bay, in 1892. After requests from farmers, in 1899 NZR agreed to carry dogs to trials under the show clause, which allowed free return within a month of competition.[14] But not all mutts were created equal. When gundog and setter clubs sought similar allowances, the Department countered that the earlier concession had been 'granted in view of the importance of sheep dog trials to the sheep raising industry'. Canary and budgie fanciers were similarly rebuffed, the Department explaining that show concessions to poultry exhibitors represented 'a measure of assistance given . . . to the primary and secondary industries of the Dominion, the object being to encourage a higher standard of production generally'.[15]

For decades sheepdogs were a part of life on rural branch lines, often to the annoyance of railwaymen. J.M. Grainger, who worked on the Oxford branch in the 1940s, recalled that at every station 'we picked up or set down passengers, cream cans, bikes, cases of fruit, crates of fowls — and dogs, always dogs . . . how we cursed them. They would get into some awful tangles; they would tie the guard's legs up in their chains, they would slip their collars while travelling.'[16]

> For decades sheepdogs were a part of life on rural branch lines, often to the annoyance of railwaymen. J.M. Grainger, who worked on the Oxford branch in the 1940s, recalled that at every station 'we picked up or set down passengers, cream cans, bikes, cases of fruit, crates of fowls — and dogs, always dogs . . .'

Trainland

## Mail by Rail

'11.40 p.m. Mail train is due . . . Right behind the engine is coupled the postal van. The sliding door opens, the mail agents push out ten to a dozen well filled bags, swelling to 25 or more at Christmas.' This brief sketch, by a postal worker at Te Kuiti in 1927, highlights another of rail's key functions, in its first century at least. Mail was carried on trains in Britain as early as 1830 and in New Zealand from 1865, initially on the Southland provincial railway between Invercargill and Makarewa. In 1878, soon after taking over the provincial systems, the government introduced the first Railway Travelling Post Office (RTPO) on the main trunk between Christchurch and Dunedin, extending the service to Invercargill the following year. RTPOs operated between Wellington and New Plymouth from 1886 (initially on the joint WMR–NZR service), Auckland and Hamilton from 1901, and on the North Island main trunk from 1909. From the 1880s to the 1960s numerous other passenger and goods trains carried mail (in their guard's vans), as did many of NZR's Road Services vehicles. For a late fee of 1d or 2d, those who had missed the mail deadline could post letters at any station where the trains stopped, through cast-iron slots on the side of RTPOs or guard's vans.

Working as a travelling mail sorter was a demanding task. The sorters spent long shifts on their feet in rocking, swaying vans, often irritated by fine coal dust and smoke (RTPOs were initially placed directly behind the locomotive to facilitate loading; for reasons of comfort and safety they were later

*Mail sorters at work inside their RTPO van, around 1939.*

ATL, Making NZ Collection, F-2091-1/2-MNZ

shifted to the rear of the train). Delivering sacks of mail at stations where the train did not stop required good timing and a well-placed lob. RTPO veterans recalled wayward sacks clattering into rows of milk cans on the platform; on one occasion, a bag carelessly tossed out at Hampden, North Otago, hooked itself around the van's lamp fitting and sped all the way to Dunedin unnoticed. As road and air competition began to bite, most of the RTPOs were phased out between the 1930s and the 1950s. The last, on the North Island main trunk, was withdrawn in 1971.[17]

## Trainland

Along with mail, the expanding rail network accelerated the spread of newspapers, books, and weekly and monthly magazines. Between 1893 and 1913 the number of locally published monthly magazines almost doubled, from 22 to 40, many of them representing recently established farming, labour, sporting and religious organisations. Ranging in scope from the *New Zealand Dairyman* to the *New Zealand Primitive Methodist*, most were produced in the main centres and benefited from swift delivery to the regions. Trains also ferried motion picture reels from city to country, or brought film-goers into town for afternoon or evening screenings. City-based merchants, manufacturers and importers used rail to penetrate rural markets, their travelling salesmen utilising season tickets, discount rates for product samples and later special concession fares. In 1920s Southland, for example, the 'small smoking cars on railway branch lines were generally fully occupied with commercial men', who whiled away slow journeys with games of poker. 'Commercial' and 'Railway' hotels sprouted around stations to accommodate the influx.[18]

> **In 1920s Southland, for example, the 'small smoking cars on railway branch lines were generally fully occupied with commercial men', who whiled away slow journeys with games of poker.**

Passenger concessions also multiplied in the late nineteenth century. In 1877 NZR set conditions and rates for excursion and special trains, and offered season tickets (for one, three, six or twelve months), half-rate school season tickets and quarter rates for school parties of twenty or more. Children under fourteen (later twelve) could travel at half rates, with free travel for those under three. By 1880 concessions had been extended to apprentices, pupil teachers, newsboys selling papers aboard trains and 'Volunteers in uniform'. In 1884 Official Season Tickets were introduced for 'Government officers travelling on public service', and every newspaper was allowed to apply for two half-rate season tickets for its reporters. Concessions were granted to theatrical companies of ten or more (who also enjoyed special luggage rates) in 1885, to football, cricket and other sports teams in 1887, and to delegates attending meetings of religious bodies and friendly societies in 1889. The Liberal government's decision to return NZR operations to direct ministerial control in 1894 prompted a further flood of requests, many of which were declined. Nevertheless, by the end of the century concessions had been extended to navy recruits, judges of exhibits at shows and Maori travelling to Native Land Court hearings.[19]

## Business and Pleasure

> NEW ZEALAND GOVERNMENT RAILWAYS.
>
> AMERICAN FLEET AT AUCKLAND.
>
> FREE RAILWAY PASS.—First-class.
>
> Issued to Miss Barber
>
> **AVAILABLE BY PARLIAMENT SPECIAL ONLY.**
>
> From Wellington to Auckland, 7th August, 1908,
> and
> Auckland to Wellington, 17th August, 1908.
>
> This Free Pass is granted by the Railway on condition that it is to be used only by the person in whose favour it is issued, and that the use of it shall be taken as evidence of an agreement with the Minister that the latter is relieved from all pecuniary or other responsibility to the holder for personal injury, or for delay, or loss of or damage to property, however caused, that may be sustained by such person while using it.
> This Pass is to be exhibited when required, and the holder of it is subject to the By-laws and other general regulations of the Railways.
>
> _____ General Manager.

*No one enjoyed more generous rail concessions than members of Parliament, whose special gold medallions entitled them to free travel throughout New Zealand and, via a reciprocal arrangement, the Australian states. This free pass, signed by General Manager Thomas Ronayne, was issued to members travelling between Wellington and Auckland on the Parliament Special in August 1908.*

ANZ, AAVL, W3493, E4620

Another significant concession, introduced in 1882, was the issue of quarter-price 'privilege' tickets to railway employees 'and their wives'. With the Department employing nearly 5000 workers in the mid 1880s and 16,000 by the 1920s, this concession enabled many working families to enjoy holidays they could not have otherwise afforded. Janet Frame, the daughter of an engine driver, recalled how at Easter 1936 'we went for our first family holiday, on the train to Rakaia, traveling in a first-class "bird cage" [balcony carriage] on our annual free ticket'. In 1943, 'as a member of a Railway Family with a privilege or priv. ticket', Frame boarded a slow mixed train bound for 'Dunedin and my Future'. Later, in 1947, the family would take advantage of a less welcome benefit granted to railway workers — free conveyance of the corpses of family members — following the drowning of Janet's 20-year-old sister Isabel at Picton.[20]

In 1900, in response to parliamentary probing, NZR reported that its suite of concessions cost £75,200 a year. In nine years of Liberal government, ordinary passenger numbers had jumped from 3.4 to 5.5 million. More dramatically, the 63,335 season tickets issued in 1899/1900 represented an increase of 480 per cent over the same period.[21] Much of that growth was in suburban rail travel. In an attempt to clean up overcrowded

# Trainland

*In the 1890s and 1900s the Liberal government looked to railways to foster suburban settlement, which politicians saw as an antidote to inner-city congestion and vice. Later governments would continue to promote the healthy joys of suburban life and cheap rail commuting, as this 1930s hoarding illustrates.*

ANZ, AAVK, W3493, E7901

inner-city 'rookeries' or slums, which were seen as breeding grounds for disease, crime and vice, the Liberals encouraged working families to move to suburban allotments on the rural fringes of cities. These spacious 'garden suburbs', brimming with clean air, veggie plots and self-reliance, would surely produce vigorous, healthy and patriotic citizens. As well as low-interest loans, politicians recognised that swift, frequent and (above all) cheap transport was the key to convincing workers to quit the city for distant suburbs.

In 1894 the government reduced fares within ten miles of Auckland, Wellington, Christchurch, Dunedin and Invercargill stations, and introduced twelve-trip (that is, weekly) 'Workmen's Commutation Tickets' and 50-trip single and family commutation tickets for distances of up to twenty miles. By 1900 workmen's tickets had been reduced again to 2s a week. That year NZR issued more than 43,000 suburban season tickets; by 1914 the total topped 221,000.[22] Even so, many workers were reluctant to live so far from their workplaces, especially if they faced a long walk at each end of the trip. Ultimately, the Liberals' hoped-for suburban push would not take off until electric tramway and bus networks stretched out in the 1910s and 1920s, and later still with the advent of Labour's state housing programme and widespread private automobile ownership after the Second World War.

Business and Pleasure

# From Tawhiao to Ratana

Concessions for Maori attending Native Land Court hearings hint at rail's longstanding role as a Trojan horse of colonisation. Nevertheless, many Maori living in areas served by rail were regular train users, including, from the mid 1870s, Ngati Whatua on the Helensville line. Te Aute College's rugby team travelled by train in the mid 1880s, as did a Wairarapa poi dancing group at the turn of the century. In August 1881, shortly after making peace with the Crown, King Tawhiao undertook a celebrated journey from Mercer to Ngaruawahia with 500 followers in a fifteen-carriage special train; he even 'stripped to the shirt-sleeves' to ride on the locomotive and sounded the whistle to general amusement. The day was marred, however, by the grisly death of a young man who fell beneath the wheels while attempting to jump off near Taupiri. Although Tawhiao blamed the victim, others apparently saw the accident as a portent of the relentless advance of Pakeha power — headed by the snorting black ngarara (monster) of Te Kooti's prophecy.

So many Maori were using the Hawke's Bay line in the 1890s that Legislative Councillor Henare Tomoana (unsuccessfully) urged NZR to provide translations of

*Waiting for the train at Otaki railway station, around 1900.*

ATL, Malcolm Ross Collection, G-17586-1/4

75

# Trainland

station names, timetables and notices. In 1900, the businessman L.D. Nathan reported that 'on our Auckland line from Mercer to the Waikato Stations right down to Rotorua, there are very often a large number of Maories, men, women and children, who travel second class'. In 1903 Land Court fare concessions were extended to delegates attending Maori Councils, and from

*This special train brought mourners to Taupiri mountain for the burial of the Maori Queen in August 2006.*

New Zealand Herald / APN

Business and Pleasure

1901 to 1907 cheap fares were also available to mourners attending tangi. Catching the 'daytime slow-train' from Hamilton to his uncle's King Country farm in the 1910s, the writer Frank Sargeson was frequently 'the only passenger who was not Maori'.

Although New Zealand trains were never formally segregated — in contrast to those in the United States, India and many other countries — the presence of Maori was not always welcomed by Pakeha travellers. In 1900 Nathan complained to Railways Minister Joseph Ward that Maori passengers on the Rotorua line were 'anything but pleasant companions for ladies and gentlemen'; in 1924, after sharing a carriage with two sick Maori children, later diagnosed with typhoid, one woman urged that 'Maoris (living in a Maori fashion) should not be put in the same carriage with European women and children, particularly on a long express journey'. The Department ignored her plea.

Just after the end of the First World War, the sleepy Wanganui village of Ratana — eponymous home of the faith-healer and prophet Wiremu Tahupotiki Ratana — suddenly became one of New Zealand's busiest railway stations. Writing in 1921, the journalist Hector Bolitho reported that Pakeha along the main trunk were astonished to see 'train loads' of Maori travelling from the King Country and elsewhere. 'Special carriages were reserved for the pilgrims . . . and a special flag station was instituted near Ratana camp.' At Christmas 1920 dozens of trains disgorged more than 3000 visitors over several days. The following year Ratana himself hired a special train to lead 300 followers to Morrinsville, although his later tours of rail-starved Northland, Bay of Plenty and East Coast were undertaken by motor car.

Ngaruawahia station on the main trunk line also hosted large numbers of Maori attending ceremonial events at Turangawaewae marae, as in 1938 when trains from Auckland, Taumarunui and Wellington delivered hundreds of travellers, two tons of apples and three tons of fresh fish to the opening of King Koroki's new house. As recently as August 2006, a special train ferried mourners up the line from Ngaruawahia to Taupiri mountain for the burial of the Maori Queen, Dame Te Atairangikaahu.[23]

Trainland

# Off to School

Education, like railways, was initially the domain of provincial governments, although only the South Island provinces had achieved much by the time of their abolition in 1876. The Education Act 1877, which introduced free, secular and compulsory primary schooling, coincided with the peak of the Vogel railmaking boom. While most city and small-town children could walk to local schools, the government looked to railways to boost school attendance in rural districts. From July 1877 NZR offered season tickets to students up to sixteen years (raised to nineteen the following year) for 10s a quarter, while noting that 'First-class carriages are not guaranteed, except in the case of girls'. School parties of twenty or more could travel at less than 1d a mile. In 1879 season concession rates were extended to apprentices and pupil teachers, and in 1882 to teachers attending Saturday training classes. In each case, NZR's losses were covered from the Education Department's budget.

Children in isolated districts received extra attention. By 1884 the offspring of railway workers living in areas lacking 'any practicable access to school by road' (a reality at settlements like Summit on the Rimutaka line) were allowed free travel to the nearest primary school. The following year free passes were granted to all children up to fifteen attending government primary schools 'from railway stations where there is no primary school in the vicinity', a privilege extended to pupils of private (including Catholic) schools in 1889. In the last five years of the century the number of school season tickets soared from 1928 to 8720, with the Education Department's annual subsidy topping £3,000 (£1,000 of which covered private-school pupils). Although the 1900 figure represented only about 7 per cent of the national primary school roll, it included a significant proportion of children in country districts.[24]

> **In the last five years of the century the number of school season tickets soared from 1928 to 8720.**

Post-primary schooling was slower to develop. Until the twentieth century few working-class or small-farming families could afford the luxury of an extended education for their children. Through the 1890s and 1900s, however, the Liberal government pressed the fee-paying grammar schools to open their doors to more free-place pupils and established new district high and technical schools offering a broader curriculum. By 1895 Premier Seddon was urging further rail concessions, declaring it 'the desire of the Government to place secondary education within the reach of the poorest man in the Colony'. In 1898 season tickets were introduced for students up to the age of twenty travelling to technical schools or classes, and by

*School's out: New Plymouth Boys' High School pupils mill about a Taranaki school train.*

ANZ, E, W2694

1909 free passes were available to all students up to nineteen holding free-place scholarships to public or private secondary, district high or technical schools. School season tickets climbed sharply to 29,705 in 1914/15, when almost one in every seven primary and secondary students in the country took the train to school.[25]

Formal agricultural training was another latecomer to the educational scene. From the 1890s the small number of students taking agricultural courses — at Lincoln College in Canterbury and at a handful of high schools — enjoyed cheap fares when travelling for field instruction in parties of at least five. Later, in 1926,

SECOND CLASS

Business and Pleasure

concessions were granted to boys journeying to the Flock House training farm near Bulls, through which a hundred British youths passed each year courtesy of the New Zealand Sheepowners' Acknowledgement of Debt to British Seamen Fund. In 1929 the recently opened Massey Agricultural College successfully sought concessions for dairy factory workers, herd testers and young farmers travelling to courses in Palmerston North. NZR's developmental mission was again evident in General Manager H.H. Sterling's comment that while he did not anticipate 'a very substantially increased traffic from the concession . . . it would be a sound investment from the country's point of view'. The privilege was soon extended to Lincoln, which in 1936 also hosted an open day for 430 farmers travelling by special train.[26]

From the late nineteenth century rail travel was a daily shared ritual for thousands of primary, secondary and technical school students. As early as 1886 a Nelson MP claimed that 'even now the railways are taken up to a great extent by the children going to the different schools'. Those who lived at some distance from the nearest station faced extremely long days. The writer Frank Anthony, who attended Hawera District High School in 1906–7, 'had to ride 6 miles, catch a train which got him to Hawera at 10 a.m., walk another mile where he arrived 3/4 of an hour late, leave school at 3 to reverse the process, reaching home in winter after dark'. And, like many farm kids, he had to collect and milk cows before and after school.

To the dismay of guards, schoolchildren often created mayhem on trains, skylarking and fighting, riding on the platforms between cars, jumping off before the train had stopped, applying the hand-brakes and smoking on the sly. Boys

*Schoolgirls from Seddonville in the Buller district on board a train in 1945. Photographer John Pascoe noted that 'Some of these children spend up to six hours a day travelling between their homes and their high school.'*

ATL, JD Pascoe Collection, F-1336-1/4

81

# Trainland

and girls were rigidly segregated, but rules were endlessly broken. A student who travelled two hours each way between Matata and Te Puke High School in the 1920s recalled how boys and girls were put in separate carriages with another in between. Undeterred, the boys would clamber onto the roof of their carriage, then 'walk along the tops and get down on to the rear platform' of the girls' car. 'None of us ever fell off,' he happily reported.[27]

Children also enjoyed regular school excursions. Keen to ingrain rail-travelling habits among the young, the Department noted in its 1895 annual report that cheap excursions for 'school-children and their parents' had not been 'initiated solely for revenue purposes, but chiefly as a means of education, and to popularise railway-travelling . . . [T]he result of this will be apparent in the future.' In her novel *The Godwits Fly*, Robin Hyde described a picnic excursion run for the poor schoolchildren of Wellington's Newtown. As they passed 'red-painted stations, stinking of freezing-works and sheds where tallow is rendered down . . . the excursionists sang lustily':

> Kaiwarra, Ngaurangha, Petone,
> Kaiwarra, Ngaurangha, Petone,
> Kaiwarra, Ngaurangha, Petone,
> The next stop is The Hutt.[28]

On occasions school trips proved too popular, especially with adults. In 1898 the *New Zealand Times* complained that recent school excursion trains had been 'so crowded with "grown-ups" that numbers of youngsters have been left behind'. Although the number of adult escorts was not allowed to exceed that of the children, on one excursion from Waimanawa to Colac 53 children were thoroughly supervised by 94 adults. Declaring that the Department 'cannot permit School Excursions to be made a pretext for Holiday Excursions by adult passengers,' General Manager Thomas Ronayne forced the school committee to fork out an extra 41 adult fares.[29] After all, he added, adults had their own generous holiday excursions.

## 'Pleasure Parties'

As the rough-hewn pioneering era was succeeded by a more settled, urbanised society in the late nineteenth and early twentieth centuries, New Zealanders sought new opportunities for leisure and relaxation. The popularity of rail travel both reflected and contributed to these changing leisure patterns. As health experts stressed the benefits of physical activity, sunshine and fresh air, people flocked to beaches and parks to picnic and paddle, frolic and fry. If city dwellers could not live by the sea or in the countryside, railways at least allowed them regular visits to recharge their batteries. Improved transport links also exposed urban New Zealanders to the fatal impact of forest clearance and agricultural development on the environment, strengthening calls for the preservation of surviving forest remnants for their scenic and scientific value. This contributed to the establishment of scenic reserves and national parks at Tongariro in 1894, Egmont (Taranaki) in 1900 and Arthur's Pass in 1929 (see Chapter 3). Accessible by rail, these parks provided city dwellers with new opportunities for sightseeing, tramping, hunting and skiing.

Sunday excursion trains were run on the New Plymouth–Waitara line as early as May 1876, despite complaints from local churchmen that 'pleasure parties going out on Sundays were the Devil's travellers'. Even before lines were completed, excursions allowed townsfolk to observe the onward march of progress, while crowded special trains ferried dignitaries and spectators to the sites of first sod, last spike or station-opening ceremonies. On the opening day of the Moeraki line in November 1876, two trains fetched more than 600 people from Oamaru. When the second was delayed at Hampden on the way back, 'sleeping youngsters, weary women and drunken men' were treated to an 'impromptu dance . . . with music provided by a tin whistle', before eventually getting home at 2.30 am. Three years later, an excursion from Invercargill ferried 479 people, including the town's brass band, to Bluff to celebrate the Prince of Wales' birthday.[30]

*As well as catering for the picnicking public, the Railways Department ran regular excursions and events for its employees and their families, like this New Plymouth 'Railway Picnic & Sports' day at Easter 1884.*

Reproduced in NZRM, Apr 1935

# Trainland

*Even bush tramways had their picnic trains. In this January 1911 image, New Year's picnickers perch precariously atop logging wagons near the King Country settlement of Manunui.*

ATL, Levesque Collection, F-84474-1/2

From 1877 NZR offered excursions where at least 120 passengers were guaranteed, while organisations like churches and friendly societies could whistle up special trains (at a rate of £1 per mile) that would wait at least five hours at their destination before returning. By 1882 the minimum excursion number and the rate for special trains had each been halved, and NZR was running regular services at Christmas, Easter, the Prince of Wales' birthday and the days of major shows and race meetings.[31]

Aside from the attractions of their destination, excursions were an adventure in themselves, offering passengers the chance to experience the novelty and thrill of rail travel, often for the first time. Crucially, they were also far cheaper than full-fare travel. In the mid 1880s, for example, a standard second-class return from Christchurch to Timaru cost 18s on the weekend and £1 7s during the week — no small change at a time when labourers on railmaking projects did well to earn 8s a day. As Minister of Public Works Edward Richardson noted in 1885, 'these trains give an opportunity of travelling to a very large class of the public who would not otherwise afford it'. The workplace, school, church, club or friendly society picnic became a New Zealand tradition, especially for larger employers like woollen mills, freezing works and the NZR's own workshops. The fatal Rakaia collision in 1899, for example, involved two special trains with 3000 passengers returning from the Islington freezing works' annual picnic at Ashburton. Even inmates of lunatic asylums could enjoy picnics by rail: from 1882 trains ferried Nelson patients to an annual picnic at Brightwater, and the Auckland asylum followed suit in the 1890s.[32]

Although the Department was aware of the promotional value of excursion fares, it kept a sharp eye on returns, especially during the depressed 1880s. Despite claims in the press that seaside trips to Caroline Bay, Timaru, had 'proved a small gold mine', in 1888 the Department decided to operate excursions on 'a more limited basis' than in the past three years, 'careful consideration having shown that as a rule this traffic has not

Aside from the attractions of their destination, excursions were an adventure in themselves, offering passengers the chance to experience the novelty and thrill of rail travel, often for the first time.

# Trainland

paid, and that the very low fares, too frequently granted, divert people from travelling at the ordinary fares'. By 1895 NZR was trying to encourage longer trips, introducing new holiday excursion tickets at a 'slightly higher' rate of 2d per mile first class and 1d second class, with 'extended' excursion tickets for Christmas and Easter holidays. To publicise the new rates, which he hoped 'will bring about a much larger holiday traffic', General Manager Ronayne authorised the printing of handbills for distribution to stations and schools and house-to-house delivery in the main centres. In 1902 Ronayne reported that new Christmas tickets (on sale from 18 December to 2 January but available for return travel until 19 February) were fulfilling 'the purpose for which they were introduced', that is, 'to place a holiday trip within reach of the masses'.[33]

Still, relatively few working people could afford long breaks from work or the cost of overnight accommodation, even if it was available. Day excursions remained the most popular form of escape. On Easter Saturday 1904, despite howling weather, trains from Dunedin station ferried more than 3000 passengers — as many as one in eight of the central city's inhabitants — to events and scenic spots near and far:

> The principal attraction for residents was the race meeting at Mosgiel, to which about 625 persons journeyed by rail; and next in public favour was the show at Middlemarch, to which place some 200 people travelled . . . Seacliff appears to be a very popular holiday resort, and no less that 260 passengers journeyed there, while about 120 travelled to Waitati, and about 40 to Puketeraki, and a similar number to Warrington. A little more than 200 tickets were issued to Mosgiel Junction, the purchasers of some no doubt going to the races, and on the branch lines — Lawrence, Catlins River, and Otago Central — about 400 people were carried.[34]

Seacliff may have been a 'popular holiday resort', but some travellers there were probably visiting relatives at the local lunatic asylum — euphemistically referred to as those who had been 'sent up the line' (or, in Oamaru, 'down the line').

On Labour Day that year 'the popular holiday resorts along the railway' were again 'well patronised', with around 1100 journeying to stations north of Dunedin and another 500 heading to Mosgiel, Milton and other branch-line stations. Races, shows and sports events remained the principal drawcards: in 1906 the '20th annual sports gathering of the Strath-Taieri Caledonian Society' at Middlemarch lured another 1200 day-trippers out of the city, 'of whom a goodly proportion visited the sports, whilst numbers of small parties could be seen in various nooks enjoying a picnic holiday'. As these reports suggest, excursions to beach, bush and racetrack were marketed to urban dwellers, offering them a temporary respite from the congested inner city with all its supposed evils. As Minister of Railways William Hall-Jones explained in 1906, the 'object of the week-end excursion tickets is to enable the people who live in the crowded areas to spend a day in the fresh air of the country. Country people do not require the issue of tickets for this purpose, as they live in healthy surroundings all the year round.'[35]

Country folk did not miss out entirely though, with numerous specials running to A&P Shows, royal receptions and other events. In 1901, for example, more than a hundred locals travelled from Ormondville (population 459) to the Palmerston North show, while in 1913 a special train brought Helensville residents to Auckland to see the visiting battlecruiser HMS *New Zealand*. Holiday excursion fares were also available on all trains to Christchurch during the six-month season of the New Zealand International Exhibition in 1906–7, when 352,753 rail travellers flocked to the city from all over the country.[36]

In 1912/13 the annual tally of excursion tickets topped one million for the first time, before falling away during the war years. Despite increasing competition from cars and buses, excursion traffic would rally in the 1920s and again in the late thirties, when NZR ran popular 'Snow Specials' to Arthur's Pass in addition to its regular picnic, beach and show excursions. As we shall see in Chapter 3, by that time rising wages, shorter working hours and smaller family sizes were putting longer holidays within reach of more New Zealand families, helping to make the interwar years the golden age of rail tourism.

*A long A$^B$-hauled picnic train, packed with Presbyterian parishioners from Timaru, drifts into Studholme on its way home from a Sunday excursion to Waimate's Victoria Park. This photograph was taken in March 1961, in the twilight years of Canterbury's summer picnic trains.*

Euan McQueen

*Wirth's Circus elephants draw a crowd of enthralled onlookers at Pukekohe in 1956.*

ANZ, AAVK, W3493, D4251

## The Circus is Coming

One of the entertainment highlights of the year in towns and cities all over New Zealand was the travelling circus, with its big-top tent, 'wild' animals, elephants, clowns, acrobats, fire-breathers and freak shows. Famous circuses like the Australian-based Wirth's (which first toured New Zealand in 1890), Ridgway's and Barton Brothers relied on special trains to transport their animals and performers, marquees and merry-go-rounds, while other trains brought circus-goers from neighbouring towns.

For a young boy in 1920s Balclutha, the arrival of Wirth's Circus — anticipated for weeks via posters and hoardings — was 'an event fit to rank with the annual Show Day'. The unloading of the trains in the early morning was almost as exciting as the main course, especially when elephants were used to shunt wagons: 'there came looming, with his great head thrust against the buffer beam, his feet shuffling the ballast of the little country station yard — my Lord the Elephant'. Other wagons served as colourful mobile homes and cookhouses for exotic performers and carnies. After the evening's performance everything was packed up and quickly railed away: 'next morning Sinclair's paddock would again be bare and empty'.

Engine-driver Rex Hercock, who drove several Wirth's trains from the 1930s, recalled how the elephants would forage trackside trees with their long trunks and terrify grazing horses. Circus trains survived until the 1970s, when the waning popularity of traditional circuses — a result of changing entertainment patterns and public concern over animal cruelty — led to their widespread replacement by newer, smaller shows transported by trucks.[37]

Business and Pleasure

## Track and Field

The popularity of excursions by families and 'pleasure parties' in the late nineteenth century was matched by a surge in participation in organised sport. Railways encouraged touring by local teams, fostered regional and national competitions, and enabled spectators to travel to matches. As in other areas, rail also helped stimulate the formation of national organisations such as the New Zealand Lawn Tennis Association (1886), the Racing Conference and the Amateur Athletics Association (both 1887), the Football Association (1891), Rugby Football Union (1892) and the Cricket Council (1894). Concession rates for touring sports teams dated from at least 1885, with rugby and cricket teams being offered return travel for single rates, Saturday fares during the week, or first-class seats at second-class prices. The system was formalised in 1887, when 'Football, Cricket, Tennis and Bowling teams' of fifteen (later twelve) members were granted first-class weekday travel at Saturday second-class rates; the same rights were soon extended to rowing, golf, rifle and other clubs.[38]

Horse races were a prime attraction for rail day-trippers. One of New Zealand's earliest European sports, racing grew from a purely local pursuit to a major national sport in the 1870s and eighties, as railways facilitated the swift and reliable delivery of racehorses (in specially designed horse wagons), trainers, jockeys and punters. In 1873–4, just days after the opening of Auckland's first railway, special trains ran to the Boxing Day and New Year races at Ellerslie, with a 3s return ticket including admission to the course: 'the whistling of the engines,

*A day at the races: this tattered 1904 poster outlines special fares and arrangements for October meetings at Wellington's Hutt Park.*

ANZ, AAVK, W3493, D48.058

# Trainland

*Those involved in individual pursuits were not as well catered for as team sportspeople, but they did not miss out entirely on rail concessions, as this advertisement for anglers' excursion tickets shows.*

ATL, NON-ATL-0157 / ANZ, AAOK, W3241, 101

and the landing on the platform at the course of the hundreds of gaily dressed passengers, all produced a very animated effect'. Private companies built lines to racetracks at Forbury Park, Dunedin (1877) and Hutt Park, Wellington (1885), while the Canterbury Jockey Club and the Manawatu Racing Club built their own sidings (in 1877 and 1904 respectively).

As well as offering concession rates for jockeys, trainers and racehorses, NZR ran frequent race-day shuttle services from central Auckland to Ellerslie and Avondale, from Wellington to Trentham, Christchurch to Addington and Riccarton, and Dunedin to Wingatui. Special trains also brought punters from further afield: meetings at Thames and Matamata were served by trains from Auckland, Trentham meetings by specials from Palmerston North and Masterton, and Oamaru races by services from Dunedin and Christchurch. Other horse sports benefited too, with the Department's concessions for '[r]acehorses, hunters, and polo ponies returned free from races, hunts, and polo matches' in 1900 amounting to £2,800.[39]

'. . . the whistling of the engines, and the landing on the platform at the course of the hundreds of gaily dressed passengers, all produced a very animated effect.'

Rail played a similar role in the development of team sports. A flurry of new football and cricket clubs in the 1880s and 1890s followed in the footsteps of the Vogel railmaking boom. Many public works and railway settlements fielded their own teams, and rural club matches were frequently timed to fit in with train timetables. Regional tours and interprovincial fixtures soon followed, promoting the codification of rules and establishment of national administrative bodies. The development of association football's Brown Shield (first contested in 1892) and Chatham Cup (1923), rugby's Ranfurly Shield (1904), and cricket's Plunket Shield

(1906) and Hawke Cup (1910) all benefited from reliable rail services. Visiting international teams also travelled widely by train, including the New South Wales rugby sides of 1886 and 1894 (which played twelve matches on each occasion), and English and Australian cricket XIs.

As well as transporting players, horses and equipment, railways allowed spectators to attend sporting events further from home and in far greater numbers than before. In 1914/15, for example, special trains ferried more than 6000 passengers to the Marlborough, Bluff and Riverton regattas, 1547 to the Caledonian sports at Timaru, 424 to watch the Australian cricket XI play Canterbury, and 8219 to Wellington's Labour Day races.[40] A Marlborough farmer recalled a boisterous crowd boarding the 7.30 am train from Ward to Blenheim to support their rugby team in a match against Buller:

> For probably half an hour before departure the passengers have been arriving at the station. Some have travelled quite a distance, picking up their neighbours on the way ... [T]he older people have come in traps, the younger ones on their hacks or bicycles ... The ladies go into the non-smokers, the men into the smoker carriages. There is continual banter among them as some want to have a bet on who is going to win. The carriages are cold. No central heating here. The young folk keep warm by wrestling and others argue the good and bad points of the local team. Many arguments get very heated.

Reaching Blenheim at 10 am, the fans crowded into restaurants and pubs before and after the game. They later trickled back to the station for the 8 pm return, the

*Exuberant Waikato rugby fans crowd aboard the 'Mooloo Special' from Frankton to Wellington, en route to a Ranfurly Shield challenge in Christchurch in August 1954. The return journey may not have been so enjoyable: Canterbury scored a last-minute try to tie the match 6–6 and retain the trophy.*

ANZ, AAVK, W3493, D1155

## Trainland

*On the first anniversary of the Gallipoli landings, 25 April 1916, a commemorative flagpole made from kauri and Australian hardwood — symbolising 'the unity of Australian and New Zealand railwaymen in peace and war' — was unveiled at Petone railway station. Although the old station has since been demolished, the flagpole was partially restored in 1985 and completely refurbished in 2005.*

ATL, AP Godber Collection, G-589-1/2-APG

last stragglers scrambling aboard 'in the traditional way of the half-drunk'. On the two-and-a-half-hour return trip, 'there was never any dearth of fun and entertainment': 'Patsy Meehan would endeavour to play a tune on his pipe, someone would fish out a mouth organ, there were recitations Banjo Paterson style. Comedy acts were put on . . . football songs, choruses.'[41] Of course, not all fans were content discussing tactics or singing songs, and from the early twentieth century NZR would face regular problems with drunken and disorderly sportsmen and supporters (see Chapter 4).

## Trouble and Strife

The steady expansion of passenger and excursion traffic since the 1880s came to a shuddering halt towards the end of the First World War. With troop trains ferrying thousands of soldiers to training camps and ports for overseas departure, overall passenger journeys initially increased, topping 24 million — the highest totals yet — in both 1915/16 and 1916/17. Dozens of temporary camps were established at showgrounds and racecourses, which offered wide open spaces and good rail links: by mid 1915 Trentham on Wellington's Wairarapa line housed over 8000 men; Hautapu, near Cambridge, handled 6000 troops and 2000 horses at its specially enlarged yards and loading banks.[42] The Department's workshops played a vital role in domestic war production, turning out ammunition carts, limbers and (at Petone) Maxim machine-guns. Railway workers were also quick to answer the call of King and Country: by March 1916 over 1728 had enlisted and 52 had been killed. Eventually, more than 5000 NZR employees served during the war, winning one Victoria Cross, two DSOs and thirteen Military Crosses; 447 failed to return.[43]

By mid 1917 NZR was struggling to cope with labour shortages, dwindling coal supplies and restrictions on overseas shipping, which strangled the flow of imported parts and slowed domestic trade. As well as suspending some express and suburban services, the Department ordered 'the abolition of all excursion trains and trains to and from racecourses, sports meetings, [and] picnics'. By March 1918, 1.7 million train-miles had been pruned from the timetable. As the chart on page 94 illustrates, the sale of holiday, school, factory and friendly society excursion tickets plummeted from 983,732 in 1916/17 to zero two years later. In another drastic move, dining cars were removed from service in an attempt to reduce costs, increase passenger capacity on existing trains, free up rolling stock for other uses and release more workers for the war effort. Like six o'clock closing of pubs, also introduced in 1917, this 'temporary' wartime measure would endure for half a century. As we shall see in Chapter 4, the subsequent reliance on station dining and refreshment rooms would become a defining feature of NZR's people's railway.[44]

# Trainland

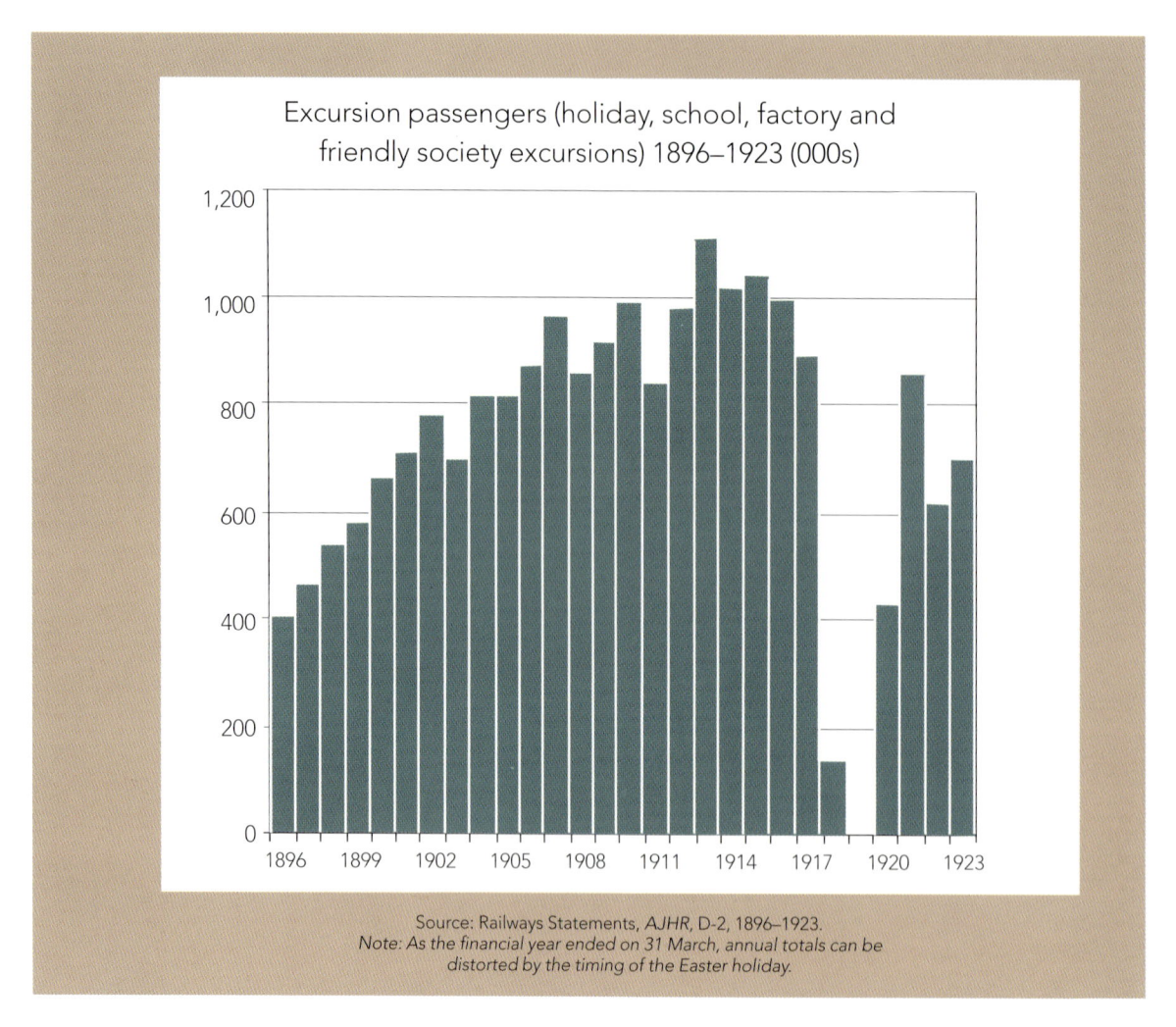

**Excursion passengers (holiday, school, factory and friendly society excursions) 1896–1923 (000s)**

Source: Railways Statements, *AJHR*, D-2, 1896–1923.
Note: As the financial year ended on 31 March, annual totals can be distorted by the timing of the Easter holiday.

Dark clouds lingered for several years after the war. The deadly influenza pandemic of November 1918 brought the whole country to a standstill, including much of the rail system, while a deepening coal crisis forced a new wave of service cuts in July 1919.[45] The Department and its workers struggled with ongoing staff shortages and deferred maintenance and improvements. Pent-up frustrations sparked a rail strike in 1920 that briefly stranded the visiting Prince of Wales in Rotorua, followed by a second, more serious stoppage in 1924. Despite industrial unrest and a short but sharp economic recession in 1921–2, passenger and excursion numbers rallied early in the decade, with total journeys topping 28 million a year from 1921 to 1924.

By that time, however, railways were facing an unprecedented challenge, as the nation's roads began to

'The end of the German sausage': Gore railwaymen celebrated Armistice Day in November 1918 by decorating locomotive F 78 and wagon with wilting greenery, imitation sausages and a blunt chalked message to the Kaiser.

NZRLS, RJ Meyer Collection, A327-1/2

fill with motor cars, buses and trucks. A notable feature of Coates' first Railways Statement in 1923 was a section on 'Motor Competition', in which he conceded that 'road-motors' undoubtedly had 'a legitimate field' but hoped that their use would be 'supplementary to, rather than competitive with, the railways'.[46] His optimism was sadly misplaced. Over the following decades, and especially after the Second World War, motor transport would lure away many key rail customers, including legions of farmers, schoolchildren, commuters and excursion day-trippers.

In the meantime, as the Minister noted, the Department was already investigating the electrification of suburban lines, the use of 'motor-trains' (railcars) and the introduction of its own motor bus services. The Coates era would also usher in a bold marketing programme centred on the activities of a departmental Publicity Branch and the publication of one of New Zealand's most popular magazines. To safeguard its uncertain prospects in volatile times NZR would embrace the so-called 'Cinderella industry' — tourism — and help thousands of ordinary New Zealanders explore their country by rail.

# Exploring New Zealand

# CHAPTER 3

# Trainland

> From the days of Marco Polo
> Down to those of Captain Cook,
> Enlightenment Opportunity Pleasure Profit
> Have been the fruits of
> TRAVEL
> Explore New Zealand:
> To travel in comfort, travel by
> RAIL
>
> — NZR advertisement, 1925[1]

The golden age of rail in New Zealand is often placed in the interwar years, especially the 1920s. Half a century after Vogel's grand vision, NZR was riding high as the country's premier land-based passenger and freight carrier, especially over longer hauls. The North and South Island main trunks, linked by the Union Steam Ship Company's Wellington–Lyttelton ferry service, formed the steel backbone of the national transport system. Almost everyone travelling between the main centres — politicians, businessmen, public servants, entertainers, sports teams, soldiers, local holidaymakers and overseas visitors — took the train. Although the war had delayed earlier development plans, the 1920s would also see a significant expansion of the national network. In 1923 the transalpine line between Christchurch and Greymouth was completed, a mere 37 years after the ill-fated Midland Company had begun work. In the North Island, rails stretched north and eastwards to link Auckland with Whangarei and Opua (1925) and Tauranga and Taneatua (1928). Gaps still remained in the national grid, but by the interwar years only the most isolated citizens lived beyond rail's reach.

PREVIOUS PAGE: U$^B$ 284 all dressed up to haul the Duke and Duchess of Cornwall's 'Royal train' between Christchurch and Dunedin in 1901, as painted by W.W. Stewart. Locomotives were often decorated on holidays and other special occasions.

Grantham House Publishing

RIGHT: The completion of the Northland, Bay of Plenty and Midland lines in the 1920s helped make the interwar years the heyday of rail tourism. An early traveller on the Auckland–Opua line was the American novelist and big-game fisherman Zane Grey, who trumpeted the Bay of Islands as an 'Angler's Eldorado'. This 1938 poster was designed by John Holmwood.

ATL, Eph-E-RAIL-1930s-02

### Exploring New Zealand

In the twelve months to March 1923 — the first of Gordon Coates' five dynamic years as Minister of Railways — NZR sold over 14 million ordinary tickets and 486,000 season tickets, altogether adding up to more than 28 million journeys — a stunning achievement for a nation of little over a million people. The same year, railways carried more than six million tons of freight — the highest total yet recorded — including almost eight million cattle, sheep and pigs, and 663,000 tons of timber.

Coates and NZR's managers presided over a vast and complex empire that included 3037 miles of track, 1120 stations and stopping places, five heavy engineering workshops, 639 locomotives, 1498 passenger carriages and 26,106 wagons. The Railways Department was New Zealand's largest employer, with a workforce of 15,728 and an annual wage bill of almost £4 million. Apart from trains, it operated its own telegraph and telephone network (with 7630 miles of wire), advertising studios, quarries, forests, sawmills, a railway-house factory at Frankton Junction, and a steamer service on Lake Wakatipu.[2]

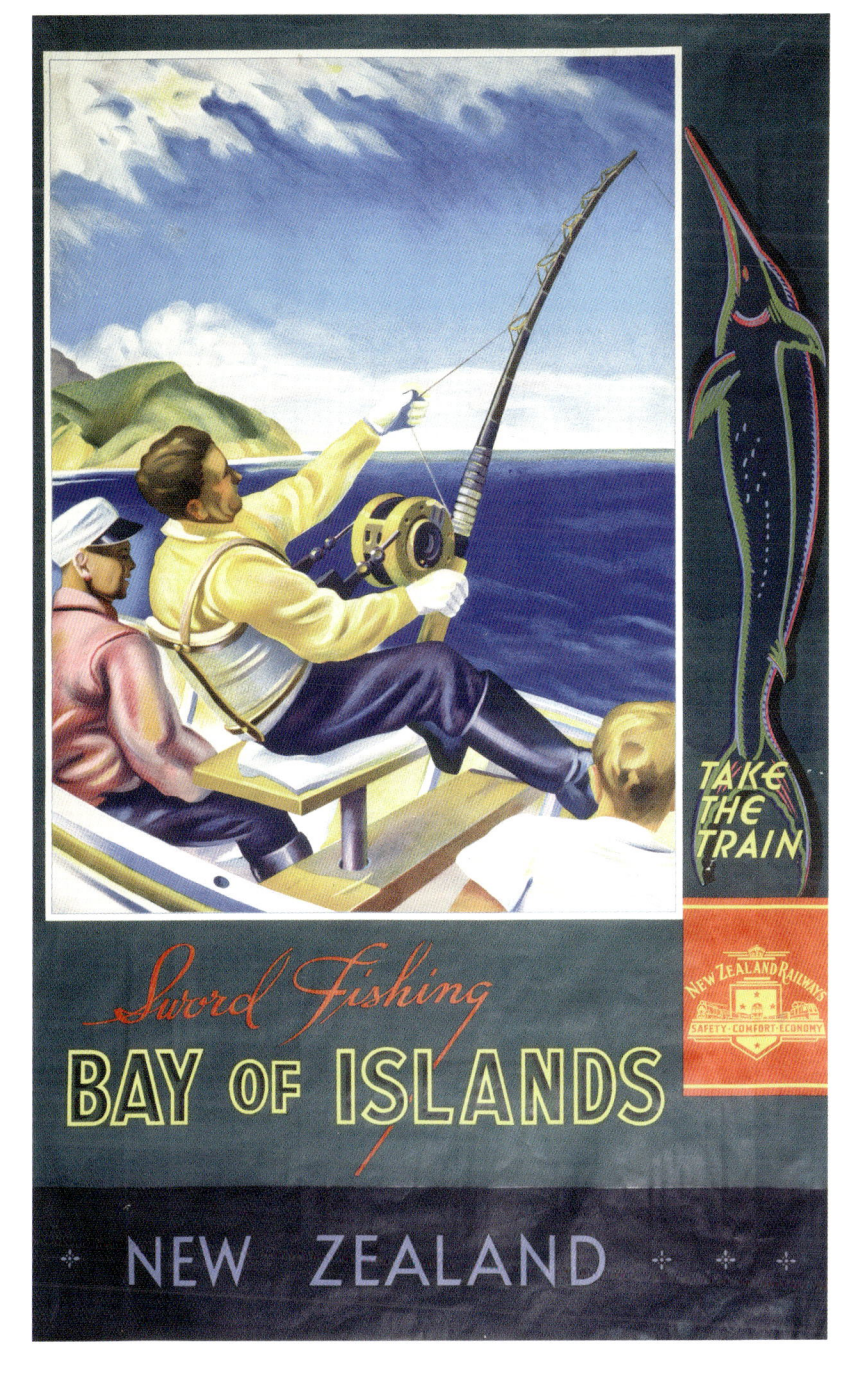

Trainland

## Rollercoaster Ride

So-called golden ages, however, are usually inventions of hindsight, evoked in part to highlight the inadequacies of a less satisfying present. Certainly, as the country emerged from the debris of war, pandemic and recession, the 1920s crackled with energy and optimism, personified by the breezy confidence of Coates himself. Later, after the tough Depression years of the early 1930s, a new Labour government resumed Reform's modernisation drive, revived rail's developmental role and breathed new life into the people's railway. Throughout the period, however, railways struggled to shake off a creeping insecurity, a fear that the good times were about to end.

The chart opposite illustrates the rollercoaster ride of NZR's passenger business during the interwar years. Total passenger journeys recovered strongly from the immediate postwar downturn to top 28 million each year from 1921 to 1924 — the highest ever achieved in peacetime, and exceeded only by the war-related surge in the mid 1940s. In 1932/3, in the depths of Depression, they would crash to 18 million, the lowest figure for more than two decades. But while the Depression slump was predictable, the slide in fact began much earlier, in the mid 1920s; by 1929/30, total journeys had already slipped to 25 million. If suburban commuters and school pupils travelling on season tickets are excluded, the decline is even more striking. From 15 million in 1920/1, sales of ordinary passenger tickets tumbled to eight million in 1929/30.[3]

> **Total passenger journeys recovered strongly from the immediate postwar downturn to top 28 million each year from 1921 to 1924.**

There was no mystery over the primary cause of rail's reversal: in the second half of the 1920s ownership of private motor cars more than doubled, from 71,403 to 150,571. With one car for every nine people, New Zealanders were among the world's most auto-mobile citizens. By 1930 there were also 1269 'omnibuses' on the roads, already carrying more than two million passengers a year, and almost 30,000 trucks. With their flexible services and competitive rates, road carriers soon captured much of rail's short-haul goods and parcels business. But the modest load-carrying capacity of trucks — and strict government regulation from the 1930s — limited their ability to challenge rail's dominance of long-distance or bulk freight. Despite increasingly intense competition, rail tonnage grew steadily through the 1920s, reaching 7.8 million tons in 1929/30.[4] Neither passenger nor freight traffic, however, would escape the impact of economic collapse in the early 1930s.

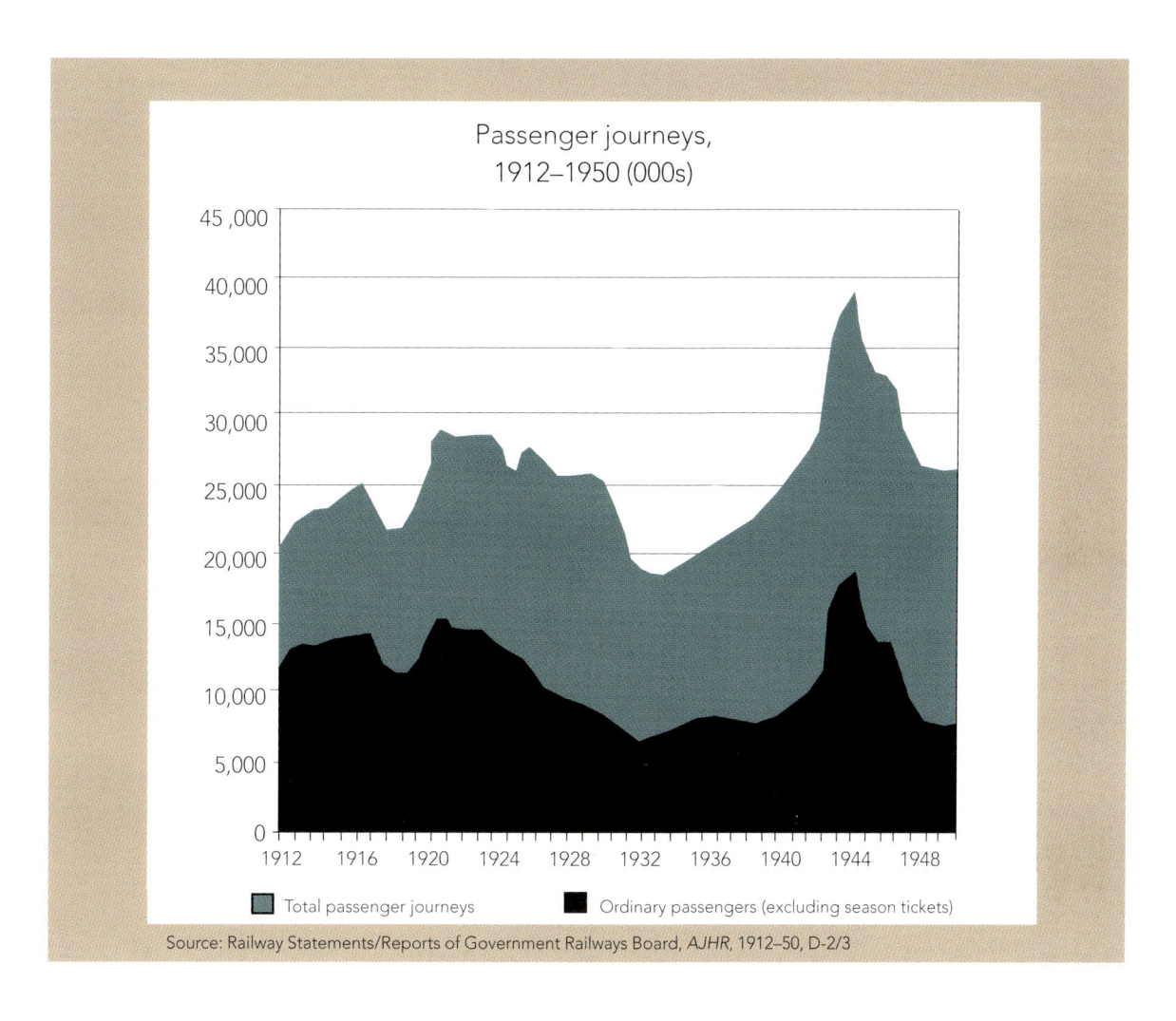

## Exploring New Zealand

**Passenger journeys, 1912–1950 (000s)**

■ Total passenger journeys   ■ Ordinary passengers (excluding season tickets)

Source: Railway Statements/Reports of Government Railways Board, *AJHR*, 1912–50, D-2/3

NZR was far from alone in facing these challenges. The automobile age threatened rail passenger numbers and profits in Britain, the United States, Australia and elsewhere. Total route mileage and passenger journeys on British railways both peaked in 1927, before beginning a long-term slide. Passenger traffic on American railroads declined throughout that decade and by 1928 had dipped below 1905 levels.[5] But unlike most American or European rail operators, NZR had enjoyed an effective monopoly for most of its history. Apart from publicising special services and excursions, it had hardly needed to advertise the benefits of rail travel, which it presumed were obvious to all. Before the First World War, trains were generally quicker, more reliable and more comfortable than their chief rivals, the coastal steamer and the stagecoach, or even the

## Trainland

early motor cars. By the mid 1920s nothing could be taken for granted.

Coates and his successors responded with a flurry of initiatives, including an invitation to two British experts, Sir Sam Fay and Sir Vincent Raven, to investigate the entire railway system in 1924/5.[6] Over the following years, the Department's management structure, staff training and financial systems were overhauled. Its outdated workshops were modernised and two completely new ones were built at Otahuhu and Lower Hutt. New services, modern carriages and larger locomotives were introduced, and massive new stations were planned for Auckland and Wellington. In an attempt to meet motor competition head on, the Department launched its own Road Services branch, and soon became one of the country's largest bus and coach operators. As well as these developments, this chapter explores two other key features of the interwar years: NZR's vigorous promotion of rail tourism, and efforts to revamp its image and performance through advertising and publicity.

RIGHT: As well as pushing day and weekend excursions, NZR actively promoted longer-distance tourist traffic from the late nineteenth century. This 1923 poster offers a four-week Tourist Ticket for each island for £10 (around $810 in today's money) or a seven-week nationwide pass for £16 5s ($1,300).

ATL, NON-ATL-0020 / ANZ, AAOK, W3241, 85

## On the Tourist Trail

NZR had run regular excursions ferrying picnickers, 'pleasure parties' and punters to beach, showground and racetrack since the late 1870s. The South Island led the way, with Timaru's Caroline Bay and Lake Wakatipu popular early destinations. It took longer for rail to reach the North Island's tourist spots, although the spa town of Te Aroha was linked to Auckland via Frankton Junction and Morrinsville in 1886. Rotorua and its surrounding 'thermal wonderland' had long been hailed as the jewel in New Zealand's tourism crown, but although the government took over work on a private railway from Morrinsville to Rotorua in 1885, construction dragged on for another nine years. In the meantime, from 1892 NZR offered cheap three-day excursion tickets from Auckland to both Te Aroha and Rotorua (with coach connections from the existing railhead). But longer holidays were harder to sell than day excursions, mainly because of the cost and scarcity of overnight accommodation. 'What would the Te Aroha people do,' a district traffic manager asked in 1892, 'with 300 young men from Saturday to Monday?' Nevertheless, the introduction in 1894 of the Auckland–Rotorua express — for a decade Auckland's only 'express' train — paved the way for a tourist boom in the region, and helped push the Liberal government towards more direct involvement in the industry.[7]

# NEW ZEALAND RAILWAYS

## TOURIST TICKETS

**TOURIST TICKETS**
ON THE
NEW ZEALAND GOVERNMENT RAILWAYS
(3037 MILES)
On Sale at the Principal Stations.

Over All Lines (Available for Seven Weeks) - - - £16 5s.
Over North Island Lines (Available for Four Weeks) £10 0s.
Over South Island Lines (Available for Four Weeks) £10 0s.

Also available on Lake Wakatipu Steamers.

These Tickets may be extended for a period up to Four Weeks at a charge of £2 10s. per week or portion of a week.

**HOLIDAY EXCURSION TICKETS**
AT REDUCED FARES
ISSUED AT CHRISTMAS, NEW YEAR, EASTER, AND OTHER HOLIDAY PERIODS AS ADVERTISED

# Trainland

From the mid 1890s NZR offered 'extended' Christmas and Easter excursion tickets and publicised them through commercially printed posters and home-delivered handbills in the main centres. At the same time, the Department teamed up with the country's two largest private tourist operators, the Union Steam Ship Company and Thomas Cook and Sons, to push combined rail/steamer trips and rail/coach tours of the North Island's 'Hot Lakes District' and the South's 'Cold Lakes and Glacial District'. In January 1901 the new Minister of Railways, Joseph Ward, established a Tourist Office within the Railways Department, and a month later convinced fellow ministers to create an independent Department of Tourist and Health Resorts — the first dedicated government tourist department in the world. As its first Superintendent, Ward picked T. Edward Donne, who had spent 25 years in the railways service, including sixteen as Wellington's Stationmaster and District Traffic Manager.[8]

> **As the Tourist Department dithered in the 1920s, the Railways Department would take the lead in promoting the 'Cinderella industry' both here and overseas.**

Donne soon set to work 'booming New Zealand' here and overseas through scenic postcards and films, magazine articles, 'lantern-slide' lecture tours, and displays at exhibitions and trade fairs. He established travel agencies in the four main centres and Rotorua to hand out maps, accommodation lists and penny railway guides. Meanwhile, the state poured investment into Rotorua, which became 'a Government Township, pure and simple'. In 1902 the Auckland express was upgraded to a daily service with modern carriages hauled by Baldwin Q- and N-class locomotives. Despite Ward and Donne's bullish predictions, however, tourism would not prove to be a 'goldmine' for New Zealand — not yet anyway. The country was located 'at the wrong end of the world' and the number of overseas visitors stagnated: in 1909 (when Donne was posted to London) just under 9000 arrived, more than half of them from Australia; in 1922 the figure was barely 8000. As the Tourist Department dithered in the 1920s, the Railways Department would take the lead in promoting the 'Cinderella industry' both here and overseas.[9]

By the 1920s the leisure and beach culture that had begun to emerge in the late nineteenth century was in full flower. Day excursions remained popular, but as in Britain, Australia and elsewhere, increasing numbers of middle- and working-class New Zealanders could now afford longer holidays of a week or more, particularly over the Christmas–New Year period. Wages were rising, especially for clerical and skilled blue-collar workers, and working hours were declining; most urban employees now worked a five- rather than six-day week, and many enjoyed paid annual holidays of at least a week.

The declining size of families — the average number of children in Pakeha families fell from 6.5 in 1880 to 2.4 in 1923 — also made longer holidays a cheaper and more manageable option. The spread of bungalow suburbs around the cities contributed to the emergence of a new concept of the family, centred on a male 'breadwinner' (who typically commuted to work by train, tram or bus), stay-at-home 'housewife', and children attending primary and secondary school. The popular vision of the 'happy home' as the bedrock of modern society encouraged a new emphasis on family-centred activities, including holidays. Tourist operators, in cahoots with the emerging advertising industry, sold the family holiday as an aspiration, an essential ingredient of healthy living and a symbol of social status. With car ownership still beyond the reach of many working people, NZR was well placed to cash in on the interwar holiday bonanza.[10]

*Railways Studios artists prepare giant portraits of the Duke and Duchess of York for display at public receptions during the 1927 royal tour.*

ANZ, AAVK, W3493, C1030

Central to the Department's tourist drive was the establishment of the Railways Studios in July 1920 (an Advertising Branch had been set up in 1915). This was the country's first outdoor-advertising studio, and led by Stanley Davis it would pioneer the development of poster art in New Zealand. As well as producing posters and other promotional material for NZR, the Studios undertook work for dozens of government and business clients that advertised at stations, inside carriages and on trackside hoardings (ironically, among their biggest customers were automobile and petrol companies).[11] With the local advertising industry in its infancy, the Studios quickly became a lucrative earner for the Department, turning a profit of £9,600 in 1922/3. That year NZR promoted 'the scenic and health resorts of the Dominion' through a series of posters

Trainland

## The Royal Wave

New Zealand's most famous and feted early 'tourists' were members of the British royal family. The Duke of Edinburgh's 1869 visit occurred in the very early days of rail, but included two short train rides between Christchurch and Lyttelton. New Zealand's first 'Royal train' appeared during the 1901 tour by the Duke and Duchess of Cornwall (the future King George V and Queen Mary), ferrying the royal party between Auckland and Rotorua and Christchurch and Dunedin. Safety was ensured by a pilot train running ahead and an emergency train following behind. After the tour the royal carriages became 'Vice-regal cars' for the Governor and his family.

The 1920s was the heyday of royal train travel in New Zealand. In April–May 1920 King George's son, Edward, Prince of Wales, travelled by royal train between Auckland, Rotorua, New Plymouth, Wanganui, Napier and Wellington, on the isolated Marlborough, Nelson and West Coast sections, and then between Arthur's Pass, Christchurch and Invercargill; the various rail gaps were filled in by motor car. At every stopover, other trains brought hordes of spectators and schoolchildren from far and wide on cheap day fares. NZR's Refreshment Branch took charge of most of the catering throughout the tour, dispatching its own silverware, china, glassware and linen, as well as chefs and kitchen staff, to hotels across the country. When the royal carriage was opened to the public at the end of the tour, more than 20,000 people nosed through it. 'Many ladies took great interest in the Royal bedroom and its crested appointments; and not a few kisses were imprinted upon the pillows.' Souvenir hunters jostled to get their hands on 'flowers from the Royal lounge, walnuts and biscuits from the Royal table and even such humble articles as wooden toothpicks or even oyster shells'.

During their 1927 tour, the Duke and Duchess of York (the future King George VI and Queen Elizabeth) travelled more than 1700 miles by train, beginning with the now traditional trip to Rotorua and ending in Bluff a month later. The couple enjoyed the

Exploring New Zealand

*The young Queen Elizabeth II on the observation platform of her Royal Car at Timaru, 25 January 1954.*

ANZ, AAVK, W3493, B4533

use of luxurious new Royal Cars (one for each island) equipped with rear observation windows, electric fans, kitchen, lounge and office. The next royal tour, by the Duke of Gloucester in 1934–5, coincided with the country's emergence from the gloom of Depression and triggered a summer boom in passenger traffic. The Duke also laid the foundation stone of Wellington's imposing new railway station. In 1939 the Otahuhu workshops turned out a gleaming new car for the planned tour by the Duke and Duchess of Kent, but when that trip was cancelled because of the war, the car was added to the vice-regal stable.

Much of the 1953–4 tour by Queen Elizabeth II and Prince Philip was undertaken by car and, for the first time, aeroplane. Royal trains travelled only between Napier and New Plymouth, Christchurch and Greymouth, and Timaru and Dunedin. Sadly, the main railway story of the tour was the Tangiwai disaster on Christmas Eve 1953, when a North Island main trunk express plunged into the swollen Whangaehu River with the loss of 151 lives. The Queen expressed her sorrow in her Christmas Day radio address and met some of the survivors, while Prince Philip attended the funeral of victims in Wellington. On her subsequent visits, Queen Elizabeth used trains less often, preferring to travel by car, air or aboard the royal yacht *Britannia*. By the 1960s the vice-regal carriages were similarly seldom used, largely because of their cost; the last was withdrawn in 1973.[12]

## Trainland

depicting Rotorua, the Waitomo Caves, Mount Cook and Lake Wakatipu, adverts in passenger carriages, and booklets of 'pictorial poster stamps illustrating scenic, sporting, agricultural, and pastoral views'. These stamps proved a hit with New Zealanders posting letters overseas, with the Department reporting that 'every mail brings letters of inquiry . . . from many different countries, thus showing that the distribution is very widespread'.[13]

By 1924 the Studios had a staff of 74, including commercial artists, signwriters, photographers and carpenters. That year the Department produced an attractive sixteen-page illustrated booklet, *Travel, Sport and Scenery*, which eulogised the country's thermal wonders, mountains, deep-sea fishing and hunting. Out of the 2150 copies printed, 100 were sent to the New Zealand High Commissioner in London, 70 to the Australian state railways and 170 to other railways around the world. Deals with the Canadian National and Canadian Pacific Railways for 'a reciprocal interchange of advertising-matter' were later followed by similar arrangements with the Indian, Egyptian, South African, Rhodesian, Belgian and Australian state railways, as well as Britain's London Midland and Scottish (LMS) company. Meanwhile, the business agents of the Department's Commercial Branch (established in August 1924) arranged the through-booking of passengers, goods and parcels to destinations throughout the country, and liaised with chambers of commerce, the Farmers' Union, A&P Associations and local progress leagues to foster new business. Passenger agents were later appointed in the main centres to meet international tourists on their arrival and help with travel and accommodation arrangements.[14]

*The Railways Department hosted its own display at the Dunedin exhibition in 1925–6, showcasing its tourist services, new passenger cars and the gleaming A$^B$ 608, recently christened* Passchendaele *in honour of the Department's Great War dead. In 1927 the same locomotive would head the Duke and Duchess of York's train in the South Island. This photograph was taken during New Zealand railways' centennial celebration at Christchurch in 1963; the locomotive is presently under restoration at Paekakariki.*

ANZ, AAVK, W3493, D8924

**The New Zealand and South Seas Exhibition at Dunedin in 1925–6 fuelled a surge in passenger traffic and gave NZR new opportunities for self-promotion. The exhibition's six-month run helped boost holiday and excursion figures from 562,122 in 1924/5 to 905,462 the following year.**

Like the Christchurch exhibition of 1906–7, the New Zealand and South Seas Exhibition at Dunedin in 1925–6 fuelled a surge in passenger traffic and gave NZR new opportunities for self-promotion. The exhibition's six-month run helped boost holiday and excursion figures from 562,122 in 1924/5 to 905,462 the following year. On a single day, 1 April 1926, eight trains delivered 5000 travellers into Dunedin. NZR offered extended South Island package tours by rail, road and steamer, and dispatched thousands of advertising booklets to newspapers, schools, chambers of commerce and organisations exhibiting in Dunedin. A further 15,000 were produced to publicise winter travel to the West Coast — 'the most invigorating time to travel South' — and promotional cards were distributed to major hotels. As well as initiating farmers' and businessmen's rail tours in the slack winter months, NZR also sought to revive the pre-First World War picnic and day-excursion traffic — much of which had been lost to cars and buses — by launching a 'Picnics by Rail' campaign and cheap Sunday excursions to beach, bush and mountainside.[15]

Rail tourism also benefited from another of Coates' mid-1920s innovations — the introduction on the North Island main trunk of a North American-style 'Limited' express, which shortened journey times by limiting

# Trainland

## Alpine Adventures

In the spring of 1926, three years after the completion of the Midland line, NZR began running Sunday specials from Christchurch to Otira in the Southern Alps. At Arthur's Pass, passengers on the first trip had a choice of continuing through the tunnel or disembarking to walk the old coach road over the pass, picking bunches of wildflowers as they went. At Otira, they lunched at the refreshment room and were entertained by the Greymouth Municipal Band, which had travelled up to meet them. For the hundreds of city factory workers, clerks, typists and shop girls who crowded aboard, the train offered a convenient and affordable means of experiencing the breathtaking scenery and fresh air of the mountains. Many had never visited the Alps before, and few could have afforded to stay at elite resorts like the Mount Cook Hermitage.

The following year, Sunday specials were extended into the winter months; on the first trip in June 1927 more than 300 passengers travelled up in steam-heated carriages. After enjoying the thrills and spills of skiing, tobogganing and snowball fights, the day-trippers were warmed by a roaring fire and cooked lunch at Otira. Soon NZR was running two trains to the Alps each Sunday with 600–800 passengers apiece. After a break during the war years, the popularity of the service peaked in the 1950s, when as many as four trains were run every Sunday, each carrying up to a thousand people.

Not everyone was thrilled at this alpine invasion. Some clergymen protested the desecration of the Sabbath with a 'riot of pleasuring', but their complaints fell on deaf ears. Others were appalled at tourism's impact on the environment. A long-time Otira resident complained that after excursions 'the road over the Gorge would be strewn with ferns, branches, moss, orchids — just abandoned. People would pick far more than they could carry, or else see better things and drop what they had, or as the day wore on, throw aside their huge bouquets of wilting lilies or daisies.' Visitors were not the only culprits. Locals 'were regularly coming up there to get the early rata flowers. They'd bring axes and chop down mature trees along the road-edge, just for a few top sprigs, which they'd later sell to tourists on the railway station.'

Concern at the impact of rail-led tourism on the mountains contributed to the establishment of Arthur's Pass National Park in 1929. But having opened up access, the Railways Department refused the park board's request to levy its passengers to subsidise conservation efforts. There were also problems with visitor misbehaviour in the late 1950s, when gangs of teenage 'bodgies' and 'widgies' reportedly ran riot in the park (see Chapter 4). After falling into decline as a passenger route in the 1970s and 1980s, the Midland line has since re-emerged as the showpiece of New Zealand rail tourism, with the TranzAlpine service currently carrying 200,000 passengers a year between Christchurch and Greymouth.[16]

*The cover of a 1950 pamphlet promoting snow specials to Arthur's Pass and Otira.*

ATL, Eph-A-RAIL-1950-01-front

## Trainland

its stops and loads. International visitors familiar with European or North American expresses had often criticised New Zealand trains for their slow speeds and frequent stops. In response, NZR introduced a 'Night Limited' on the Auckland–Wellington run in December 1924. Hauled by the celebrated A$^B$-class 'Pacifics' (and W$^{AB}$ tank engines over the mountainous central section), it made the trip in fourteen and a quarter hours — three hours 45 minutes quicker than the regular express. Instead of the normal fifteen stops, the Limited paused only at Frankton Junction, Taumarunui, Ohakune, Taihape, Marton and Palmerston North. By the 1930s better-off travellers could enjoy the journey in plush new sleeping cars or first-class carriages with comfortable reclining seats. Locomotive power was also upgraded: following an unfortunate experiment with British-built Garratt articulated locomotives, in the mid 1930s the A$^B$ class was superseded on the main trunk by the giant 4-8-4 K class — the pinnacle of steam power on New Zealand's railways.

While the Night Limited flourished, the introduction of a fifteen-and-a-quarter-hour Daylight Limited in November 1925 proved less successful. Poor patronage forced its cancellation the following June and a brief revival in 1929–30 was doomed by the Depression. Despite its discomforts, most business, government and tourist travellers preferred overnight travel, which allowed them to avoid

*Although the Daylight Limited never achieved the iconic status of its overnight counterpart, it was a popular fixture of NZR's summer timetable in the 1950s, when this leaflet was issued.*

NZRLS

112

accommodation costs and delivered them to their destination in the early morning. Thereafter, Daylight Limited services were confined to the Christmas–New Year and Easter holiday periods, when main trunk traffic swelled to bursting point, especially in the mid to late thirties. On Christmas Eve 1934, for example, five trains — Night and Daylight Limiteds, the regular express, and two 'relief' expresses — carried 1800 travellers from Wellington to Auckland; two years later, seven were needed, while on Christmas Eve 1938 eight expresses carried more than 3000 passengers north. Easter traffic also boomed in these years, peaking on the Thursday before Easter 1939, when eight expresses ran each way between Auckland and Wellington.[17]

## Selling Rail

Two of the most visible products of Coates' modernisation drive were the striking posters produced by the Railways Studios and the *New Zealand Railways Magazine*, which appeared monthly from May 1926 to June 1940. Although the Studios had produced promotional material since 1920, the quantity and quality of its work surged as road competition intensified later that decade. During his trip to the Imperial Conference in 1926, which included a North American stopover, Coates was impressed by 'the great use made of modern publicity methods to attract business to the principal railways of the world'. At his urging, in October 1927 the Department established its own dedicated Publicity Branch, which would be able to call on 'trained publicity experts and journalists' as well as the skilled artists of the Railways Studios.[18] The Branch worked closely with the Tourist Department, local authorities and chambers of commerce to publicise tourist travel, accommodation and sightseeing packages, while the Studios produced a series of bright, attractive lithographic posters highlighting the scenic and therapeutic charms of the Bay of Islands, Tauranga, Rotorua, Napier, National Park and Timaru ('Best Reached by Rail') and combined rail/motor trips to Lake Wanaka, Mount Cook and Fiordland.

Local commercial advertising in the early twentieth century, as in Britain and Australia, generally lacked the sophistication and punch of American marketing or the modernist élan of French rail publicity. Mimicking

**Local commercial advertising in the early twentieth century, as in Britain and Australia, generally lacked the sophistication and punch of American marketing or the modernist élan of French rail publicity.**

EASTER
SAVE 6/- IN £
APRIL
15
TO
21
AVAILABLE
FOR
RETURN
24
MAY
BY RAIL
RAILWAY STUDIOS' DESIGN & PRINT

## Exploring New Zealand

RIGHT: *'Right Away for School Holidays': the influence of modernist design trends is evident in the bold shapes and lettering on this 1935 poster.*

ATL, Eph-E-RAIL-1935-01

LEFT: *Stylised 'bathing belles' and other female figures featured prominently in interwar railway advertising, as this 1930 poster demonstrates. As well as seeking to catch the eye of male viewers, advertisers recognised that wives and mothers made many families' decisions about domestic expenditure, including holiday travel.*

ATL, NON-ATL-0099 / ANZ, AAOK, W3241, 69

the style and tone of British railway advertising, most NZR posters in the 1920s featured sun-drenched beaches, soaring mountains, lush forests, exotic Maori, or symbolic figures like the 'bathing belle' or 'seaside girl' — whose scantily clad form and purposeful pursuit of pleasure appealed to both male and female audiences — with lettering and other information arranged around the edges of the central image.[19]

By the early thirties, however, the artists of the Railways Studios were moving away from simple pictorial representations towards more daring abstract designs that often used a montage of images and skilfully integrated text into the overall design. Promotions were often aimed at women, as advertisers recognised that wives and mothers made many of the key decisions about family spending, including holidays (even though, for many homemakers, the reality of vacations was simply the same domestic drudgery in different surroundings).

NZR adverts also frequently stressed the safety of rail travel compared to the perils of the road. As car numbers soared in the late 1920s, so did the road toll, with 178 deaths in 1929 — an increase of 127 per cent since 1921 and, on a per capita basis, even worse than today's road carnage.[20] Prospective travellers were regularly reminded that 'The Railways are the Safe Ways', while NZR's motto in the 1930s — 'Safety, Comfort, Economy' — emphasised its priorities.

Many of the Studios' posters and outdoor adverts were reproduced in the *Railways Magazine*. Throughout its fourteen-year run the magazine was edited by G.G. Stewart, who had joined the Department in 1898 and became the inaugural

Trainland

## The 'Aesthetic Agony' of Advertising

Not everyone was impressed by the Railways Department's enthusiasm for outdoor advertising in the 1920s. In 1924 the Christchurch *Press* attacked the 'confusion and ugliness' of New Zealand railway stations, where travellers were bombarded with images of 'flat wine and flatter women, and somebody's mustard and everybody's motor-cars'. Not even the 'prisoners of a railway carriage' could escape the 'aesthetic agony' of onboard adverts pushing 'somebody's butter or clothes or bacon'. Later that decade the Christchurch City Council, Canterbury Progress League and the local Beautifying Association complained to Minister Coates about the 'hideous crop of hoardings . . . flashing all round the city'. Although it agreed not to erect hoardings in 'scenic beauty spots', the Department maintained a rigorously commercial approach to one of its more lucrative activities, even exploiting the Crown's exemption from liquor licensing laws to advertise whisky and beer at stations in 'dry' (no-licence) districts.

Public hostility to the barrage of trackside adverts took an unexpected turn in 1930. One lazy Sunday afternoon in Clyde, Central Otago, a startled track worker spied

manager of the Publicity Branch in 1927. Many of the magazine's striking covers were designed by Stanley Davis, including the stylised view of a train soaring high over the Makohine Viaduct that adorned the first six issues. Based on British and American railway company magazines, the publication was originally intended as a 'shop organ' for the Department's 18,000 staff and major customers, and was delivered free to all NZR employees, MPs and 'the leading firms, shippers and traders doing business with the New Zealand Railways'. Reflecting contemporary interest in 'industrial psychology', it also aimed to enhance departmental esprit de corps at a time

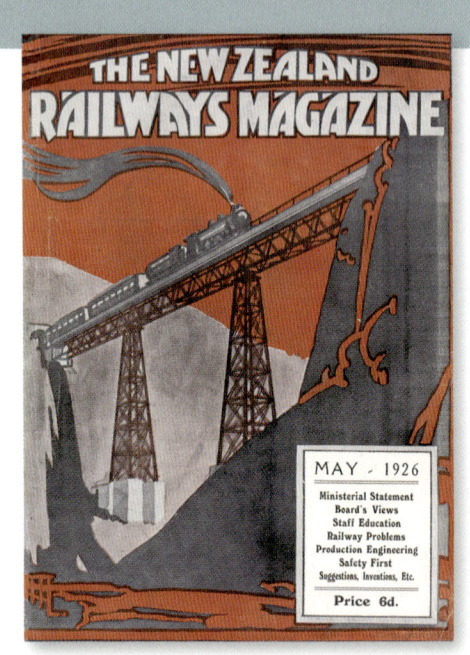

*Advertisements at Wellington's old Thorndon station in the 1930s.*

ANZ, AAVK, W3493, D10153

two men in suits hacking down a trackside Texaco hoarding with an axe. Several other signs in the Kawarau Gorge met the same fate. Tracked down via their getaway car, four prominent Dunedin doctors were subsequently hauled before the courts. Under headlines such as 'War on Hoardings', the press revealed that the docs' 'voyage of destruction' was intended as 'a protest against the despoiling of the countryside by large and unsightly advertising hoardings'. The four were convicted and ordered to pay £5 each in fines and compensation. Their plucky protest against visual pollution apparently did not extend to concern for the environment — the toppled hoardings had been heaved into the Kawarau River.[21]

**LEFT:** *This striking image, designed by Stanley Davis, appeared (in different colours) on the cover of the first six issues of the* Railways Magazine *in 1926.*

ATL, PUBL-0190-1926-05-cover

of strained labour relations.[22]

Alongside railway news and technical articles from New Zealand and overseas, the magazine pushed domestic tourism through numerous travel stories, photo spreads, advertisements and accommodation listings. It soon expanded its menu to include 'New Zealand Verse' and short fiction, 'Wit and Humour', sports news, historical yarns, biographical sketches, and a frothy books page ('Among the Books') edited by journalist Pat Lawlor. In 1927 the magazine introduced a regular column 'Of Feminine Interest' (later entitled 'Our Women's Section') featuring recipes, fashion tips, society gossip and notes on children's health. This column, Stewart explained, was directed towards the 'lady members of the service, of whom there are now eighty-five' (out of 18,000); more significantly, he hoped the wives and

# Trainland

daughters of the 12,000 married railwaymen would also 'appreciate the regular appearance of a page devoted to feminine and household matters'.[23]

In 1933, apparently at the urging of Lawlor (now advertising manager), the *Railways Magazine* further widened its brief to become a 'general interest' monthly for all New Zealanders; in the mid 1930s its circulation reached 26,000. The historian James Cowan, probably its most prolific contributor, wrote a series of 48 sketches of 'Famous New Zealanders', along with 75 other historical and travel features. Lawyer Archie Treadwell authored a series on famous legal cases, and in 1935–6 Robin Hyde penned a lively travel serial entitled 'On the Road to Anywhere: Adventures of a Train Tramp'. Several serialised features were republished as booklets, notably Cowan's two illustrated 'six-penny books', *The Romance of the Rail*, which traced the history and scenic delights of the North and South Island main trunk lines, and his 1936 guide to Maori *Railway Station Names and Their Meanings* (although his more creative interpretations were questioned by Sir Apirana Ngata and others).

The *Railways Magazine* weathered the difficult Depression years but failed to survive the Second World War. After producing a propaganda-laden 'Flags for Freedom' issue in March 1940, it ceased publication without warning in June — a victim of wartime economies, paper shortages, and Stewart's imminent retirement. Over fourteen years the magazine had blossomed from a house journal into a hugely popular general interest monthly. While critics like Eric McCormick sneered at Stewart and

RIGHT: *A range of NZR promotional material can be seen in this 1930 view of the Rotorua station booking hall, including an advert for James Cowan's* Romance of the Rail *guides (on the column at left), large tourist maps (either side of ticket booth No. 3), and posters advertising Sunday trains and 'Half-fares for Whole People'.*

ANZ, AAVK, W3493, E769

*Advertisers often harnessed the 'power' of rail imagery to sell other goods and services, as this announcement in a mid-1930s* Railways Magazine *illustrates.*

NZRM, Apr 1935

Exploring New Zealand

Lawlor's conservative editorial policy, which avoided any hint of controversy and favoured established literary figures, the *Railways Magazine* was a crucial outlet and source of income for numerous New Zealand writers, poets and freelance journalists. During the interwar years no other monthly magazine matched its commitment to promoting a popular literary culture in New Zealand.[24]

Trainland

# Dark Days

The Great Depression of the 1930s blighted thousands of lives and put the prospect of rail travel and holidays beyond the reach of many. In 1932/3 passenger journeys tumbled to 18.4 million, the lowest for twenty years. Freight tonnage, which had continued to grow through the 1920s, was equally hard hit, sliding from 7.8 million tons in 1929/30 to 5.5 million three years later. Although the volume of some agricultural produce like wool, butter and meat actually increased, the tonnage of timber, coal, cement and other commodities more than halved. NZR's gross revenue slumped from £8.3 million to £6 million, forcing savage cutbacks. In three years the Department's workforce plummeted from 19,410 to 14,696. More than 760,000 train-miles were shaved off the timetable in 1930/1, and a further 1.1 million the following year. A number of daily expresses were reduced to weeklies, and passenger services were removed from several rural branch lines, mostly in the South Island. Some lines or sections were closed completely, prompting the first significant reduction in route mileage in the country's history. At the same time, construction work was suspended on several projects, including the long-delayed route between Nelson and the West Coast. It would never be revived.[25]

Inevitably, the Depression reignited debate over transport competition. NZR had offered low rates and special concessions to farmers, miners, timber-millers and manufacturers since the 1870s, its losses being cross-subsidised by the higher rates charged for general merchandise and imported goods. In the 1920s these high-rated goods proved a soft target for trucking companies, which could offer a more convenient door-to-door service and undercut NZR's rates over short distances. As the Depression began to bite, longstanding rail customers began shopping around. In 1930 General Manager H.H. Sterling complained that it was 'becoming increasingly evident that certain persons and companies are prepared to exploit the railway tariff in their own interests' by 'sending all their low-rated goods by rail while sending their higher-rated goods by competitive [road] services'.[26]

The worst 'offenders' were farmers, who enjoyed generous rail subsidies on lime and fertiliser, but when it came to shipping their produce and other goods regarded NZR as just another business competing for traffic. From the Department's viewpoint, the farming community appeared selfish and ungrateful. After all, hadn't railways opened up their lands and fostered their export industries? During the Depression, however, loyalty was a luxury few could afford.

RIGHT: 'Thousands of feet above worry level!': NZR continued to push holiday travel, with some success, during the depths of the Great Depression. This poster was one of a series produced in 1932.

ATL, NON-ATL-0155 / ANZ, AAOK, W3241, 1

"Thousands of Feet above worry level!"
The Hermitage
MT. COOK
LOW
COMBINED
RAIL & MOTOR FARES
ISSUED BY N.Z. RAILWAY PUBLICITY BRANCH
NEW ZEALAND

## Trainland

As in the 1880s, one of the government's first responses to economic downturn was to call for a Railways Royal Commission. Its 1930 report condemned 'wasteful' transport competition and prompted Parliament to pass the Transport Licensing Act 1931, providing for the strict regulation and licensing of motorised passenger and goods services. In an attempt to woo customers, NZR adopted a system of flat rates for distances up to 200 miles and introduced new services, including overnight goods express trains, night stock trains, and combined rail and road through-booking for door-to-door deliveries. The Royal Commission also called for NZR to be 'depoliticalized', and when Sterling retired in 1931 he was replaced by an independent five-man Government Railways Board.[27] Once again, as in the 1880s, when times got tough ministers were only too happy to distance themselves from their troublesome department. Transport regulation and board control would give rail valuable breathing space during the slump years, but neither would offer a long-term solution.

> **During the 1933 Christmas holidays, the *Evening Post* heralded the annual flood of 'bach-dwellers' to the Kapiti Coast as though the Depression had never happened.**

Life for many better-off New Zealanders meanwhile continued much as before. Holiday and pleasure travel predictably declined during the slump, but even at its lowest point in 1931/2 almost three million holiday and excursion tickets were sold. The Publicity Branch and Railways Studios continued to churn out attractive posters to lure holidaymakers to beach, mountain and spa resorts; 1931's crop included a series of 'Winter Sports' posters, large contour maps of the North and South Islands ('Seeing New Zealand by Rail'), and a fold-out pamphlet on the Raurimu Spiral. The following year the Branch joined with local bodies and the Tourist Department to promote a 'See New Zealand First' campaign — an early version of the 1980s 'Don't leave town till you've seen the country' promotion — through newspaper advertisements, booklets and posters.

During the 1933 Christmas holidays, the *Evening Post* heralded the annual flood of 'bach-dwellers' to the Kapiti Coast as though the Depression had never happened: 'there is scarcely any section, creed, or profession that does not supply its quota. And once the holiday-makers have quitted the train, distinctions which previously existed disappear.' While it is unlikely that the sullen ranks of unemployed and relief workers filled their 'quotas' at the country's beaches, rail tourism continued to provide welcome income for NZR throughout the worst years of Depression.[28]

# The People's Railway Reborn

The economy was already improving by the time M.J. Savage's Labour government was elected in November 1935. Labour's vision was articulated in *Railways Magazine* advertisements championing 'Railways for National Welfare' and 'The People's Railways for the People's Profits'. As the new Minister of Railways, Dan Sullivan, declared:

> Probably no country owes more to its railway system than does New Zealand, and certainly no country has made greater use of railways in the furtherance of general development. From the year 1863, when the first lines were opened for traffic, until the present day our railways have been and still are our first line of communication. They constitute, in fact, the economic foundations of our national life.[29]

In keeping with Labour's faith in state enterprise and central planning, the Railways Board was abolished in April 1936. Direct ministerial control resumed, with the energetic Garnet Mackley (who had headed the Board since 1932) becoming General Manager. The government also tightened transport licensing rules by imposing a 30-mile limit on all truck operators competing against rail.[30] Meanwhile, in an effort to reduce unemployment and promote regional development, Bob Semple's Public Works Department resumed work on track improvements and realignments, and restarted several stalled construction projects, including long-planned lines between Parnassus and Wharanui (linking Christchurch with Picton), Dargaville and Tangowahine, Putorino (northern Hawke's Bay) and Gisborne, and Westport and Inangahua.

Once again, the Railways Department hummed with activity. With the restoration of pre-Depression services and the adoption of a 40-hour week,

*'Power to Serve': in the late 1930s big K-class locomotives frequently appeared in NZR advertising as a symbol of the revitalised people's railway.*

NZRM, May 1938

# Trainland

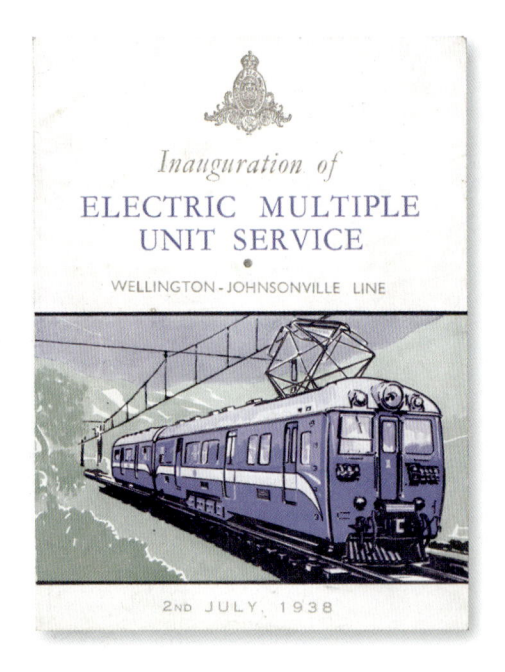

*Aotea (RM 30) was the first of six Hutt-built Standard railcars introduced in 1938–9 and named (following a public competition in the Railways Magazine) after a Maori ancestral waka.*

AJHR, 1938, D-2

*An invitation to the opening ceremony of the Johnsonville electric multiple-unit service in July 1938, presided over by Railways Minister Dan Sullivan and Wellington Mayor Thomas Hislop.*

ATL, Eph-B-RAIL-1938-01-front

NZR's workforce expanded rapidly to reach 25,885 by the end of the decade. The workshops poured out new rolling stock and locomotives. Commuter traffic in Wellington was boosted by the opening of a grand new station close to the city centre in June 1937. Following the completion of the Tawa Flat deviation that year, the old Johnsonville route out of the city became a suburban line, served from July 1938 by the country's first English Electric multiple-units. By 1940 the main trunk line out of Wellington had been electrified as far as Paekakariki.[31]

The late 1930s also saw the introduction of New Zealand's first regular railcar services. For decades NZR had hoped that petrol- or diesel-powered 'motor trains' could replace mixed trains and compete with bus services on routes where passenger patronage was flagging, but early experiments were discouraging. In 1936 the Hutt workshops built two Leyland-engined railcars for service on the Midland line (where their main task was to deliver copies of the *Press* to Greymouth), followed by nine Wairarapa-class 'tin hares' for the Rimutaka route. In April 1939 the first of six 'Standard' 52-seat diesel express railcars entered service between Wellington and New Plymouth. The Hutt-built Standards, which reached 74 miles per hour on trials, proved a huge success, and were joined in the 1940s by nine British-built Vulcan 50-seaters for use on South Island lines.[32]

124

# On the Road

One of the successes of the 1930s was the bold expansion of NZR's Road Services branch. Although the Department had operated some motor buses as early as 1907, the branch's origins lay in the 1926 purchase of a service between Napier and Hastings. Two others near Oamaru soon followed, and in 1927–8 NZR purchased six bus companies in the rapidly growing Hutt Valley. It acquired its first long-distance coach service (between Wellington and Wanganui) in 1934, and was soon promoting tourist trips to Franz Josef, Fiordland and elsewhere. Road Services grew dramatically under the Labour government, taking over long-distance coach services between Auckland, Waikato, Rotorua and the Bay of Plenty, Christchurch and the West Coast, and in Central Otago, and launching its first extensive goods operations.

By 1940 NZR was operating 138 coaches, 111 suburban buses and 218 goods vehicles, and carrying over five million passengers and 100,000 tons of freight a year. A decade later road passenger journeys topped 24 million, just two million short of the total for rail passengers. After the Second World War the Department further expanded its non-rail operations,

*As well as running suburban and intercity bus and coach services, NZR's Road Services branch promoted motor tours to scenic destinations like the 'Southern Lakeland'.*

NZRM, May 1938

# Trainland

> launching an air-freight service (1947) and introducing the first Cook Strait rail ferry, *Aramoana* (1962). Long before the label became fashionable, NZR was a pioneer of 'intermodal' transport services.
>
> While its foray into road transport proved a success for the Department, it was hardly a triumph for rail itself — many of its passenger and freight customers simply shifted from trains to vehicles. After the war, Road Services, railcars, and private buses and trucks helped seal the fate of the last rural mixed train services and a number of struggling branch lines. In the mid 1960s Road Services had almost 800 buses and coaches — a fifth of New Zealand's total fleet — and was carrying around 23 million passengers a year, but patronage fell away in the 1980s. Road Services would not survive the rigorous rationalisations of the following decades: in 1991 the Railways Corporation's long-distance coach operation and Speedlink parcel service were sold to the private InterCity Group and New Zealand Post Ltd respectively. Intermodal transport continues to flourish, however, with current rail operator Toll running a large and profitable fleet of trucks, as well as the Interislander ferries, and promoting itself as 'New Zealand's leading multimodal freight transport and distribution company'.[33]

The Labour government was especially keen to 'democratise' internal tourism and put holidays back within reach of 'the masses'. Holiday travel had grown steadily since the summer of 1934–5, when glorious weather and the Duke of Gloucester's visit had boosted passenger numbers. In the late thirties, following the restoration of Depression wage cuts and the introduction of a 40-hour week, they rocketed to new levels. At Easter 1936 more than 21,000 travellers poured through Wellington Station (not counting local commuters), with 2380 bound for Auckland, 2943 for Manawatu, 1959 for Taranaki and 1543 for Hawke's Bay. During the Christmas break, more than 32,000 left the city by train for holiday destinations around the North Island. In 1938, 11,160 travellers departed on Christmas Eve alone, crowding aboard sixteen express trains bound for Auckland, New Plymouth, Napier and Wairarapa. The *New Zealand Herald* described the bustle and clamour of Auckland station at Christmas time:

## Exploring New Zealand

**At Easter 1935 the Christchurch Corsair Social Club filled sixteen carriages for an excursion to Queenstown via Dunedin and Kingston, boarding the Lake Wakatipu steamer *Earnslaw* for the final leg.**

Throngs of people in the most diverse kinds of holiday attire, people laden with suitcases, bags and parcels of every conceivable shape and size, and above all children, armed with buckets and spades, toy aeroplanes, squeakers and a hundred and one other toys, all hurried or were hurried down the platforms, until it seemed that everyone in Auckland was bent on leaving the city.

According to the *Evening Post* in April 1936, New Zealanders' enthusiasm for rail travel made them on a per capita basis 'the greatest travellers in the world' — long before the era of mass car ownership, air travel and the big 'OE'.[34]

NZR also revived excursion services that had fallen away during the Depression, such as farmers' and businessmen's tours, and launched new ones, including springtime 'Daffodil Specials' to Lawrence in Central Otago. At Easter 1935 the Christchurch Corsair Social Club filled sixteen carriages for an excursion to Queenstown via Dunedin and Kingston, boarding the Lake Wakatipu steamer *Earnslaw* for the final leg. The following year nine special trains ferried 3764 rugby fans from Invercargill to a Ranfurly Shield challenge in Dunedin, while the 1937 Springbok tour sparked another surge.[35] Subsequent promotions included the introduction of Railway Travel Savings

*From the late 1930s thrifty New Zealand families could buy Railway Travel Savings Stamps, which offered 5 per cent interest on savings towards rail holidays.*

NZRM, May 1938

**TRAVEL SAVINGS STAMPS**

Assuring Needed Holidays

*Another Good Railways Service*

"If I only had the money for the trip!" How often have you had that yearning when you have seen pictures of famous scenes of New Zealand or have heard friends or relatives talk about them?

You know, too, that you had the money, but it vanished in fractions on all manner of trifles.

Now comes your chance to have that trip of heart's desire. The Railway Travel Savings Stamps (1/-, 2/-, 2/6d. and 5/-) will help you to build up the fare conveniently.

*Stamps and Free Booklet at Stations*

Radio on rails: in April 1939 the mobile radio station 5ZB embarked on a 79-day promotional tour of the North Island. More than 15,000 people inspected the carriage during its travels from Whangarei to Masterton.

ATL, NON-ATL-0108 / ANZ, AAVK, W3493, E6870

Stamps, an arrangement with the Group Travel Association to promote 'cheap travel for wage-earners' and the construction of a mobile Railway Broadcasting Studio.[36]

Rail tourism was one of the success stories of the interwar years, and a major contributor to NZR's strong recovery in the late thirties. In 1938/9, the last full year of peace, passenger journeys climbed to 23.3 million, freight tonnage to 7.5 million tons, and gross revenue to £9.3 million. Despite the predictable slump of the early 1930s, in the years from 1922 to 1939 holiday and excursion journeys had risen from 610,000 to 3.4 million — or, as a proportion of total passenger traffic, from about 2 per cent to a sizeable 15 per cent.[37] With a further flood of travellers expected to visit Wellington for the New Zealand Centennial Exhibition in the summer of 1939–40, NZR's prospects looked bright. After the grim days of the Great War and Depression, rail seemed to have recaptured the verve and vitality of its 'heroic' pioneering days. The powerful K- and J-class locomotives, sleek railcars and electric units, grand urban stations and stylish Art Deco advertising posters epitomised the glamour, power and modernity of Labour's revitalised people's railway. But the rollercoaster ride was far from over.

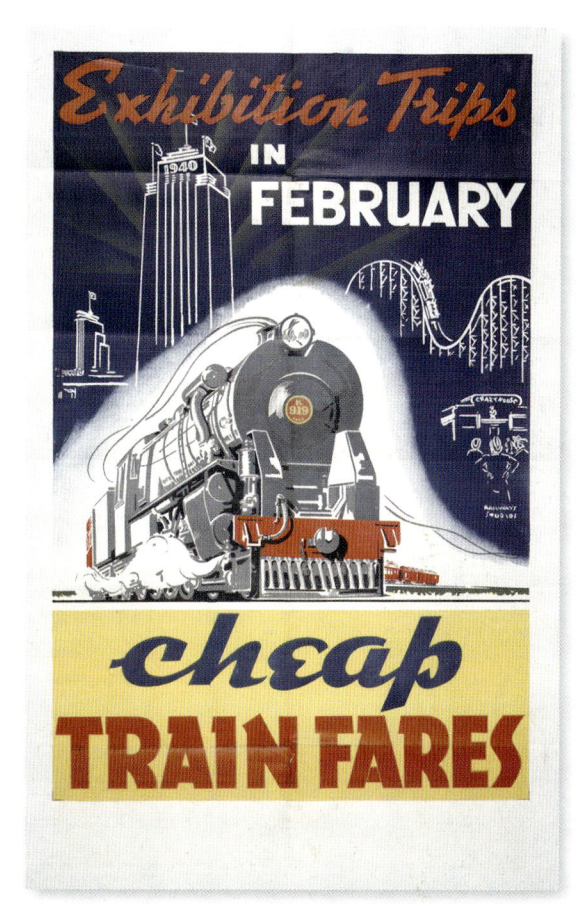

*The New Zealand Centennial Exhibition in Wellington attracted more than 2.6 million visitors during its six-month run in 1939–40, including tens of thousands of rail travellers from all over the country.*

ATL, NON-ATL-0154 / ANZ, AAOK, W3241, 36

## The End of the Golden Weather

In September 1939, just 21 years after the guns fell silent in Europe, New Zealand again went to war. Once again, the rail system was overstretched, coal stocks were exhausted, and NZR would end the conflict in a weary, dishevelled state. Once again, thousands of railway workers served overseas, including more than 800 in two volunteer Railway Operating Companies that performed with distinction in the North African desert. Despite losing a third of their staff to the services, the

## Trainland

*The Second World War generated record passenger traffic but placed enormous strain on NZR's staff and services. As this photograph suggests, soldiers were not the tidiest or best-behaved of rail passengers.*

ATL, F-61218-1/2

Department's workshops poured out everything from Bren-gun carriers and bomb casings to camp kitchens and marine engines for minesweepers.

In July 1942 the government declared all railway occupations 'essential', but the damage was already done. By the following March, 6876 NZR employees — 26 per cent of the 1939 workforce — were serving in the forces, compared to just 15 per cent of British and 8 per cent of Canadian railway workers. The Department plugged some of the gaps with recently retired railwaymen, while the number of women workers increased from 627 in 1939 to more than 2000 four years later. Previously confined to refreshment rooms and clerical work, women now took up duties as ticket collectors, car cleaners, porters and baggage attendants. In the Wellington Station luggage room, 'porteresses' were 'doing a full-sized man's job . . . receiving, checking, stacking and delivering luggage — no light task'. Despite this, they were paid a fifth less than their male colleagues.[38]

As in 1917, pleasure travel was drastically curtailed, with all excursion trains and extra holiday services cancelled at Christmas 1941. Unlike the First World War, however, overall passenger numbers continued to climb, reaching an all-time high of 38.6 million journeys in 1943/4 (see chart on page 101). The 1939/40 surge was partly a result of the Centennial Exhibition in Wellington, which attracted 17,500 rail visitors in

In July 1942 the government declared all railway occupations 'essential', but the damage was already done. By the following March, 6876 NZR employees — 26 per cent of the 1939 workforce — were serving in the forces, compared to just 15 per cent of British and 8 per cent of Canadian railway workers.

## Trainland

February 1940 alone, but the boom that followed was largely driven by wartime demands. With thousands of New Zealand and American troops travelling to camp, shuttling back and forth on leave, or heading to ports for overseas embarkation, in 1943/4 military movements accounted for a third of rail passenger traffic and a tenth of freight tonnage.[39]

The expansion of war-related manufacturing in rail-served areas like the Hutt Valley and south Auckland boosted commuter traffic, while the severe restrictions imposed on private motoring (especially rationing of petrol and rubber) forced many car-owners back to rail. The enforced rationalisation of trucking and coastal shipping further boosted rail revenue, but piled more pressure onto NZR's hard-pressed services. By 1944, with its workforce 3000 short of prewar levels and coal stocks dangerously low, the Department was forced to make further cuts to non-essential services.

Amid the record traffic and revenue statistics of the forties, rail travellers and workers endured overcrowded trains, careworn carriages, long working hours, refreshment room food rationing and frequent delays, cancellations and breakdowns caused by deferred maintenance. The war years were also marred by tragedy on the tracks: in June 1943, 21 passengers were killed and 47 injured in an accident at Hyde, Central Otago; five months later, three Upper Hutt commuters were killed and twenty injured in a derailment largely attributed to overdue track maintenance.[40] As in 1918–20, coal and staff shortages lingered after the war and various 'temporary' restrictions, including the suspension of excursion and group concession tickets, remained in force until the end of the 1940s. The prestigious Night Limited did not return to its pre-war timetable until November 1948, and the reinstatement of a full main trunk timetable took another year. With substantial military traffic for several years after the war, passenger numbers remained high until 1947, but by 1952 they had dipped under 22 million, similar to pre-war levels.

The tourism industry was in equally poor shape. Hopes of a post-war flood of international arrivals were

*By the early 1960s, when this pamphlet was produced, NZR was promoting the scenic delights of daytime travel on the North Island main trunk.*

NZRLS

## Exploring New Zealand

*This 1974 Silver Star advertisement evokes the sleek sophistication of NZR's 'luxury overnight express'. But despite the quality of its accommodation and marketing, the service was doomed by competition from NAC's Boeings.*

ATL, Eph-D-RAIL-1974-01

hampered by accommodation shortages and neglected infrastructure, including the rail system. In 1948 the *Mercantile Gazette* reported that tourists were dismayed by the 'seating accommodation, sleeping berths, and ventilation of the cars', which 'has been described as primitive'.[41]

As the wartime hangover began to clear in the 1950s, NZR sought to exploit the tourist potential of daytime rail travel. A diesel-hauled Scenic Daylight summer service was introduced on the North Island main trunk route in 1963, followed by the Blue Streak (1968) and Silver Fern (1972) daytime railcars. Meanwhile, the arrival of the sleek Japanese-built Silver Star trainset in 1971 revolutionised overnight travel between Auckland and Wellington. With its bowtie-wearing stewards, buffet car, on-board alcohol sales, shoe-shine service and stainless steel exterior, this air-conditioned all-sleeper train offered main trunk business and tourist travellers a new level of service and luxury.[42] The same year, NZR launched its own heritage steam operation specifically aimed at the tourist market. The Kingston Flyer, which used restored A[B] locomotives and passenger cars on a section of the Lumsden–Kingston branch line, soon became the country's best-known train.

*TranzAlpine travel: New Zealand rail operators have long sought to exploit the visual appeal of spectacular scenery to attract international and local tourists.*

Tranz Scenic

By the 1970s, however, rail was facing a potent new threat — air travel. Regular passenger flights between major cities dated back to the mid 1930s, but were largely curtailed during wartime. From 1958, when the state-owned National Airways Corporation (NAC) introduced turbo-prop Vickers Viscounts on main trunk routes, aviation began to chip away at rail's dominance of long-distance travel. NAC carried half a million travellers that year, compared to NZR's 3.2 million long-distance (that is, non-suburban) passengers. A decade later, when the first Boeing 737 jets entered service, the airline (1.1 million passengers) was closing the gap on NZR (2.1 million).[43] If rail could not match air travel for convenience and speed, trains were still considerably cheaper than planes, at least until the late 1980s. In 1971, for example, a one-way trip on the luxury Silver Star cost $18, the equivalent of about $210 in today's money, compared to a whopping $65 ($760 today) on NAC's jets. Even so, the Silver Star would not survive the decade, making its last trip in September 1979.

The postwar expansion of air travel, together with the increasing affordability of cars, highway improvements and the introduction of larger inter-city coaches, saw NZR's long-distance passenger traffic tumble from 6.5 million (1950) to 999,000 (1980). In the volatile years of the late 1980s and early 1990s the New Zealand Railways Corporation and its successor, New Zealand Rail Limited, would again look to tourism to restore flagging patronage. A suite of new tourist-oriented services included the TranzAlpine between Christchurch and Greymouth, the Coastal Pacific (later TranzCoastal) on the Christchurch–Picton route, the daytime Overlander on the North Island main trunk, the Bay Express between Wellington and Napier, and the Geyserland and Kaimai Expresses out of Auckland. By 1993, when New Zealand Rail was privatised, long-distance journeys had slumped to 391,000. Riding on the popularity of the flagship TranzAlpine service — promoted as one of the 'great train journeys of the world' — patronage rallied later in the decade, topping half a million in 2000/01.[44] At the same time, private operators like Otago's Taieri Gorge Railway and various rail heritage groups ran their own highly successful tourist excursions.

By the early twenty-first century tourists were an essential market for rail operators around the world. But despite the success of the TranzAlpine, New Zealand railways' private owners — preoccupied with their profitable 'multimodal' freight operations — have been reluctant to invest in improving and marketing passenger services. Tourist traffic could not save the struggling Geyserland, Kaimai and Bay Expresses, all of which closed in 2001, or the Southerner, which followed in 2002, ending 123 years of passenger travel on the Christchurch–Invercargill route. On the North Island main trunk, the overnight Northerner — successor to the legendary Night Limited — was axed in 2004. Two years later the daytime Overlander, reportedly carrying barely 50 passengers a day, nearly met the same fate.[45] Despite its subsequent reprieve, and its supporters' confidence in the route's tourist potential, the long term future of the service remains uncertain. Seven decades after Christmas Eve 1938, when sixteen long express trains swept 11,000 travellers out of Wellington on a single day, the clatter of holidaymakers and children 'armed with buckets and spades' had become a distant memory at New Zealand's railway stations.

CHAPTER 4

# Citizens of Trainland

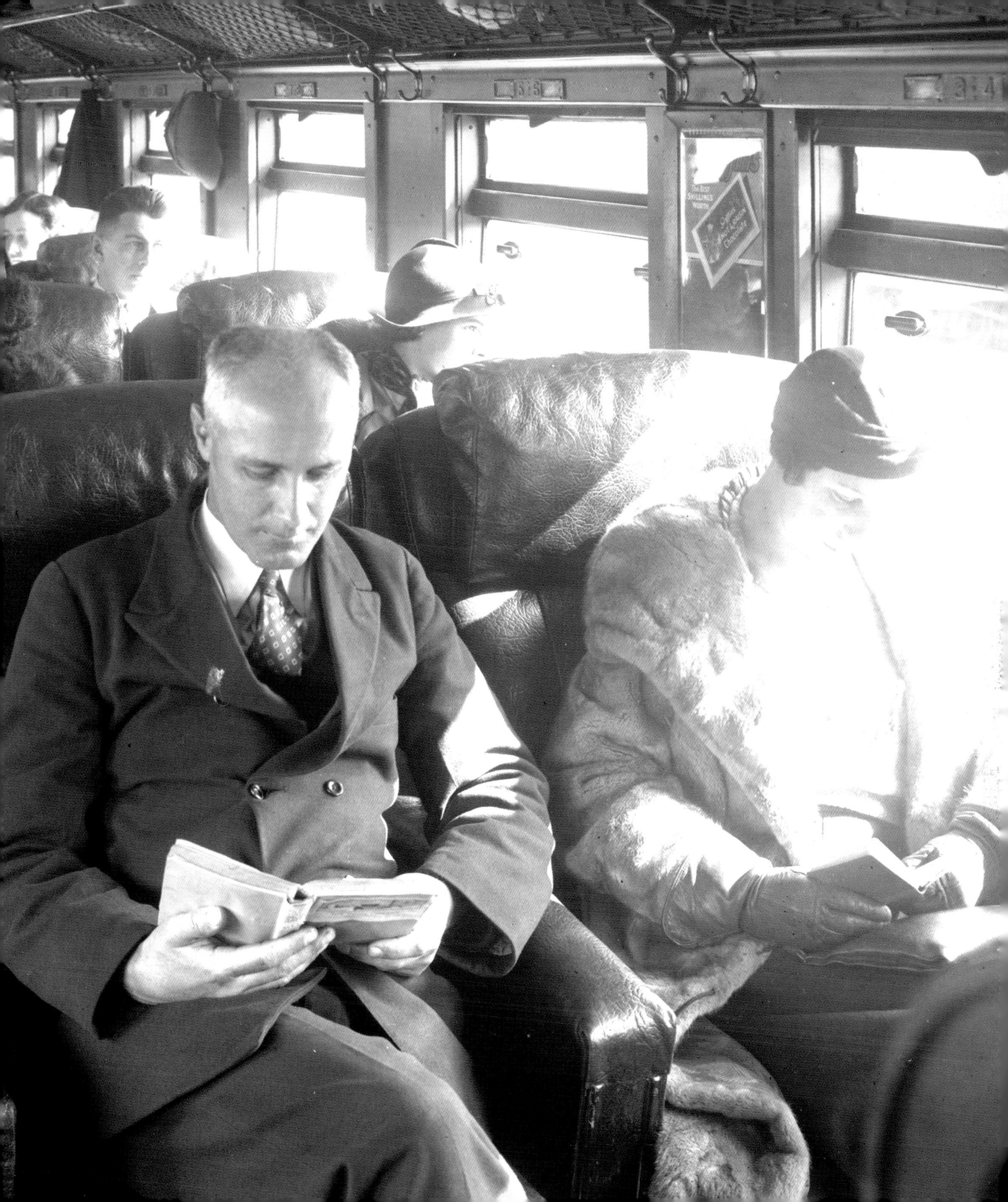

# Trainland

> For a few hours we are all, consciously or otherwise, naturalised citizens of Trainland, lost in a warm, lamplit limbo of strange places and strange faces . . . Warmth, change, comfort, the possibilities of adventure, dark dream-blue fields slipping quietly past.
>
> — *Robin Hyde*[1]

Between the 1870s and the Second World War the power, speed and utility of railways, once a startling novelty, became a familiar fixture of New Zealand life. While freight transport was always NZR's core business, most people's rail experience centred on the passenger train and the railway station. In the enclosed space of the passenger carriage the traveller entered a self-contained, rolling world — a 'limbo of strange places and strange faces' — temporarily detached from the landscapes 'slipping quietly past' the window.

Train travel provided rich possibilities of adventure, escape, relaxation, or a warm homecoming; 'a train is, above all things, a leisurely-minded vehicle'. Of course, reality rarely matches expectation: 'If you come in the train you are always disappointed because it never takes you where you would like to go.'[2] And while the separation of first- and second-class, ladies' and smoking cars reflected real social differences, the train offered a meeting place for New Zealanders of all ages, races, backgrounds and beliefs. It was also, variously, a lounge, dining room, bedroom, playground, theatre, library, crime scene and bar. The same was true of the second familiar element of the people's railway: the station. Whether grand urban monument or tiny weatherboard shed, from the late nineteenth century to at least the 1950s the station was a prominent and reassuring landmark in most cities, towns and rural districts. Like a family home or school, the station possessed a social as well as a physical fabric. Its ticket office, waiting rooms, refreshment rooms and platforms embodied the memories, emotions and experiences of all who had passed through them.

But familiarity breeds contempt. Just as they were avid users of NZR's passenger (and freight) services, stations and refreshment rooms, the 'citizens of Trainland' took these facilities for granted, complained about them and often abused them. In short, they treated the railways as if they owned them — which

PREVIOUS PAGE:

*Secluded in the comfort of a late-1930s first-class carriage, 'citizens of Trainland' pass the time reading, chatting or gazing out the window.*

ANZ, AAVK, W3493, C106

## Citizens of Trainland

*Like many suburban stations, Opawa on the electrified Christchurch–Lyttelton line had its share of problems with youthful mischief and petty vandalism. This 1957 publicity photograph was used to warn the public of the dangers of crossing the tracks in front of trains — a common occurrence on New Zealand's informal people's railway.*

ANZ, AAVK, W3493, B1068

in many ways they did. Public behaviour aboard trains and at stations therefore reveals much about New Zealanders' social interactions, their attitudes to class and gender, food and cigarette smoking, leisure and entertainment, and their often turbulent relationship with alcohol. For all their positive contribution to economic and social development, railways also reflected a darker side of New Zealand society, and were often the focus of public anxiety over drunkenness, crime, indecent behaviour, graffiti and vandalism. Squalid tales of grog, violence and vice along the rails seldom find a place in the selective nostalgia that glorifies the 'good old days', but they are nevertheless part of our rail story.

### 'All Aboard!'

In the Vogel era the adventure and novelty of rail travel outweighed its many discomforts. Just as well. The standard passenger carriages of the 1870s were tiny four- or six-wheel wooden boxes with rigid axles, 'longitudinal' (lengthways) bench seats and gloomy colza-oil lamps. Heating, toilets and passageways between carriages were non-existent. Passengers had the choice of travelling first or second class (often in a partitioned composite carriage), with the price of a first-class ticket typically 50 per cent higher. But apart

## Trainland

from horsehair cushions, coir floor mats, brass spittoons and the 'quality' of one's travelling companions, the advantages of first class were relatively slight; one late-nineteenth-century immigrant dismissed it as 'barely up to an English 2nd'.[3]

In contrast to the small private compartments and side corridors of many British and European trains — so familiar to readers or viewers of railway murder mysteries — almost all New Zealand carriages were American-style open 'saloon' cars. Slow speeds and frequent stops added to journey times but at least gave passengers a welcome respite from the bone-jarring (and often stomach-churning) rattle and roll. But if early rail travel was frequently a trial, it stacked up well against the alternatives of horseback, stagecoach, and coastal steamer or schooner.

Improvements came slowly. For the introduction of its South Island express in 1878, NZR fitted some six-wheelers with smoother-riding 'bogie' undercarriages. Five years later the Addington workshop began building American-style bogie cars, most of them composite-class hybrids.

RIGHT: These well-dressed passengers (and guard) in a 56-foot second-class car are posing cheerily for a 1950s publicity photo. New Zealand's open 'saloon' carriages were cheaper to build, maintain and operate than European-style compartment cars, and also offered travellers more opportunities for social interaction.

ANZ, AAVK, W3493, B7755

**In contrast to the small private compartments and side corridors of many British and European trains, almost all New Zealand carriages were American-style open 'saloon' cars.**

Later in the 1880s, the bold-as-brass Wellington and Manawatu Railway Company (WMR) set new standards with American bogie cars featuring large windows, electric lighting and upholstered seats — even in second class. NZR responded in the 1890s with new 44-foot carriages fitted with Pintsch compressed-gas lighting, padded bench cushions in second class and lavatories in first. A more curious innovation was the balcony car or 'birdcage', with its six-seat British-style compartments and exterior corridor or viewing 'gallery' enclosed by a metal grill — ideal for the celebrity traveller sweeping into town, although less suited to winter rain and snow. The 1909 debut of the North Island main trunk express saw the introduction of 50-foot carriages with chair seating (for 30 in first class and 44 in second) instead of the old benches, lavatories in both classes and connecting gangways and gates.

By the mid 1920s steam heating was widely fitted to mainline trains, electricity was superseding gas lighting, and 'Midland red' had become the standard livery. The 1930s saw further advances, with the

Citizens of Trainland

introduction of 50-foot steel-panelled first-class day cars (accommodating 27 in nine rows of three) and, from 1936, a class of standard 56-footers with fully upholstered seats (seating 31–35 in first and 56 in second), ladies' and gents' lavatories at opposite ends, and enclosed vestibules, which facilitated easier and safer movement between carriages and also helped exclude locomotive smoke and cinders. Overseas visitors were impressed: in 1937 an Australian politician described NZR's new cars as 'the most comfortable he had ever seen'; two years later, the British photographer Angus McBean stated that 'for comfort, cleanliness, modernity, window space and general design the present rolling stock in the Dominion out-classed that in the fifteen or twenty states in which he had travelled'.[4]

As with other elements of the rail system, the frugal Vogel legacy cast an enduring shadow over carriage

Trainland

## Smoke-drinkers and Fire-eaters

The numerous tunnels on New Zealand's mountainous lines posed a particular smoke hazard for unwary travellers, especially in the hot summer months. A window carelessly left open when the train entered a tunnel would see the carriage engulfed in acrid smoke and cinders from the locomotive (or in later years, unpleasant diesel fumes). Janet Frame recalled the railway ritual of 'the passengers coughing, shutting and opening and shutting the windows' as 'the carriage filled with smoke'. Writing in the *New Zealand Railways Magazine* in the mid 1930s, Robin Hyde wondered:

> why there is always someone who leaves train windows open when a tunnel is drawing nigh, and who therefore has to wrestle simultaneously with the spirit and the window-catch? For so it is. There is absolutely no teaching these smoke-drinkers, and one can only suppose they are first cousins to the family of fire-eaters. Tunnel number one appears on the horizon, is passed. Reproachful but forgiving, the other occupants of the carriage survey the offender, who beams charmingly . . . The instant that the train has cleared the tunnel, up goes her window once more. Nor does it descend in time to escape the vengeance of tunnels two, three, four, or five. Everybody's patience wears thin except that of the lady with the passion for fresh air who comes smiling through it all.[5]

design. The distinctive tubular or 'bullet' shape of the 1930s carriages was a product of the network's restricted loading gauge and tight, rounded tunnel profiles. Through numerous upgrades and refurbishments, the 157 carriages built between 1936 and 1945 have provided the country's standard long-haul passenger stock ever since. The railcars and suburban multi-units introduced from the late 1930s maintained NZR's solid reputation for passenger accommodation, for a few decades at least, but away from the glamour of the main lines, comforts remained elusive. On rural branch lines and isolated sections like Nelson, where mixed trains

*An excursion train headed by Mainline Steam's K$^A$ 942 bursts out of a tunnel north of Kaikoura in 1997, while a dense column of smoke still pours from the tunnel in the background.*

Peter McGavin

predominated, longitudinal seating, spartan upholstery and gas lighting were common until the 1950s.

Long-distance travel frequently required an overnight journey, especially on the North Island's main trunk. From the beginning of the service in 1909 main trunk expresses included one or two sleeping cars, each with twenty berths in five compartments, which cost an extra 10s on top of the first-class fare. From 1927, travellers on the Night Limited — at least those who could afford to pay the equivalent of more than $300 in today's money — could enjoy the trip in 'de luxe' 56-foot steel-panelled sleeping cars, with sixteen berths in eight

# Trainland

compartments, a steward, kitchenette, vestibules and electric lighting. By the 1930s the 'high-backed, stoutly padded' reclining seats of the first-class day cars also offered a reasonable level of comfort. Travelling first class in 1935, Robin Hyde recalled 'Lights out on the Limited': 'perhaps it's eleven o'clock when the last page is turned and the last yawn yawned. The game then . . . is to curl up in such a way that your sleeping-partner can't object, and lapse into the arms of Morpheus.' For the less fortunate in second class, the straight-backed throw-over seats made for a long, often sleepless ordeal, as 'all night long they sought elusive comfort with the NZR pillow' (which from 1925 main trunk travellers could hire for 1s).[6]

## Class Action

As elsewhere in the world, rail passengers were sifted into 'classes' from the outset. In stark contrast to Britain, where there were as many as seven classes, New Zealand never had more than two (plus sleepers). In keeping with the egalitarian ethos of colonial society, the difference between first and second class was often modest, especially compared to the vast gulf between cabin and steerage accommodation on nineteenth-century immigrant ships or grand ocean liners. But the issue cannot be dismissed completely. Second-class carriages were considerably more cramped, had less comfortable seats, and for some years lacked toilets and other amenities. They were also marshalled at the front of the train, and therefore more affected by the noise of the locomotive and irritating intrusions of smoke, cinders, coal dust and fumes. This fore-and-aft arrangement reflected centuries-old maritime tradition, and was similarly determined by considerations of passenger comfort — and safety. On most occasions, cinders and smoke were all that second-class travellers had to worry about, but in a head-on collision or derailment they were much more likely to suffer injury or death.

The reality of this class arrangement was starkly demonstrated by New Zealand's deadliest train disaster, at Tangiwai in 1953. When a volcanic lahar fatally weakened the bridge over the Whangaehu River, the first

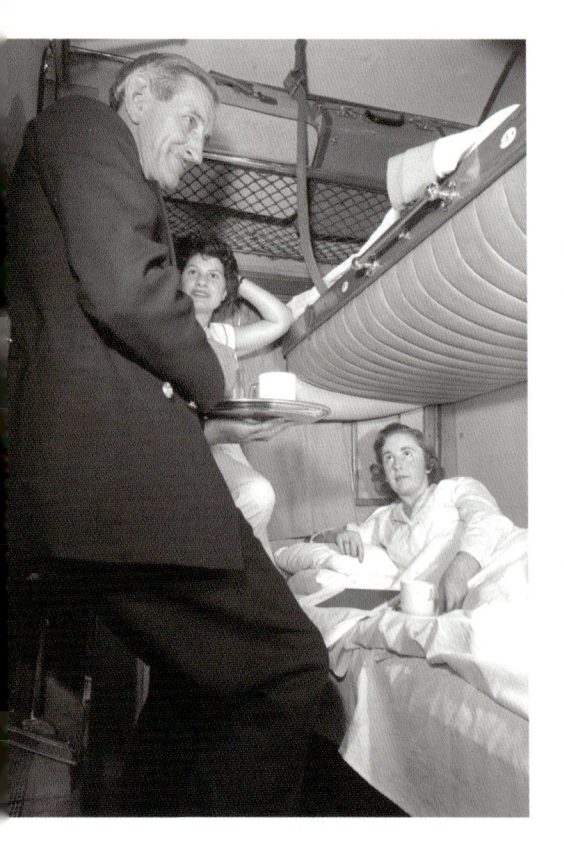

*A sleeper attendant delivers refreshments to two pyjama-clad travellers in this cosy 1950s publicity shot.*

ANZ, AAVK, W3493, B7767

*An A-class compound locomotive heads a typical early main trunk express out of Wellington in 1909, banked by another A (at rear) for the steep climb up to Johnsonville. The RTPO van directly behind the locomotive tender is followed by second-class carriages, a dining car, first-class cars and sleepers.*

ANZ, AAVK, W3493, C1530

half of the Wellington–Auckland express — locomotive $K^A$ 949, its tender, and all five second-class carriages — plunged into the raging waters. The leading first-class car teetered on the brink for a moment before tumbling in, and all but one of its occupants was saved; the other three first-class cars and two vans (including the Railway Travelling Post Office) remained on the track. In all, 151 of the 285 passengers and crew on board were killed: out of more than 170 second-class passengers, only 28 survived; in contrast, just one first-class passenger was lost. Among the numerous suggestions considered by the commission of inquiry into the accident was the placement of vans directly behind the locomotive to provide more protection to passenger cars, but this was rejected as impractical.[7] Although the context and situation were quite different, it is sobering to reflect that life and death at Tangiwai was determined by 'class' (or the price of a passenger's ticket) to an even greater extent than on the *Titanic* — where three-quarters of steerage (third-class), three-fifths of second-class and just over a third of first-class passengers died.

# Trainland

*The shattered hulk of car 'Z', the only first-class carriage to topple into the Whangaehu River at Tangiwai. It was swept onto the riverbank and all but one of its 22 occupants was rescued. Most of those travelling in the five second-class cars were not so lucky.*

ANZ, AAVK, W3493, D1952

As well as class, trains in Britain and other countries were frequently segregated by gender through the provision of 'ladies' cars'. Although trains, trams and other forms of public transport offered women greater mobility and new opportunities for social interaction outside traditional conventions, they also increased the possibility of harassment by male travellers. From the 1870s New Zealand, like other countries, provided ladies' waiting rooms at many stations. In the 1880s NZR briefly ran ladies' cars on Christchurch–Dunedin expresses, but self-reliant colonial women seemed to regard them as an unnecessary luxury and they were soon withdrawn. In the decade before the First World War, the Women's Christian Temperance Union (WCTU) and other groups revived calls for 'separate accommodation' for women and children, largely because of concern at drinking by male travellers. Reluctant to add extra weight to his trains, General Manager Thomas Ronayne told the WCTU that because New Zealand carriages were 'not divided up into a number of small compartments' like those in Britain, there was less 'risk of ladies being molested or annoyed by objectionable passengers'.[8]

In mid 1917, however, NZR had a change of heart. When dining cars were withdrawn (see 'Meals on Wheels' on page 148) ten of them were converted into ladies' cars. The first entered service on the overnight North Island main trunk express in December that year. Divided into first- and second-class saloons, seating thirteen and 24 respectively, the car was staffed by a female attendant and provided a gas-ring for heating children's drinks. Ladies' cars (minus the attendant) were reintroduced on the South Island main trunk two years later, and from 1923 appeared on trains from Wellington to New Plymouth, Napier and Woodville.

Although they were initially popular — in 1922 the *Auckland Star* reported that the ladies' carriage was 'beautifully sweet and clear, [with] no odours of smoking or drinking about' — patronage soon fell away. In 1929 the cars were removed from the southern and secondary North Island lines, and attendants were withdrawn from the main trunk express as a cost-cutting measure in 1933. By that time, ladies' cars were leaving Wellington with, on average, just six passengers a night. Most women without children preferred

Citizens of Trainland

*Well-dressed ladies chat on the platform at Christchurch station around the turn of the twentieth century. For a time in the 1880s, and again from 1919 to 1929, NZR ran ladies' cars on the South Island main trunk.*

ATL, F-38597-1/2

to travel elsewhere in the train, as did the increasing number of female smokers; the ageing ladies' carriages also compared poorly with NZR's sleek new day cars. In October 1938 the last ladies' cars were withdrawn and converted for use on suburban lines. The following decades saw repeated calls for their reintroduction, not so much from women but from other travellers who preferred not to be disturbed by crying babies. The Department, however, staunchly resisted their reinstatement on economic grounds.[9]

A more enduring distinction, which for many years provided a de facto gender segregation on trains, was the separation of smoking and non-smoking

# Trainland

passengers. With their wall-mounted match-strikers, brass spittoons and enamelled notices asking passengers not to 'expectorate' on the floor, 'smokers' were exclusively male bastions until the 1920s, when women began to light up in larger numbers. Indeed, the WCTU's earlier demands for ladies' cars were partly based on the fact that 'men enjoy the privilege of smoking compartments'. In 1912 Wellington's *Dominion* complained of 'lurid obscenity in a packed smoker'; the Department itself admitted that 'undesirable characters generally travel in the second [class] smoker'.

Initially, mainline expresses carried a similar number of smoking and non-smoking cars, but by the 1950s the demand for smokers was so great that four or five were needed for every non-smoker. Even then, there were frequent complaints of travellers lighting up in non-smoking cars, especially on crowded excursion trains or racing and rugby specials. On branch line mixed trains, smokers and non-smokers were often segregated into compartments within the same car. The railcars of the 1940s were similarly divided into two compartments, with smokers allocated three-fifths of the seats. As recently as 1975, NZR reported that two-thirds of its customers requested smoking reservations, but the popularity and social acceptability of smoking was to decline sharply over the following decades.[10]

The 1970s and eighties saw the removal of longstanding passenger distinctions in favour of universal accommodation. First and second classes were abolished in 1978, and between 1980 and 1985 suburban and long-distance trains progressively became smoke-free; the last sleeping cars were removed (from the Northerner) in 1987. By that time, however, the problem was not so much how to arrange passengers on New Zealand trains, but how to get them on board.

## Meals on Wheels

There is one area where New Zealand's rail experience diverged from most of its overseas counterparts. In the years before 1899, and again from 1917 to the 1970s, NZR's trains lacked onboard dining facilities, forcing passengers to rely on station refreshment rooms or their own supplies. In contrast, the private WMR ran dining cars for almost all of its short history. The first, introduced in 1887, was a tiny four-wheeler that could only be boarded when the train was stopped, but it was soon replaced by a 28-foot American-style diner with end-platform access. WMR later upgraded its service with a 31-footer seating twelve (1890), a 43-footer with refrigerator, electric lights, coke stove and seating for seventeen diners (1894), and finally a 52-footer capable of seating eighteen (1904). In these years the company earned an outstanding reputation for the quality of its food, which included fresh trout loaded at Waikanae, strawberries and pears from Paekakariki, and whitebait, flounder and oysters from Horowhenua.[11]

NZR's first 'refreshment car', an Addington-built 44-footer, entered service on the Christchurch–Dunedin run in December 1899, followed two years later by others on the Wellington–New Plymouth route. The latter service was then a joint operation with WMR, and until 1905 NZR dining cars on the Palmerston North–New Plymouth leg were leased to WMR's caterer. By that time NZR had dining cars on its prestigious Auckland–Rotorua express, and from February 1909 the service was extended to the North Island main trunk. By 1917 the Department had a fleet of 22 dining cars, including nine new 50-footers with seating for 25. For a cost of 2s per meal, the breakfast (8–9.30 am) and tea (5–7 pm) menus offered fried or boiled fish, grilled chops, sausages, bacon and eggs, cold meats, and coffee or tea; at dinner time (12–2 pm), passengers could enjoy hot joints and grills, steak and kidney pie, ham or ox tongue, fish, potatoes, seasonal vegetables, salad, cheese, plum pudding, custard and fruits. For morning and afternoon tea, 3d would buy tea or coffee, bread, butter and jam, biscuits and cake. The cars were manned by a chef, second cook, head waiter and second waiter, with an extra man during holidays. Known as the 'sea-going' staff, they were all former cooks and stewards from merchant ships, and initially wore their own ships' uniforms (with NZR brass buttons).[12]

> **NZR's first 'refreshment car', an Addington-built 44-footer, entered service on the Christchurch–Dunedin run in December 1899, followed two years later by others on the Wellington–New Plymouth route.**

Despite their lavish decor, fine food, silver service and attentive waiters, dining cars had severe limitations. For a start, no more than 80 passengers could usually be fed during each sitting, a small portion of the 200 or more carried on main trunk expresses. The 'first in, first served' arrangement led to long queues through adjacent carriages and complaints from latecomers about cold food. It was also hard work for the 'sea-going' staff, who toiled in cramped, swaying and often unbearably hot galleys (windows had to be kept shut to keep out dust and smoke); despite their sea-legs, many succumbed to motion sickness. To make matters worse, dining cars haemorrhaged money, losing as much as 1s a meal.

In mid 1917, as wartime coal and staff shortages began to bite, the Department announced a 'temporary' withdrawal of all its dining cars, the last of which ran between Wellington and New Plymouth on 20 August.

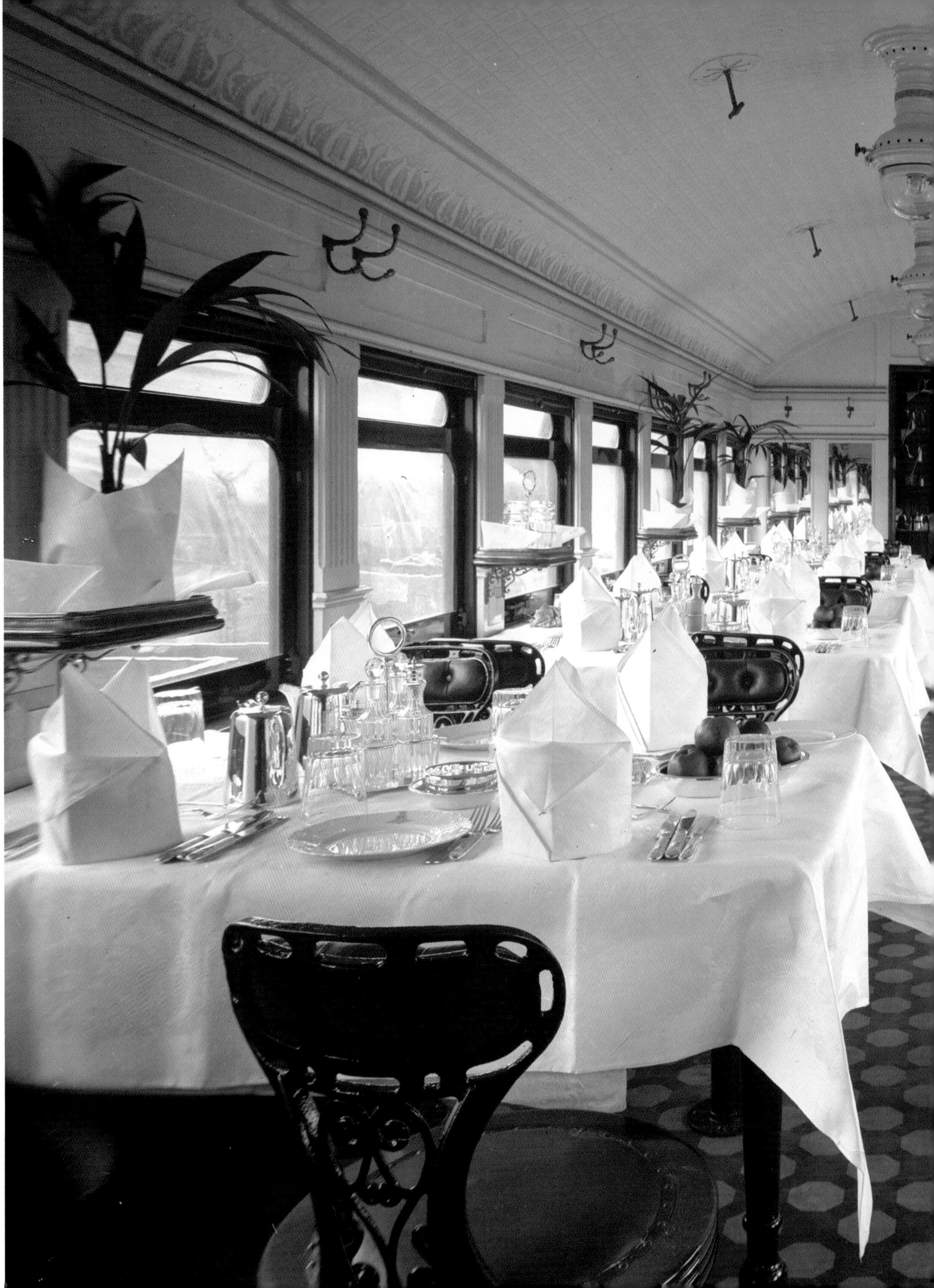

*A view inside one of the elegantly appointed dining cars that ran on the North Island main trunk between 1909 and 1917. Initially, they were only attached between Wellington and Ohakune, as the remainder of the trip in both directions occurred at night; from 1914 dining cars were picked up or dropped off at Taumarunui or Waiouru to lighten the load during the night-time slog over the central section.*

ANZ, AAVK, W3493, C608

# Trainland

The decision was partly financial, but mainly prompted by pressing wartime need: it would enable an extra passenger car to be added to overcrowded expresses, free up rolling stock for refitting as ordinary carriages (including ladies' cars), and release more male workers for the war effort.[13] From now on, NZR would rely on largely female-staffed station refreshment rooms, which — as we shall see below — were to become an iconic feature of twentieth-century New Zealand life.

## Songs and Stories

Cocooned in the 'warm, lamplit limbo' of their carriages, most passengers passed their journeys gazing out the window, chatting, reading, knitting or playing cards. Others amused themselves and fellow passengers with songs, stories and poems, while some brought banjos, mandolins, mouth organs, guitars or transistor radios aboard. On an Otago train in 1905, an 'old man, over 80 years of age . . . produced an ancient-looking fiddle and proceeded to enliven the tedious journey with reels, hornpipes, and country dances'. A Marlborough farmer recalled 1920s rugby supporters playing the mouth organ, bellowing 'football songs', improvising comedy skits and performing 'recitations Banjo Paterson style'. This free entertainment was not always welcome, as in 1929 when a group of sailors 'along with their lady friends', heading south from Auckland on leave, annoyed fellow passengers by loudly 'singing along with a Banjo and Mandolin the usual Music Hall songs'. Robin Hyde described an 'extraordinarily sociable' journey from Auckland to Waitomo in the mid 1930s, with 'footballers playing a ukulele and

*Station bookstalls, like this one at Frankton Junction, catered to travellers' needs by selling newspapers, magazines and paperbacks, cigarettes and matches, playing cards, stationery, postcards and confectionery.*

ANZ, AAVK, W3493, D658

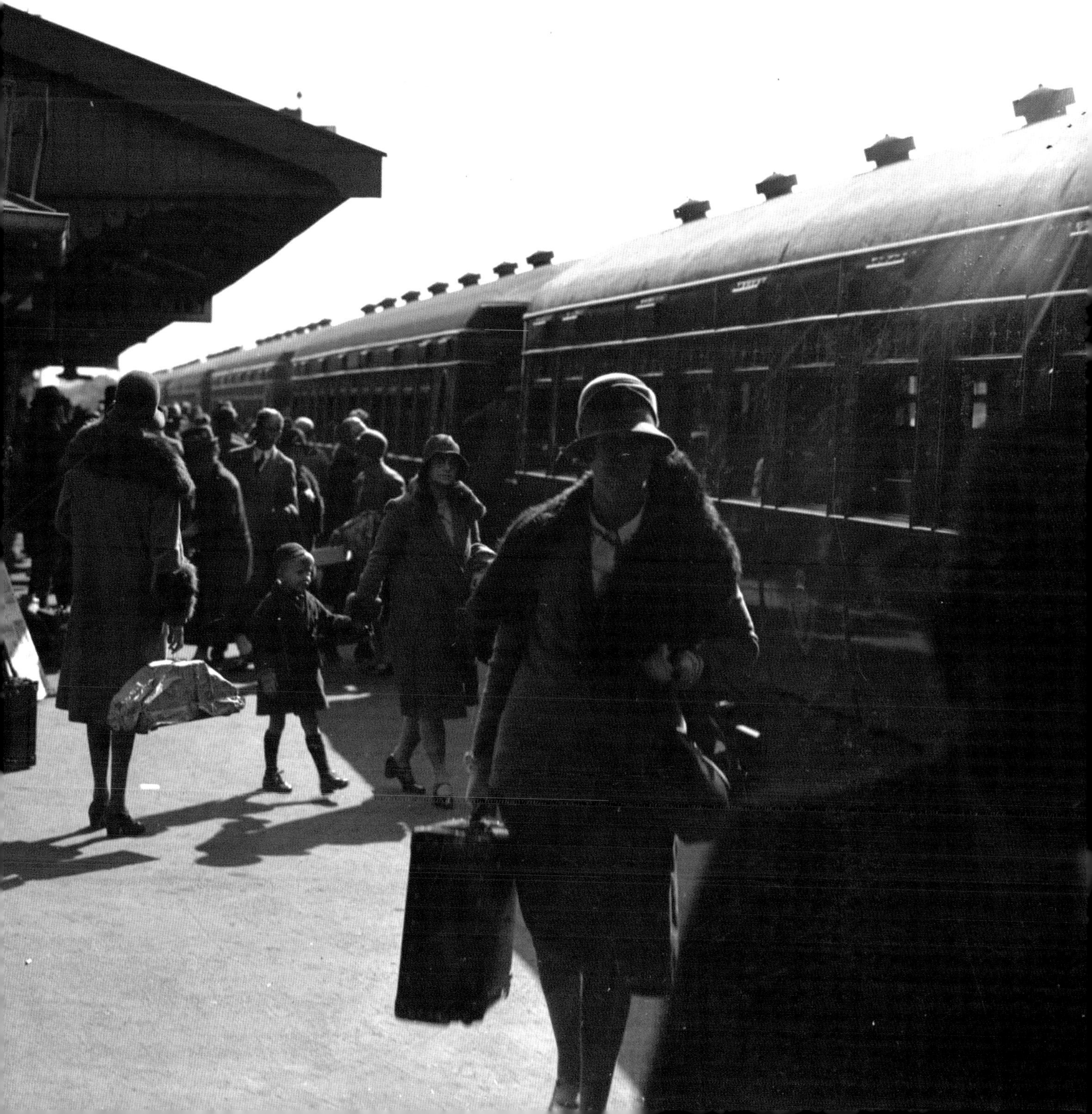

## Trainland

crooning in a nearby carriage', and a train-wide 'treasure hunt' which saw dozens of passengers 'crawling about and looking under the pillows of the few old stagers who, far from joining in, had gone peacefully off to sleep'.[14]

Reading was naturally a popular way to pass the time. Many travellers brought their own books or magazines, or purchased them from the well-stocked station bookstalls. Passengers on express trains could also buy newspapers and magazines from newsboys or 'runners', who were granted half-rate concession fares to peddle their wares on board. As runners were allowed to sell anything stocked by bookstalls, their satchels soon bulged with tobacco, cigarettes, matches, postcards, pens and popular books.

The dubious quality of the 'pulp fiction' circulating on early-twentieth-century trains appalled the country's moral guardians. In 1908 Reverend R.H.W. Bligh of the 'White Cross League' complained that 'literature of a degrading order such as "Police Budget" and the "Wellington Truth", papers given up to stories of lust and murder, are being sold on the trains'. Three years later a traveller on the Christchurch–Dunedin express complained of 'newsrunners barging through the carriages and pestering passengers to buy doubtful books' such as *The Story of the Escaped Nun* and the saucy works of 'Victoria Cross' (Vivian Cory). According to a Manawatu passenger, boys as young as fifteen were peddling 'lurid' books, which they 'insidiously thrust on the attention of travellers . . . with the remark "This is really spicy" or "This is just red hot"'. After manfully struggling to the end of one, he declared it 'absolutely the filthiest book I have ever read'. 'In the smokers,' another passenger agreed, the 'most putrid literature is offered for sale, besides indecent post cards.'[15]

**The dubious quality of the 'pulp fiction' circulating on early-twentieth-century trains appalled the country's moral guardians.**

In 1912 there was another flurry of complaints about 'filthy, immoral, literary "hogwash"' circulating on the country's trains. A group of Feilding churchmen, apparently well-informed 'by a person who has specially interested himself in this matter', claimed that 'a very large proportion of the purchasers of these books [are] women, and many of them women of such standing as would not care to be seen asking for such publications from reputable booksellers'. The Department took the matter seriously enough to instruct district traffic managers to probe the moral hygiene of local trains. The Wanganui manager reported that runners representing Books and Papers Ltd, the *New Zealand Times*, *Wanganui Chronicle* and *Dominion*

*Wellington station's bookstall in the 1960s, its rear shelves stocked with paperbacks, pocket combs, mints and 'Kiwis' milk caramel toffees.*

ANZ, AAVK, W3493, B2234

were peddling books such as Elinor Glyn's *Three Weeks*, Victoria Cross' *Anna Lombard*, H.W.C. Newte's *The Lonely Lovers*, and *The Diary of My Honeymoon* by 'Lady X'. His Wellington counterpart added *The Harlot in Heaven*, *Confessions of a Princess* and *The Secret History of the Mormons* to the rail library of shame.

To modern eyes, the scandal over books like Glyn's 1907 bestseller *Three Weeks* seems ridiculous rather than shocking, but their frank discussion of adultery and female sexuality caused a sensation across the Empire in the years before the Great War. In 1914 the Department tightened bookstall lessees' contracts to prohibit the sale of 'immoral, indecent, or doubtful literature', but officials conceded that unless publications had been proscribed under the Indecent Publications Act there was little they could do to prevent their sale to rail travellers.[16]

The storm in a paperback calmed after the war, only occasionally resurfacing. In 1926 a correspondent

## Trainland

denounced Robert Keable's war novel *Simon Called Peter* as 'a foul thing treating sex ideas with a freedom only done in brothels', but NZR officials disagreed, considering it a 'faithful portrayal of life at the front'. Five years later the Department asked bookstall lessees to remove the American magazine *Breezy Stories*, condemned by complainants as a 'moral cesspool' filled with 'suggestive drawings of semi-nude figures'.[17] By that time, however, tales of lust had been largely ousted by stories of violence and villainy, in the form of the murder or crime mystery. In 1935 Robin Hyde advised travellers:

> Follow the example of your fellow passengers and equip yourself with not fewer than three detective novels. These will have paper backs and purple contents. The predominance of detective stories at all railway bookstalls (love limping home a very poor second, and the rest of literature nowhere at all), shows how thin is our veneer of civilisation. The book which sustained me from Marton to Frankton Junction sported no fewer than thirteen corpses, and I must confess I could have done with more.[18]

Even the thoroughly respectable *New Zealand Railways Magazine* got in on the act, publishing a serialised murder mystery, 'The Thirteenth Clue' (see Chapter 5). From the 1960s, NZR's rarer brushes with morality were confined to the indefatigable Patricia Bartlett's campaign against the sale of *Playboy* on the Cook Strait ferries.

## Drunk and Disorderly

Pulp fiction was not the only target of early-twentieth-century moral evangelists. If complaints to the Railways Department are to be believed, the country's trains were awash in a sea of grog, profanity and vice. Alcohol was never sold in WMR or NZR dining cars, and sales at refreshment rooms ended in 1905. Nevertheless, for many passengers the 'reviving' hip flask of spirits was an essential travelling companion. Although drunkenness in any public place (including railway carriages) was a criminal offence, the Department tolerated passengers bringing personal supplies aboard trains as long as they were 'consumed in a reasonable and decorous manner'.[19]

Often, as the carnage of a 1904 Easter trip to Christchurch by Dunedin's Alhambra and Union rugby teams illustrates, the reality was anything but decorous. After the train disgorged its passengers at Dunedin, the carriage floors were reportedly littered with broken glass, food, rubbish and cigarette butts. Cleaners emptied one car of 28 discarded beer bottles and three whisky bottles. Vomit crusted in a corner, blocked the lavatories, and streaked the paintwork outside the windows. A window pane was broken, a water filter damaged and a door wrenched off its hinges. Players and supporters had earlier left a similar trail of destruction at the Ashburton refreshment rooms, throwing cups, saucers, sugar, sandwiches and tea across the floor; the lessee and another man were assaulted and two offenders were nabbed by the local constable. The Alhambra team's manager staunchly denied any wrongdoing, blaming 'strangers' for the damage and implausibly suggesting that the lads' beer bottles contained nothing stronger than lemonade. Club officials were later hauled before the Otago Rugby Football Union, but with the help of the legendary Dunedin lawyer Alfred Hanlon eventually got off scot free.[20]

**When the bustling seaport of Port Chalmers briefly went dry in 1902, thirsty seafarers, wharfies and locals packed the evening trains into Dunedin and turned the 11.40 pm return service into the 'drunkenest train in Australasia', nicknamed the 'Royal Soaks Express'.**

The Railways Department and the privately leased refreshment rooms that operated at its stations were largely exempt from the web of restrictive liquor licensing laws passed in the late nineteenth century. As a result, refreshment rooms like Dunedin's stayed open for an hour and a half after hotels closed at night, and also opened on Christmas Day, Good Friday and Election Day, when hotels were forced to shut. 'On those days,' the *Otago Daily Times* complained in 1904, 'drinking to a great extent takes place at the Railway Station, and disorderly scenes are often enacted there.' From 1895 the Department agreed not to issue licences to rooms in 'dry' (no-licence) areas, but that only shifted the problem. When the bustling seaport of Port Chalmers briefly went dry in 1902, thirsty seafarers, wharfies and locals packed the evening trains into Dunedin and turned the 11.40 p.m. return service into the 'drunkenest train in Australasia', nicknamed the 'Royal Soaks Express'. Eventually, following a spate of fights and arrests at Dunedin station, Railways Minister Joseph Ward banned the sale of liquor at all refreshment rooms from 1 April 1905.[21]

Again, the decision backfired. A year later, the Chief Traffic Manager reported that '[s]ince the abolition of the sale of liquor at the refreshment rooms drinking on the train has become a common practice, especially at holiday times', when passengers frequently brought their own flasks and bottles aboard. There was regular

There was regular trouble with touring sports teams and race-goers, while late-night trains to ports like Lyttelton and Bluff earned a particularly unsavoury reputation.

LEFT: *Touring sports teams and their supporters were often troublesome train passengers. This image shows the mess left by rugby players on the Silver Star in 1973.*

ANZ, AAVK, W3493, D24456

trouble with touring sports teams and race-goers, while late-night trains to ports like Lyttelton and Bluff earned a particularly unsavoury reputation. In 1904 two drunken passengers died after falling off Bluff trains; another was killed in the Lyttelton tunnel while trying to urinate from the open platform between carriages. Miners' trains to Waihi and West Coast towns were equally notorious. In 1909 the Paeroa Stationmaster reported that carriages on the Waihi miners' special 'were bespattered from end to end with vomit, blood and hair', while trouble spilled into the streets with reports of brawling, public urination and window breaking. The following year, behaviour on the Saturday night train from Westport to Granity was said to be 'simply disgusting', with 'half drunken youths' singing, swearing and playing two-up. 'It was perfect bedlam.'[22]

Elsewhere, trains were used to subvert the longstanding alcohol ban in the King Country district. During the later years of main trunk construction a large, thirsty workforce smuggled vast amounts of grog into the area. The trip from 'wet' Frankton down to 'dry' Taumarunui could be particularly high-spirited: a 1907 correspondent reported that the 'drunkenness which is carried on, both by Whites and Maoris, is a menace to public convenience. Last evening, friends assured me, men and women were drinking to excess and were most disgusting — even vomiting over the floors of the cars.' A local guard confirmed that the 'trouble is mostly with labourers coming up to the co-operative works'.[23] The problem receded as the navvies moved on after 1908, but settlers, sawmillers, local Maori — and frequently train crews — continued to smuggle alcohol into the King Country until the district's prohibition was lifted in 1954.

Emergency regulations prohibited liquor on troop trains during both world wars, but despite intense lobbying from temperance groups the Railways Department concluded that an outright alcohol ban would be extremely unpopular and impossible to enforce without searching passengers and their luggage. By-laws against 'riotous, disorderly, indecent, or offensive' behaviour on trains were toughened in 1922, but by that time the moral crusade against drink was beginning to ease.[24] In part, this reflected the evangelists' success in entangling society in a web of laws and restrictions. In fact, public drunkenness and disorder had been declining for decades, largely due to the demise of the old frontier communities of seamen and whalers, kauri bushmen, goldminers, agricultural labourers and navvies. Rather than the all-male worlds of pub, work camp and racecourse, the new model of urban masculinity, the male 'breadwinner', increasingly spent his

# Trainland

leisure hours in family-oriented pursuits — a trend NZR sought to exploit in the interwar years through its promotion of family holidays, Snow Specials and other excursions.

Together with West Coast mining settlements and port towns, one of the last bastions of frontier masculinity was the PWD's dam-, road- and railmaking camps. In the late 1930s and forties the spirit of the old main trunk lived on aboard the special trains that ferried workers on the Parnassus–Wharanui line into Christchurch once a month. Known as the 'Bob Semple special' after the PWD's garrulous minister, the return train left the city at 11 pm. As engine driver J.M. Grainger explained, 'with these people an army of officials and police would have been needed to prevent liquor from being taken aboard'. When the guard tried to collect tickets he found many of the passengers 'in a befuddled state' or fast asleep. 'From all sides the guard was being pressed to join his passengers in a glass of beer or a nip of whisky. Pies, saveloys, crayfish, oysters and fish and chips were offered.' He resisted all temptation, only to find his young assistant had taken a different approach: 'In the centre of the car was a keg of beer and . . . around it was a group of young people, including the assistant, singing.' The older man 'slipped his ticket punch into his pocket' and joined in.[25]

While they battled the demon drink, the Railways Department and eagle-eyed evangelists were constantly on the lookout for other breaches of public order. Sexual acts on trains appear to have been relatively rare, probably because NZR's open saloon carriages denied travellers the privacy of European-style compartments. Some British and French lines, for example, were notorious for onboard prostitution, a problem that does not appear to have troubled New Zealand rail authorities. In a rare incident in 1908, a guard stumbled upon a couple having sex in a 'birdcage' compartment on the Dunedin–Christchurch express:

> **I saw them committing a most indecent act in full view of anyone that might have passed along at the time. I told them this was not allowed and in any case they might have pulled down the blinds. They never shifted their position when I went in but he cooly handed me both tickets saying it's all right old man.**

Although the male offender refused to give his name, he was later tracked down, convicted of indecency and ordered to pay court costs. In the general absence of compartments, other than on sleeping cars, amorous travellers had to make do with the cramped discomfort of toilets, the fleeting darkness of tunnels or the flimsy cover of blankets — as in 1931, when a married painter from Addington workshops was caught in the act under a rug with a woman who was not his wife.[26]

Far more common were complaints of men 'casting offensive matter' (urinating) off platforms between carriages, especially on crowded race or excursion specials and suburban trains, which usually lacked toilets. Troop trains were often unruly, especially during both world wars, although even in the mid 1920s Christchurch pedestrians complained of Territorials en route to Burnham Camp exposing themselves from train platforms. More serious sexual offences were rare: in 1938 a seventeen-year-old boy was accused of raping a girl in the toilet of a Timaru–Christchurch excursion (he was later convicted of indecent assault, with the judge recommending 'a sound thrashing'); in 1955 an intoxicated man exposed himself to passengers and urinated on seats; and in 1972 a 53-year-old indecently assaulted a nine-year-old girl on a Midland line railcar (he was committed to Sunnyside Psychiatric Hospital).[27]

The 1950s moral panic over 'teenage' delinquency, breathlessly detailed in the 1954 report of the Mazengarb committee, highlighted mounting public anxiety over social disorder. Teenage tearaways hit the headlines soon after when 30 or 40 boys terrorised passengers on an Auckland suburban train, smashing windows, pulling the emergency cord, uncoupling carriages and reportedly reducing the guard to a quivering wreck. In 1960, 'teenage riots' at the staid Hastings Blossom Festival were widely blamed on the 5000 Wellington and Hutt Valley youth who travelled north on five special trains. There was also trouble at Arthur's Pass, with 'gangs of youths and girls' aged thirteen to fifteen reportedly 'running riot' on a 1957 Snow Special, breaking four carriage windows

*Give it a whirl: young Wellingtonians dance on the station platform before boarding a special train for the Hastings Blossom Festival in September 1955. Five years later this popular event would be marred by so-called 'teenage riots', blamed on train-travelling youths from Wellington and the Hutt Valley.*

ANZ, AAVK, W3493, D1421

## Trainland

and sending two of their number to hospital. Two years later, a gang of more than a hundred 'bodgies, widgies, and louts' abused fellow excursionists, pelted cars with snowballs, assaulted a motorist and broke more carriage windows. In response, NZR increased supervision by guards and police, segregated 'youthful parties' at the front of the train, and reserved adult and family cars at the rear. But the Department refused to derail popular excursions just 'because some teddy boy might kick up a shindy'. 'We can't ask them to come along and prove something before letting them on,' an official explained. After all, 'the railways belong to the people'.[28]

Although media reports of teenage delinquency were undoubtedly exaggerated, drinking and disorderly behaviour aboard trains remained a major concern. In the 1950s and sixties the Department fielded frequent complaints of abusive language, drunkenness, underage drinking, minor assaults and passengers throwing empty beer bottles from trains. Guards often had to call police to remove offenders — although on at least one occasion police were the culprits. In July 1968 main trunk passengers complained of a group of policemen drinking, shouting abuse and 'breaking wind with childish glee' between Auckland and Palmerston North; one vomited in the toilets and another on the platform at Taihape.[29] More often, however, the troublemakers were soldiers travelling to and from Waiouru (especially during the era of compulsory military training), groups of apprentices on trade training courses, and — as in 1904 — touring sports teams and their followers.

## Station to Station

In an era before widespread access to automobiles and telephones, let alone television and the Internet, the railway and its station provided many communities with their primary (sometimes only) connection to the outside world. The station was the 'front counter' of local commercial activities, many of which were timed to coincide with the arrival and departure of trains. It was also a vibrant hub

*Big-city railway stations like Wellington's were potent symbols of civic pride and prosperity. Although motor competition had already begun to undermine*

*rail passenger traffic by the time it opened in 1937, the capital's station remains a thriving passenger hub.*

Paul Hamer

of social life, a place of welcomes and farewells, joy and sadness, hope and disappointment. In addition to their station and refreshment rooms, and the surrounding complex of yards, sheds, signal boxes and water towers, many towns boasted a string of railway workers' houses and huts (see Chapter 1), a 'Railway Hotel' and a cluster of nearby shops, stables and eateries.

City stations were embodiments of civic pride, power and prosperity, much

# Trainland

*The railway 'brand' carried considerable prestige in the first half of the twentieth century and was often adopted by businesses and other amenities. Many towns boasted 'Railway' bakeries, butcheries, stores, theatres and especially public hotels — like this one in Woodville, photographed in 1999.*

Paul Hamer

like modern sports stadiums or airport terminals, although rail hubs usually occupied a more prominent, central location. Perhaps the clearest evidence of the prominence of rail in early-twentieth-century New Zealand is Dunedin's stunning station, completed in 1906. In the 1930s Auckland and Wellington erected even larger (if less elegant) stations, imposing monuments to the power of rail — at a time when its ascendancy was already being challenged by road transport. At main trunk towns like Taumarunui and Taihape large crowds would often gather on Saturday nights to meet the Limited and the express, even in the early hours of the morning. Strategic junctions like Frankton, Palmerston North and Marton also bustled with constant activity. In the 1930s Robin Hyde suggested that Marton Junction contained, 'at a rough guess, more newsboys, cups of tea and large ham sandwiches to the square inch than any place else in the world'.[30]

At the other end of the spectrum, John A. Lee's sketch of small-town Southland

## Citizens of Trainland

rang true for hundreds of rural settlements: 'Riversdale was, and still is, a one-street village with shops on one side of the street and the railway station on the other. The social events of the day were the daily arrival of the railway train with its delivery of mail, [and] the synchronised departure of the mail coach to Waikaia.' On the isolated Moutohora section in the 1920s, the arrival of the daily mixed train from Gisborne was 'one of the highlights of community life':

> Swinging hurricane lamps as they came down bush tracks, people walked from near and far to meet the evening train, often late because of the steep gradient between Waikohu and Matawai. While waiting for the train on cold winter nights they gathered around a fire in the station building and exchanged the gossip of the day. To them, the railway was the lifeline of the community.[31]

The opening of a new station was a huge event for a community of any size, brimming with the promise of progress and prosperity. Amid a riot of flags, bunting and greenery, crowds thronged to greet special trains of bigwigs and officials, followed by the traditional smorgasbord of food, speeches and self-congratulation. For the local mayor and MP, it was an opportunity to bask in the railway's reflected glory and ensure re-election.

> **The opening of a new station was a huge event for a community of any size, brimming with the promise of progress and prosperity.**

Stations were also the scene of public welcomes for royal visitors, governors-general, prime ministers and other celebrities, who often swept into town in their own special carriages or plush 'birdcages' — the stretch limos of their day. Thousands turned out to salute soldiers bound for or returning from war, greet touring artists like the Australian soprano Dame Nellie Melba in 1902–3 and the Polish pianist and statesman Ignace Paderewski in 1927, or welcome conquering heroes like world champion sculler Billy Webb, who was mobbed on his return to hometown Wanganui in 1907. Wedding and funeral parties, family, friends and lovers, and well-stuffed sacks of mail, magazines and parcels also passed from station to station.

Stations, sheds and yards were magnets for children, especially rail workers' kids. Bob Stott, whose father worked on the Hawke's Bay line, recalled the absorbing activity of Waipukurau station in the 1940s:

## Trainland

There were always dozens of people on the platform even in a town of less than 3000 . . . I can recall goods trains with a van so full that a roadsider would be added. Tin cans of movie film, racing pigeons, boxes of wet fish, bicycles, dogs, papers and magazines, cases of fruit, always sacks of mail and wicker hampers of fragile parcels, as well as anonymous bits and pieces by the dozen.[32]

Like many others, Stott spent 'a good slice' of his school holidays on or around trains. Engine-driver J.M. Grainger recalled holiday time in North Canterbury just after the Second World War:

The yard was overrun with children . . . and when they found that the new guard always had his pockets full of sweets and that he encouraged the children to go for a ride they descended on him in droves . . . My mate would take one of the bigger boys on the engine and the guard would turn the points in the yard. The rest of the children would be put into the cleanest wagon we could find (and it wasn't always too clean) and I would ride with them to see that no one got hurt. We would travel up and down the yard until we were heartily sick of the whole idea but the children, of course, never got tired of it.[33]

*Railway stations have always been places of arrival and departure, anticipation and longing. As this 1941 image suggests, farewells took on an extra poignancy during wartime.*

ATL, F-28405-1/2

Looking back from the early 1960s, Grainger noted that this 'free and easy attitude' was already a thing of the past.

Behind the hustle and bustle, the waving dignitaries and cavorting kids, there was a seamier side to station life. Like other public facilities, stations attracted less celebrated and often less welcome visitors: loafers and drunks, people with time on their hands or lonely souls seeking human contact. Some became local identities, like the enigmatic Catherine Hill, who frequented the Frankton station for decades from

Citizens of Trainland

the Second World War. Locals dubbed her 'Coffee and Bun' after her regular purchases from the station refreshment rooms, and speculated (erroneously) that she was waiting for a fiancé who had never returned from the Great War. An early resident of Ormondville recalled local youth regularly 'gathering at the station to see the last train come in', because there was little else to do in the town.[34]

At city stations in the early 1900s 'the rough element' was reportedly 'strongly in evidence . . . during the departure of trains after 10.0 pm'. The 1905 refreshment room prohibition was supposed to improve matters, but in 1912 a 'gang of young ruffians' was found fighting and drinking at Wellington's Lambton Station. The aftermath of the First World War brought regular complaints of men 'loitering' and drinking around station lavatories, with returned soldiers reported to be 'frequent offenders'.[35] In the early twentieth century some busy stations gained unsavoury reputations as unsafe places for women travelling alone. In the 1910s one women's group even alleged — without much evidence — that Frankton was the centre of

*This platform scene seems innocent enough, but in the early twentieth century bustling Frankton Junction earned a reputation as a potentially perilous place for women travelling alone.*

ANZ, AAVK, W3493, B5292

# Trainland

a 'white slave traffic', in which young women were kidnapped and forced into prostitution. Later, in the early 1950s, Maori girls as young as fourteen were alleged to be 'frequenting' Frankton railway huts (home to a large workforce of Maori track labourers) 'for immoral and other undesirable purposes'.[36]

The darker side of station life was also reflected in longstanding problems with graffiti and vandalism. In 1908 the intrepid Reverend Bligh poked his nose into the grimy corners of Temuka's railway urinals, noting the 'very indecent drawings and writing on the walls' and carefully jotting down various 'immoral suggestions'. He was still on the job a decade later, reporting that 'in nearly every case where I have to use a flag station I see a great deal of obscene writing and drawing'. The Department acknowledged the problem, experimenting with resilient paint finishes for toilet walls as early as 1922, and even offering anti-graffiti advice to the Victorian state railways. Outdoor advertisements at stations and along railway tracks were also easy targets for vandals. In 1928 the Advertising Branch complained that 'for some time past a number of advertising signs have been wilfully damaged by stones, shot-guns and rifles'; the problem was apparently 'prevalent throughout the whole of the Dominion' but especially bad in South Island rural areas. Although rewards were routinely offered for information, few convictions were ever secured.[37]

Suburban stations were often popular night-time gathering places for local youth. At Opawa in Christchurch, 'hooligans' scratched obscene words in the walls, defaced posters and notices, stole light bulbs, urinated on the floor, set rubbish on fire and broke windows with depressing regularity in the early twentieth century. Few were ever caught, although in 1935 a thirteen-year-old boy was hauled before the Children's Court for smashing a station toilet bowl with a rock; two years later two boys and a girl, aged fourteen and twelve, were nabbed breaking windows. In 1938 vandals reached a new low by smearing cow dung over all of the station's door handles.

*Station or trackside advertising hoardings have always been easy targets for vandals. Despite departmental efforts like this 1906 reward notice, the usually youthful offenders were seldom caught.*

ATL, Eph-C-RAILWAYS-1906-01

# Citizens of Trainland

*As New Zealanders turned away from rail travel in the 1970s and 1980s, many suburban stations shared the desolate fate of Puhinui in South Auckland, photographed here in 1978.*

ANZ, AAVK, W3493, D39536

In the 1950s and sixties the Department struggled with a spate of rock-throwing from overbridges, trespassing and vandalism in yards, pilfering from wagons and attempts to derail trains by wedging rocks in points. The offenders were not always troubled teens: in 1956 two seven-year-olds and a five-year-old were caught firing rocks at passing trains with shanghais; three years later, a flurry of vandalism and theft in the Addington yards was pinned on two nine-year-olds.[38] It was a sign of things to come. By the 1970s and eighties many unattended suburban stations had been boarded up and reduced to tattered, graffiti-covered eyesores. As rail's heyday became an increasingly distant memory, so too did the station's status as vibrant hub and 'lifeline of the community'.

## 'The Refresh'

Few aspects of New Zealand's railway history have seized the public's imagination quite like the station-side Railway Refreshment Rooms (the 'RRR' or 'refresh'). For much of the twentieth century, and especially in the four or five decades after the removal of dining cars in 1917, the five- to ten-minute dash from the train into the refresh — with its crisply uniformed 'girls' offering rows of pies, sandwiches and cakes, and

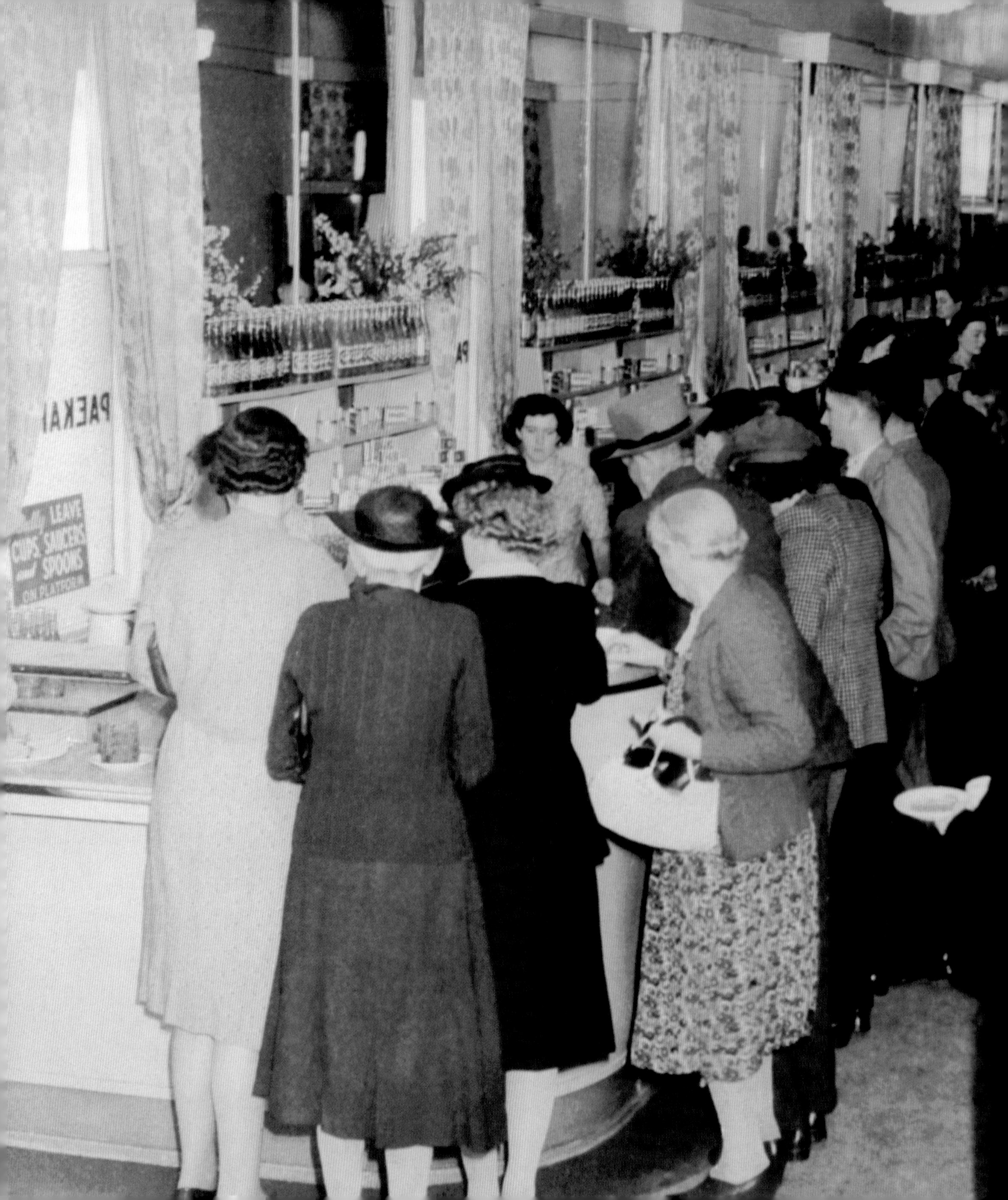
LEAVE
CUPS
SAUCERS
SPOONS
ON PLATFORM

## Citizens of Trainland

steaming tea and coffee in thick railway cups — was one of the central rituals of New Zealand travel. In many ways it was a teetotal equivalent to the equally infamous 'six o'clock swill' in pubs which, coincidentally, began life as a 'temporary' wartime measure in 1917 and survived for 50 years.

Everyone, it seemed, had an opinion about this curious Kiwi tradition, and it was seldom flattering — the visiting American writer Henrik Van Loon thought our refreshment rooms were 'an example of how mankind ought not to live'.[39] The quality and variety of the rooms' refreshments and the standard of their service were constantly scrutinised and frequently condemned. The 'unseemly scramble' for refreshments at main trunk rooms, especially at holiday times, was compared to a battlefield, or a rugby scrum or maul; some wags even identified it as a key to the All Blacks' international success.

Refreshment rooms have featured in folksongs like Peter Cape's 'Taumarunui (on the Main Trunk Line)' and Rod Derrett's 'Kiwi Train', and in novels like Janet Frame's *Owls Do Cry*:

> He looked out the window at the throng of people struggling at the counter of the refreshment room, and the triumphant line of them outside, fulfilled and rested and dreamy, leaning upon the wooden bench beside their empty cups and fizz bottles and strewn crusts of sandwiches, and he thought, in his rising fear, It isn't civilised.

'A pie at Paekok': the refreshment room at Paekakariki was a popular stopover for travellers heading in and out of Wellington.

ANZ, ABIN, W3337, box 44

171

## Trainland

They have also been immortalised in verse, ranging from the doggerel of James Claridge's *The Iron Horse* ('At Frankton Junk., a lively spot, | Awaits coffee-tea all piping hot') to Rex Fairburn's satirical 'Note on N.Z.R.' ('The thought recurs to those who are entrained: | The squalid tea of Mercer is not strained') and Hone Tuwhare's 'Steam Loco on Siding':

> REFRESHMENTS. For most, a journey not yet concluded.
> Time out for the wet-lipping of thick railway mugs
> of yellow tea. In it, the sugar spoon stands upright
> and perfectly still. I point to an adhesive jam roll;
> a hardboard meat pie. The lady behind the counter looks at me sadly
>     and grunts.
> Indifferently, I grunt
> back — and pay up. A whistle shrills. The scrum
> breaks up in the Refreshment Rooms.[40]

Initially, the location of refreshment stops was determined by the locomotives' thirst for water as much as passengers' needs. From the 1870s a number of private lessees secured the right to operate refreshment rooms or stalls on railways land, usually erecting tiny wood and corrugated iron lean-to shacks alongside station buildings. The Department opened several of its own rooms prior to the First World War, but its main involvement dated from 1917, when dining cars were withdrawn from service. That year, the newly established Refreshment Branch took over privately run rooms at Mercer, Frankton, Marton, Palmerston North, Hawera, Ashburton and Oamaru, and opened a new facility at Christchurch. The rooms offered a standard menu of ham or beef sandwiches (8d full slice, 4d for half), bread and butter or cheese (4d), tea or coffee (4d), a bun or roll (3d), a glass of milk (3d), aerated waters or milk and soda water (6d each), plus a range of cigars priced from 4d (Swiss) to 9d (Havana). The legendary railways meat pie and sausage roll joined the bill of fare in the 1920s.[41]

Other private rooms soon came under the Department's umbrella, including Woodville (1921), Helensville

*Ohakune's refreshment room — seen here all dressed up for Peace Day in 1919, with proprietor Leslie Bradcock at left — was one of a number of privately run facilities taken over by the Railways Department in the 1920s.*

Author's collection

and Waipukurau (1923), Taumarunui (1924), Clinton (1925), Ohakune (1926), and Paekakariki and Kaitoke (1927). By the mid twenties the Branch was catering for over a million customers a year. Over the four-week summer holiday period in 1928/9 the six rooms in Auckland province served 51,700 cups of tea, 18,300 cups of coffee, 49,900 sandwiches and 56,600 pies and cakes, churning through 3819 pounds of ham and 1380 pounds of butter. This was the fastest of fast food: at Waipukurau in 1925, 260 hungry travellers (a volatile mix of rugby supporters and Woodford House schoolgirls) were served in ten minutes; in the 1940s the Ashburton room regularly served 600 in seven minutes. By 1935 the Department was running 30 counter rooms and four sit-down dining rooms (see 'Dinner at Oamaru' below), plus eighteen station bookstalls. With eleven smaller rooms still in private hands, New Zealand boasted one refreshment room for every 80 miles of railway. During the demanding years of the Second World War, Refreshment Branch patronage peaked at over eight million counter customers annually, plus another half a million in the dining rooms.[42]

## Dinner at Oamaru

Although its counter refreshment rooms attracted most of the attention, and customers, the Railways Department also operated a number of sit-down dining rooms. These enabled travellers, especially better-off ones, to enjoy a substantial three-course meal at a slightly more leisurely pace. From the end of the First World War the Department ran dining rooms at the busy junctions of Frankton and Marton, where travellers often spent time in transit waiting for connecting trains, and Oamaru, where the Christchurch–Dunedin express made a regular 22-minute 'dinner' (lunch) stop. A room was opened at Otira in the mid 1920s, and others were later established at Auckland, Napier, Taihape, Wellington and Christchurch (until the 1920s there were also private dining rooms at Woodville and Clinton). Most famous of all was Oamaru, which was capable of seating 250 diners at long tables; on occasions the train was delayed to squeeze in a second sitting. For a set price of 2s 6d (1s 3d for children), diners could sample delights like 'stewed tripe and oysters', 'smoked fish with butter sauce', 'roast sirloin of beef with Yorkshire pudding' and 'compote of pears with boiled custard', with the added bonus of 'unlimited returns'.

At Easter 1926, during the New Zealand and South Seas Exhibition's season in

## Citizens of Trainland

LEFT: *A 1930s view of the dining room at Marton, which shared the long tables, crisp linen and prim decorations of its famous Oamaru counterpart.*

ANZ, AAVK, W3493, E8271

Dunedin, more than 5000 passengers passed through Oamaru's dining and counter rooms in a single day, chomping through 400 pounds of meat, 200 pounds of vegetables and 3000 loaves of bread, plus hundreds of pies, rolls and cakes. Visitors heaped praise on the dining room's gastronomic delights: in the mid 1920s a party of North Island wool buyers claimed it was 'the best dinner we've had in New Zealand'; a Northland visitor thought it 'the best in Australasia'. In 1928 the captain of the touring Australian cricket team went even further, declaring that 'in the whole of his travels in New Zealand, Australia, and the Old Country he and his team had never been provided at a railway station with a meal to equal that supplied at Oamaru'.

After the Second World War, as rail passenger numbers began their long, steady decline, NZR's refreshment services — and in particular the expensive sit-down rooms — struggled to make ends meet. The 1952 Royal Commission on Railways, noting that dining rooms had lost £30,471 the previous year, recommended that hot meals be discontinued. The Frankton and Marton rooms were closed in 1954, followed by Oamaru in March 1963. In 1980 the station's counter refreshment room would meet the same fate.[43]

*Oamaru's long wooden station was designed by George Troup and completed in 1900. The dining room was at the southern (far) end of the building.*

Gavin McLean

In 1947 the *Evening Post* feigned surprise that 'the Mercer sparrows have, almost incredibly, grown sleek and radiant upon the remains of railway pies'.

## Citizens of Trainland

*The other side of the counter: travellers crowd forward to catch the waitress' attention at Palmerston North's new station cafeteria in 1963.*

ANZ, AAVK, W3493, B11404

While its dining room meals earned praise, the Department's counter refreshments garnered decidedly mixed reviews. As elsewhere in the world, railways food and drink had a reputation for blandness and poor quality, much like school or prison fare, or airport and airline food in later decades. Among the hundreds of complaints in the Department's files, a couple of examples will suffice. In 1928 a Wanganui traveller likened his tea to 'a bad disinfectant or a mouth-wash that had deteriorated', and was bemused by 'half-hot pie crusts, surrounding the appendages of sundry animals, named and unnamed'. In the 1940s an Otira customer wondered if his tea had been 'made from the washing-up water, for it tasted and smelt like it'; another complained that the 'coffee was cold' and 'the pies barely warm, greasy and unappetising'. In 1947 the *Evening Post* feigned surprise that 'the Mercer sparrows have, almost incredibly, grown sleek and radiant upon the remains of railway pies'.[44]

Others leapt to the defence of the NZR 'cuppa and pie'. In 1920 one traveller insisted that 'nowhere in New Zealand, hotels included, is the tea and coffee of a higher standard'. The Department naturally agreed. In 1949, the Comptroller of the Refreshment Branch noted that 'Inspectors of the Department of Health have informed us frequently that privately conducted tea rooms, restaurants and hotel kitchens generally compare very unfavourably with Departmental standards.' In fairness, from the 1920s to the 1950s refreshment room fare was probably as good as, if not better than, that offered in most local cafeterias, tearooms, pubs and restaurants. Given the state of New Zealand's hospitality and tourist industry, however, that did not necessarily mean much. In 1950 the Automobile Association labelled the general standard of meals 'a national calamity', while a hotel workers' union leader claimed that there was only one formally trained chef in the whole country.

Nevertheless, the rooms' limited menu seemed to satisfy the requirements of most New Zealand travellers. After the Second World War the Plunket Society, Women's Food Value League and other groups urged the Department to stock healthier fare. The Refreshment Branch demurred, explaining that 'in the past we have tried out stocking special foods and also wholemeal bread, but the demand has always been so poor that only a few rooms still consider it worthwhile having a few brown bread sandwiches on sale' — a sobering comment on New Zealanders' eating habits at the time.[45]

Visitors and locals alike were equally shocked by the 'unseemly' stampede for refreshments when crowded

# Trainland

trains stopped. One traveller claimed that 'a gentleman lost all trace of quality, femininity disappeared, as men and women clawed to reach the counter'. 'The present rule I have heard as Rafferty Rule' (that is, no rules at all), wailed another unhappy customer. 'More correctly it is Pig Rule.' An article in the *New Zealand Farmer* magazine advised a hesitant traveller to 'Use your King Country elbows, Bill!' This was Social Darwinism in action, with women and children last. 'It is a great embarrassment to a woman to have to elbow her way in amongst a lot of men.' In the late 1940s the *Dominion* complained:

> Long before the train has stopped the more agile travellers, men and boys, swing onto the platforms and when the elderly folk, mothers with children, and those who are reluctant to alight from a moving train finally reach the refreshment counter, it is already two to five deep with customers . . . Each successive row gets cooler, weaker and more watered-down tea, till the final customers get a pale, cool beverage devoid of flavour or reviving quality.[46]

Barry Lineham crammed a jumble of battlefield and rugby metaphors into his 1959 song 'Wellington Express':

> 10 minutes for refreshments is the signal for the rush
> As the famished hordes exterminate the feeble in the crush
> No battlefield is grimmer, where battered heroes die than the bloody
> Railway battle for a cupper and a pie.
> In a scrum All Blacks would envy
> Only hardy souls remain
> To grab a bun and sandwich is the saviour of the train
> But every second station the milling hundreds press for gourmet treats
> Refreshments on the Wellington Express.[47]

Acknowledging public concern, the Department explored alternatives to the counter crush. Mobile 'refreshment barrows' were trialled at Palmerston North and three other stations in 1926, but the narrowness of New Zealand platforms made them more of a nuisance than a solution. Takeaway lunch cartons were offered for sale at major stations the following year. Advertised with the slogan, 'To avoid the rush, buy a

## Citizens of Trainland

carton', they cost 1s and contained an apple, two pieces of fruit cake, a shortbread biscuit and two sandwiches (ham, tomato or egg and lettuce). In 1928 the Branch introduced a more lavish 'luncheon hamper' for main trunk travellers. Available for 3s at Frankton and Marton, these wicker baskets contained cold ham, tongue, mutton or corned beef, salad, bread and butter, biscuits and cheese, an apple, orange or banana, a thermos flask of tea, and their own condiments, crockery, cutlery and serviette. Sales of both cartons and hampers were 'rather disappointing', however, and they were withdrawn in 1929 and 1931 respectively. More successfully, in 1937 a number of rooms were fitted with sliding hatches to enable patrons to be served directly on the platform. After rejecting various self-service options, the sale of food vouchers on trains, and proposals for rails or 'races' to corral patrons into queues, the Branch agreed in 1949 to reserve sections of the counter for women with children and disabled travellers (notably war invalids).[48]

If the refreshment room scramble was often a trial for rail travellers, spare a thought for the counter staff. Elva Houghton, who worked at Ohakune in the 1940s, recalled the daily (or nightly) grind of the main trunk refresh: 'most of our work was at night with the expresses and the Limiteds arriving after 10.30 pm going south, and again at about 3 am, going north; four trains each night, often interspersed with troop trains. Three or four hundred were on each train.'[49] Once the train had left, the refresh girls had to clean up the mess of half-eaten pies, sandwich crusts and spilled tea, wash all the dishes, and tally the food, crockery

*From 1928 NZR offered luncheon hampers like this one to North Island main trunk travellers who wished to avoid the refreshment room crush. Sales were disappointing, however, and the service was withdrawn three years later.*

ANZ, AAVK, W3493, D10277

## Trainland

*Helensville 'refresh girls', (from left) Nell Stewart, Isabel Hunter, Ruth Ellis, Adelia Davis and Elsie Leader.*

Helensville Pioneer Museum

and cutlery; often a box of dirty cups collected from the carriages would be offloaded for washing, sorting and redistribution to their rooms of origin.

Although expected passenger numbers were wired ahead from preceding stations, the arrival of overcrowded race-day, excursion or troop trains made the job even harder. In 1920 the Frankton rooms were overrun by more than a thousand punters off a race special: 'The crowd is stated to have been the most drunken and unruly that the staff has had to deal with, there being also much bad language.' When the train was subsequently delayed at Mercer, 'the drunken mob took charge of the rooms where only women were in attendance, stealing both food and property'. In 1949 an 'Ex-RRR Girl' described the experience from the other side of the counter: 'believe me, that is the place to get an insight into people and their natures. They seem to think the waitresses are animals by the way they shout and whistle and also hammer their fists on the counter.'[50]

Despite the trying conditions and strict discipline, many refresh girls spent decades in the same rooms, which often became family operations. Rhoda Johnson, for example, worked at Helensville for three decades, sharing the counter with five sisters and a niece, as well as the Hunter, Curtis and Morris sisters. Millie Christensen, who served at Paekakariki, Taumarunui and Mercer, and had sisters in the Frankton and Ohakune rooms, recalled that a 'lot of refresh girls married railwaymen. We were used to hard work and we knew all about the odd hours people worked on the railway.'[51]

**Despite the trying conditions and strict discipline, many refresh girls spent decades in the same rooms, which often became family operations.**

# Citizens of Trainland

## 'Like Lumps of Lard': The Legendary Railways Cup

The thick white railways cup is perhaps an even more celebrated symbol of the old NZR than the refreshment rooms themselves. Indeed, the cups are arguably more popular today than in their heyday: early examples fetch high prices in antique shops and auctions, and some intrepid collectors even scour the scrub along railway lines in search of long-discarded items. Earlier consumers were less enthusiastic. Like the refreshment room scramble, 'cups one-quarter of an inch in thickness . . . were a source of dismay to many women visitors'; one traveller thought they 'felt and looked like lumps of lard'. According to Rod Derrett's 'Kiwi Train', the cups were 'so strong that if you collected them all / They'd make a good foundation for a new town hall'. An old joke warned passengers against throwing them out the carriage window in case they derailed a following train. Ignoring this advice, New Zealanders seem to have instead made railway-cup tossing into something of a national sport.

For much of the twentieth century the Railways Department was New Zealand's biggest crockery purchaser. Its stocks needed constant replenishment: in 1933 more than 14,000 cups were lost or broken; five years later the total topped 28,000. Attrition was greatest on night trains, where crockery taken aboard from rushed refreshment stops was carelessly left beneath seats and kicked over in the dark. Other losses were more deliberate: numerous cups and saucers found their way into passengers' bags or out the carriage window. In 1939, a search along the few miles of track between Ohakune and Horopito recovered 103 cups (79 of them broken), 116

*An NZR cup made in Temuka after the Second World War.*

Alex McGowan

# Trainland

saucers (88 broken) and four teaspoons. Railway workers were far from blameless. In 1928 the Refreshment Branch complained that cups were 'frequently being found in station offices, porters' rooms, huts, goods sheds, workshop premises, [and] on engines'. A search of the Frankton offices in 1940 recovered twenty purloined cups; others were being used as water bowls in dog kennels and baskets 'containing poultry, racing pigeons, and domestic pets'.

Crockery losses peaked during the Second World War, when thousands of cups and saucers were accidentally broken on overcrowded troop trains, spirited away to military camps or hurled out carriage windows. In the year to March 1942 no fewer than 101,257 cups were lost or broken, virtually emptying the Branch's reserve stocks. That very month, the *Dominion* reported that 'passengers in a south-bound train were seen to fling dozens of cups and half a dozen pillows into the Wanganui River'. Between 1940 and 1946 the Department's losses totalled a staggering 674,641 cups and 163,635 saucers.

*Broken crockery litters Ohakune's platform following the departure of a crowded express in 1949.*

ANZ, AAVK, W3493, B1246

In the 1950s the Refreshment Branch revamped many of its rooms, prompting the *Auckland Star* to declare in 1956 that 'Railway Food and Service are Good Now': 'station buffet restaurants gleam with new enamel and are bright with fluorescent lights. Staff are spruce, young and quick.' But in an era of declining passenger numbers, the closure of secondary line services, and newer, faster trains that required fewer stops, many rooms haemorrhaged money. Following the recommendations of the 1952 Royal Commission, the Kaitoke and Woodville rooms were shut immediately. The once thriving Marton room, which lost over £9,300 in 1952,

Before the war all NZR crockery was imported from leading British manufacturers such as W.H. Grindley & Co, John Maddock & Sons and Royal Doulton. But in 1942, with supplies strangled by the German U-boat menace and the demands of British wartime production, the Department had to turn to local producers in Auckland and Temuka. Unfortunately, the first 'cane-coloured' Auckland-made cups were 'of high porosity, low durability, bad in colour and finish', and produced without handles because no one knew how to attach them. With the Labour government determined to promote domestic manufacturing, local production continued after the war, even though the Branch described a 1951 batch of Temuka crockery as 'absolute rubbish'. Within a few years, limited imports resumed and Crown Lynn in Auckland began successfully producing the chunky white cups that became familiar to thousands of postwar rail travellers.[52]

> **RAILWAY REFRESHMENT ROOMS**
> Would passengers who take counter-room cups, saucers, and teaspoons from the Railway Refreshment Rooms please place same on the platform **IN A POSITION OF SAFETY** before the train departs.
> Crockery should not be taken away in the train when time permits of the refreshments being partaken of before departure.
> The **CO-OPERATION OF PASSENGERS** with a view to conserving stocks of crockery held in the Railway Refreshment Rooms will be appreciated, as replacement from overseas in these difficult times is uncertain and costly.

A wartime notice imploring rail travellers to help conserve the Department's dwindling crockery stocks.

Author's collection

closed two years later, followed by Maungaturoto (1956), Mercer (1958), Paeroa (1959) and Ohakune (1960).

That still left the Department with 26 counter rooms, four dining rooms (at Wellington, Taihape, Christchurch and Oamaru), nine bookstalls and two hairdressing salons (at Auckland and Wellington), but as passenger traffic dwindled and additional services were axed further closures were inevitable. Helensville shut its doors in 1967, Ashburton in 1971 and Waipukurau in 1972. The iconic Frankton and Taumarunui rooms sold their last pies in 1975, followed by Clinton and Oamaru in 1980. The last survivors — at Otira,

## Trainland

Springfield, Kaikoura and Taihape — closed in the late 1980s, bringing to an end one of New Zealand's most distinctive dining experiences. 'Never again', the *Waikato Times* lamented in 1975, would 'the motley crowd in various states of dishevelment' press forward 'to catch the fickle eye of the lady with the beige enamel teapot.'[53]

## Back to the Buffet

Since 1917 NZR had fended off continual demands to bring back dining cars, which many saw as a more civilised alternative to the refreshment room maul. Any thoughts of reintroducing dining cars after the First World War, however, were stymied by lingering coal shortages, the conversion of the previous cars to other uses and doubts over their economic viability. In 1925 the Department reported that dining cars rarely made money in the United States, where their prices were comparatively high, or Britain, where they sold alcohol. The same held true after the Second World War, when a Canadian Pacific Railway executive advised that 'dining cars could not be operated except at a loss', and US railroad companies reported a US$25 million deficit in their dining-car operations for 1947. By the 1960s, however, NZR was exploring cheaper 'buffet service' options, as well as onboard sales of alcohol, long absent from the (theoretically) sober New Zealand railway scene. Alcohol sales appeared for the first time on the experimental 'Blue Streak' Auckland–Hamilton railcars in April 1968, followed in December by the new Auckland–Wellington railcar service.[54]

The six 'prestige' passenger services of the early 1970s — the Northerner, Blue Streak, Silver Star, Silver Fern, Endeavour and Southerner — each provided buffet cars or counters and alcohol sales, although drink could only be consumed in smoking sections. The luxurious but shortlived Silver Star offered a 'buffet car' with sit-down tables, waiters and meals cooked on board, room-service drinks until 11.30 pm, and even breakfast in bed. Perhaps inevitably, alcohol sales fuelled longstanding problems with drunkenness on trains, especially among sports teams and spectators. In the worst incident, the Northerner was delayed for an hour near Feilding in 1985 when a drunken brawl broke out in its buffet car. 'I think it's a disgrace that the stewards serve so much alcohol to people who are obviously very, very drunk,' one passenger complained. 'After 10 o'clock several drunken people just started a brawl . . . I was very, very frightened, and the so-called stewards all took off and

RIGHT: *After an absence of half a century, in the late 1960s and early 1970s NZR reintroduced refreshments on its 'prestige' passenger trains. This image shows the buffet car on the new Southerner during its trial run in November 1970.*

ANZ, AAVK, W3493, D19766

Citizens of Trainland

# blue streak

**DAYTIME RAILCAR BETWEEN WELLINGTON & NEW PLYMOUTH**
Each way Monday to Saturday • Hostess Service

Railways

book now at any Railway Booking Office or Accredited Travel Agency

left us passengers just there.'⁵⁵

With the growing availability of prepackaged foods and microwave ovens in the 1980s, onboard catering was gradually reduced to 'Snacks on Tracks' counters, which survive on the country's remaining long-distance trains. A journalist travelling on the threatened Overlander service in August 2006 was far from impressed with the state of onboard refreshments, describing a cheese and tomato sandwich as 'possibly the worst' she had ever eaten.⁵⁶ Passengers can at least enjoy a leisurely lunch break at the National Park cafeteria, where the train stops for 45 minutes — a far cry from the old ten-minute dash — and in early 2007 Toll announced plans to introduce a new menu, reportedly showcasing top-quality local food and wine.

But it will take more than a facelift to recapture the silver-service luxury of the early-1900s dining car or the bustle and buzz of the mid-century refreshment room. Over the last half-century most New Zealanders have turned their backs on the people's railway, emptying its passenger trains, stations and long-gone refreshment rooms. Robin Hyde's 'naturalised citizens of Trainland' have abandoned the 'warm, lamplit limbo' of the railway carriage for the supposedly sunnier climes of 'Carland' or 'Planeland', consigning the once-familiar NZR pillow, meat pie and tea cup to the realms of folklore.

*In the early 1970s NZR sought to lure customers on to long-distance services like the Blue Streak railcar by providing refreshment counters, alcohol sales and hostesses in 'chic' uniforms.*

ATL, NON-ATL-NZRLS-013
(Courtesy NZRLS)

# The Long Train Journey

**CHAPTER 5**

# Trainland

> The long train journey is remembered as a dream of strangeness and strange landscapes: a rocketing over countless railway bridges, past swamps of flax with their tall black-beaked flax flowers, clumps of willows, the towns, their names borne along within the rhythm and the sound of the train — Clinton, Kaitangata, Milton, Balclutha — each a cluster of houses around its railway-coloured railway station.
>
> — *Janet Frame,* To the Is-land[1]

'What is it about railways,' wondered the *Auckland Star* in 1959, 'that can stir the emotions or befuddle the senses of otherwise normal and rational adults? Railways rank with pet cats and dogs in their ability to arouse enthusiasm and orgies of sentimentality.'[2] The article was prompted by threats to close unprofitable branch lines, a political flashpoint in the 1950s. Still, 'orgies of sentimentality' were perhaps premature at a time when the national rail network boasted over 3400 miles (5470 km) of track, steam locomotives were still widely used, and 2.3 million New Zealanders racked up 25 million passenger journeys a year.

Over the next four decades, as branch closures reduced the length of the national network to 3900 km and total passenger journeys slumped to about half their 1959 levels, our rail story would be dogged by a sense of decline and neglect. Certainly, the railway has remained a major carrier of bulk and containerised freight, hauling record tonnages in the early 2000s. But in per capita terms only about a third as many people travel by train today as in the 1950s (and less than a sixth as many as in the early 1920s), and over 95 per cent of them are commuters on Wellington and Auckland's subsidised suburban networks.

Increased productivity, mechanisation, the withdrawal of services and other changes have reduced the rail workforce — once the country's largest — to a

PREVIOUS PAGE:
*Commuter capital: Wellington's Tranz Metro trains carried more than 11 million passengers in the year to June 2006.*

Paul Hamer

RIGHT: *New Zealand's grandest railway 'cathedral', Dunedin station, fittingly celebrates the glories of rail in stained glass.*

Gavin McLean

# The Long Train Journey

fraction of its former size. The same processes of change have led to the closure (and typically demolition or sale) of hundreds of railway stations, refreshment rooms, sheds and other structures, while many surviving stations no longer handle regular passenger services. Huge chunks of railway land have been sold off; apartments, retail outlets, stadiums and other amenities have sprouted where rail lines, wagons and sheds once stood. Many older New Zealanders have seen their country's rail heritage literally disappear before their eyes.

Yet nostalgia and enthusiasm for railways is as strong as ever. Given the central role of rail in this country's economic development, the expense and effort the state devoted to railmaking, and the ongoing appeal of rail heritage, we might also expect railways to have taken centre stage in New Zealand arts and culture. Certainly, there is no shortage of railway books and magazines; dozens of historians and enthusiasts have wistfully chronicled the perceived decline of the once great rail enterprise and systematically catalogued the country's locomotives, rolling stock, viaducts, tunnels and stations. But has the romance or reality of rail inspired the creative minds of New Zealand writers and artists? A glance through the standard anthologies and surveys is somewhat discouraging. New Zealand would not necessarily be alone in

## Trainland

this regard: it could be argued that Britain, the birthplace of the railway, has produced a surprisingly meagre crop of railway novels, paintings, songs and films.[3] If we look a little deeper at the work of key novelists, poets, songwriters and artists, however, a rich vein of local railways culture can be uncovered.

## Expressions of Rail

In 1938 the poet O.N. Gillespie penned an article for the *New Zealand Railways Magazine* entitled 'New Zealand Railway Lines in Prose and Verse'. Drawing on his extensive knowledge of the subject and 'weeks of search' at the Alexander Turnbull Library, he glumly reported 'that the total output of imaginative literature inspired by our railways is quite small, amounting to one collection of short stories, and a few scattered platoons of verse' — and that one 'sparkling' short-story collection, C.A. Jefferies' *By Rail and Semaphore*, has not stood the test of time as well as Gillespie might have hoped. Although puzzled 'that so little of this gripping epic of human endeavour has been preserved in our literature', Gillespie was confident that rail writing would flourish in New Zealand: 'There is a novel in every journey of a night goods train; there is a poem in every white jet of steam as a "K" locomotive climbs to Horopito. They will be written.'[4]

Subsequent generations of writers and artists, it seems, have failed to deliver the goods. Part of the reason no doubt lies in this country's unusually strong dependence on Anglo-American cultural influences.[5] Like many other aspects of our social and cultural history, local rail imagery has been overshadowed by British and American imports. A random list of key 'texts' could include Agatha Christie's *Murder on the Orient Express* and other railway crime mysteries, Wilbert and Christopher Awdry's *Thomas the Tank Engine* series (and subsequent merchandising empire), Edith Nesbit's *The Railway Children*, Hornby and Lionel model trains, Heath Robinson's eccentric cartoon creations, David Lean's *Doctor Zhivago*, J.K. Rowling's magical Hogwarts Express, the great train robberies of American westerns, *The Little Engine That Could*, Buster Keaton's *The General*, Arthur Hiller's *The Silver Streak*, images of hobos riding boxcars, and a hit parade of great American railroad songs: 'I've Been Working on the Railroad', 'This Train (Is Bound for Glory)', 'The Wabash Cannonball', Elizabeth Cotten's 'Freight Train', Lead Belly's 'Rock Island Line', Curtis Mayfield's 'People Get Ready', Steve Goodman's 'The City of New Orleans', Tom Waits' 'Downtown Train', REM's 'Driver 8', and dozens more.

Has New Zealand produced anything to compare with this stellar rail roll-call? A good place to start is the work of this country's best-known novelist, Janet Frame, who has been quoted several times earlier in

*Like many small settlements, Janet Frame's sometime childhood hometown, Edendale in Southland, featured a 'watertank painted railway hut red on its railway-hut-red stand beside the railway line'. This freshly painted water tower was photographed at Parnassus, North Canterbury, in 1970; like most such structures, it is now long gone.*

Euan McQueen

this book. In her three-volume autobiography Frame traces her upbringing in the 'railway country' of interwar Otago and Southland and her lifelong identity as one of the 'Railway People'. Her father had joined the Railways Department at eighteen — lured by the prospect of job security — and rose through the ranks from cleaner to engine driver. He also became secretary of the local branch of the engine drivers' union and encouraged Janet's childhood writing by bringing home blank, marble-edged 'railway notebooks'. Both Janet and her mother had poems published in the *New Zealand Railways Magazine*.

While many writers have imagined the train as a means of 'escape', Frame knew 'there was no use escaping anywhere, from family or frost or land, the escape made impossible anyway because, as the daughter of a railway worker, I had to accept the possession of and by every inch of railway track in the country: an iron bond of mutual ownership'.[6] The colours and sounds of the railway world held a particular fascination. One of Frame's childhood hometowns, Edendale, Southland, features a 'watertank painted railway hut red on its railway-hut-red

# Trainland

**She hears '[t]he train struggling up the hill, its groan, hiss, joyous whistle, Got it, Got it', and imagines within its steady rhythms the repetition of placenames: 'Kaitangata, Kaitangata, Kaitangata, Winton, Winton, Winton, Kakanui, Kakanui, Kakanui.'**

stand beside the railway line and the spindly red-painted little house high up where the signalman lived and hung out his signals'; small towns are 'a cluster of houses' around their 'railway-coloured railway station'. She hears '[t]he train struggling up the hill, its groan, hiss, joyous whistle, Got it, Got it', and imagines within its steady rhythms the repetition of placenames: 'Kaitangata, Kaitangata, Kaitangata, Winton, Winton, Winton, Kakanui, Kakanui, Kakanui'.[7]

In *An Angel at My Table*, Frame recounts a trip from Auckland to Tauranga in the mid 1950s. The journey 'lasted most of the day' and 'was so much a part of the natural surroundings of bush, waterfalls, fern, wet clay, a glistening world of wet, that the heart of the land entered the railway carriage and there was the feeling of the loneliness and strangeness of a personal exploration'. Here, New Zealand's 'developmental' railways are not the all-conquering master of nature we have come to expect. The barriers separating the self-contained bubble of the traveller's carriage from the outside world have become fluid. After a long delay while workers cleared a trackside slip — more evidence of rail's tentative ascendancy over nature — the journey continues:

> [W]hen the train at last began to move, creaking slowly around narrow bend after narrow bend where the rainwater oozed from every pore of earth and bark and leaf and fern, there was the privilege of knowing, like being favoured with a secret, that this was not the 'main trunk line', accepted by use, with refreshment stops and cities along the way, this was a 'branch line' with all its mystery, neglect, vague atmosphere of exile which is the nature of branch lines everywhere, even in dreams, thinking, and history.[8]

Railway journeys and stations also featured in Frame's New Zealand-based novels. Her description of the 'uncivilised' refreshment scrum in *Owls Do Cry* has been mentioned in Chapter 4. In *Scented Gardens*

*Lonely rural flag stations like this one at Inchbonnie, Westland (photographed in 2001), have featured in a number of New Zealand novels, including Robin Hyde's* The Godwits Fly.

Paul Hamer

for the Blind, a character waits 'on the platform of the railway station among the discarded sandwich crusts and the sea-gull droppings' as another trainload of passengers 'make their stampede for the refreshment rooms'. In *State of Siege* Frame conjures a trip in a Night Limited sleeper, a 'dimly-lit, meat-pie journey to Auckland, in a shelf-like top bunk':

> Breath soot-high; voices when the train stopped, voices sharp and clear as footsteps walking the platform of the station; steam clouding like cottonwool; heavy-eyed sleep, eyelids sealed with specks of soot. Then early morning, cold clothes with too many arm and feet holes, a fawn railway-coloured, blanket-coloured biscuit; tea; a newspaper. And then, at the end of the jolting, heaving journey over railway lines that had surely been cut on the bias, a slow, measured halting, and in the scatter of people waiting, promising cars and warm homes, crying welcome from Auckland Station.[9]

## Trainland

No other New Zealand fiction writer has portrayed the world of the railway with Frame's devotion. An obscure work set during the great railmaking era, Herman Foston's *At the Front* (1921) — subtitled *A Story of Pluck and Heroism in the Railway Construction Camps in the Dominion of New Zealand* — captures something of the colonists' clamour for rail and rough-and-tumble camp life. One of New Zealand's best interwar novelists, Robin Hyde, penned a vivid travel series for the *Railways Magazine* in the 1930s, but did not feature railways prominently in her novels. Her account of a school picnic excursion from *The Godwits Fly* (1938) has been mentioned earlier; elsewhere in the same novel she evokes a typically lonely rural station, 'one of those little shows where you never see anything but a red tin shed, a tank, and a train gulping down water, her steam ghostly, her passengers, drugged with sleep and their own vapours, staring out of the window like doped flies. None of them ever got off at Raupo.' Later, when a character is due to leave Raupo by mixed train, he hesitates, discomfited by the plight of the doomed livestock that were to share his journey: 'suddenly and strongly, he didn't want to board his train, which was already in the station. The string of sheep-trucks packed with bodies like dirty fawn rugs, bodies alive and bleating until they reached the slaughter-yards and were reduced to a black jelly of blood, joints on iron hooks, raw hides and a stink of fertilizer, decided him.'[10]

Others writing during the interwar or early postwar decades similarly employed trains and stations as avenues of arrival and anticipation, departure or escape. In John Mulgan's *Man Alone* (1939), Johnson flees Auckland's Depression riots by hitching a ride — 'riding the blinds' in the American hobo tradition — in empty fertiliser and cattle wagons as far as Ohakune. 'Night came on as the train took its slow way, climbing through the bush-hills to the high plateau that runs across the centre of the island . . . The air grew colder and a steady rain was falling on the roof. Johnson, remembering the line, felt the curve of the spiral as the train climbed, and felt it straighten out again as it reached the plains.'

In Bill Pearson's *Coal Flat* (1963), the train to Stillwater delivers a new schoolteacher, who has 'still hardly recovered from her emotion on emerging from the Otira tunnel and seeing mountains and bush: she couldn't imagine country more wild and she was surprised to find she was the only passenger in the carriage who seemed to be affected'. Later, four recruits leave Dunedin for the Second World War aboard a train 'full of loud excited young men, kissing their girls and their wives on the platform, shouting, swigging beer from bottles to the connivance of a railway guard powerless to stop them, singing aggressively and playing cards'. Published the same year, Ronald Hugh Morrieson's *The Scarecrow* evokes the sleepy world of the rural branch line in 1950s Taranaki. When their truck breaks down the young narrator and his father hitch a ride to 'Klynham' in the guard's van of a lumbering 'goods with car'. The only passengers in the solitary, ancient passenger carriage, with its 'narrow bench seats' and windows that 'all refused to open', are the aunt and niece of murder victim Daphne Moran — and the murderer himself, the sinister Hubert Salter.[11]

More recent writers have also used trains and stations as avenues of arrival or escape. But with railways no longer the commonplace feature they once were, their appearance instantly locates a story in time. In Maurice Gee's *Plumb*, the eponymous clergyman travels from Auckland to Wellington in a Night Limited sleeper, passing the 'small hours' in a 'moon rayed closet full of dead air and burnt coal', with a 'swaying circular motion that set my stomach floating as though on oil'. In *Going West*, Gee describes the rail journey from the fictional West Auckland town of Loomis into the city of 'opulence and commerce, bright lights, sin'. As the line began to curve 'the impression one had was of worming into Auckland', but '[o]nce across the spindly bridge there was no creeping, you stabbed like a knife'. Childhood memories and myths are evoked as the train enters:

> Newmarket Tunnel, with men's cigarettes in the dark, and kids making ghost yells, and the smell of sulphur — and once in there, the big kids said, a Seddon Tech boy rooted his sheila and they both had their pants pulled up and were sitting as though nothing had happened by the time the train came out the other end.[12]

Similarly, blacked-out troop trains and expectant station crowds help locate Patricia Grace's novels *Cousins* and *Tu* in their wartime setting, as does her description

*O.N. Gillespie's bold declaration that 'there is a poem in every white jet of steam as a "K" locomotive climbs to Horopito' may not have eventuated, but these impressive machines remain a powerful symbol of rail's golden age. This drawing by Allan Paterson captures the restored $K^A$ 935 in action at the Hutt Valley's Silver Stream Railway.*

Allan Paterson

## Trainland

of a family's arrival in Wellington: 'the train slowed, laying back white smoke, sounding its whistle and creaking along the tracks past the dirty sheds, over oily, broken rock to where the yards began. This was the end of the line.'[13] Here, the railway is presented as history, an evocation of the way things were.

Railways rarely appear in Katherine Mansfield's New Zealand-based short stories, although 'The Escape', 'Father and the Girls', 'The Little Governess' and other stories contain vivid descriptions of European train journeys. In late 1907, during her travels around the North Island, Mansfield confided in her journal that she found rail travel 'inexpressibly charming': 'I lean out of the window, the breeze blows, buffeting and friendly, against my face, and the child spirit, hidden away under a hundred and one grey city wrappings, bursts its bonds, and exults within me.' She 'peered into the long wooden saloon' of the Kaitoke refreshment room, 'where a great counter was piled with ham sandwiches', and described Woodville's dining room as 'a great barn of a place — full of primly papered chandeliers and long tables — decorated with paper flowers — and humanity most painfully in evidence'.[14]

> '. . . the train slowed, laying back white smoke, sounding its whistle and creaking along the tracks past the dirty sheds, over oily, broken rock to where the yards began. This was the end of the line.'

Frank Sargeson's most evocative rail story is not 'Conversations on a Train' (which does not mention railways other than in its title), but his account of a journey to Northland in the autobiographical *Never Enough!* In the mid 1920s Sargeson and a friend travelled along the newly opened line from Auckland to the Bay of Islands, where they holidayed in a tent. Gazing out the carriage window, Sargeson is struck by the unfamiliar landscape of mangroves, kauri and (especially) nikau palms — so different from his uncle's King Country farm — that he drifts off into one of his 'most lively and vivid daydreams'. His mood soon changes, however, as 'the sluggish train' begins 'to traverse areas where forest had long been extinct, so that all that remained was the barren wilderness known as gumland . . . such a dead-looking place'. When Sargeson retraced his journey (by bus) half a century later, he was moved 'to see that rail journey as memorable beyond anything I could have been likely to imagine'.[15]

Railways have long been a popular subject for children's literature. While generations of New Zealanders have been brought up with British and American railway stories and characters, there has also been a sporadic

## The Long Train Journey

local output. In 1938, perhaps mindful that rail's place in youthful imagination was already under threat from the automobile and aeroplane, the Railways Department published an illustrated propaganda booklet, *Your Own Railway*, subtitled 'For New Zealand Children — A Story Showing How Fairy Tales Become Real'. In 1950 the Education Department produced a 40-page 'primary school bulletin', *The Steel Road*, which showed 'How a "K" locomotive works', explained the intricacies of the tablet system and took readers for a ride on the Night Limited with driver 'Big Jim' Barn and fireman Wiremu Paku. Along with a list of suggested activities, the booklet included a bibliography of children's railway books — all of them British. Prior to the 1980s, it seems, the only fictional story with a local setting was a delightful illustrated tale of the Rimutaka Incline, *Freddy the Fell Engine* (1966), although it too was published in England.[16] Despite a handful of more recent rail stories and activity books, the globalised marketing empire of Thomas and his friends continues to overshadow all local endeavours.

New Zealand lacks Britain's strong tradition of crime writing, in which the railway — especially the long-distance night train and the secluded first-class compartment — has often featured as the setting for romance, murder and mystery. As we have seen in Chapter 4, from the interwar years New Zealand railway station bookstalls overflowed with paperback whodunits of British origin (although they were often set on the notoriously decadent Continent). The

*The cover of* The Steel Road, *an Education Department booklet for primary school children published in 1950.*

ATL, B K 743-COVER

Trainland

# Weeping Waters

Of all the moments in New Zealand rail history, none match the drama of the Christmas Eve tragedy at Tangiwai in 1953. Alongside *Wahine* and Erebus, the very name remains a byword for disaster. With a death toll of 151, it was at the time the eighth deadliest rail accident in the world (although it should be noted, by way of comparison, that 279 people died on the country's roads that year). The horror was magnified by its terrible timing, as most of the victims were heading north to spend Christmas Day with family and friends; the Nicholls and Benton families each lost five members, and the Fitzgeralds four. The nation woke to the terrible news on Christmas morning, and searchers later found dozens of battered, mud-soaked presents, toys and teddy bears downstream. The New Zealand cricket team was playing a test match in Johannesburg at the time, and the brave Boxing Day batting effort by fast bowler Bob Blair — who had just learned that his fiancée, Nerissa Love, was among the victims — caused a sensation in South Africa. The literal translation of the Maori placename, 'weeping waters', and the presence in the country of the young Queen Elizabeth II, only added to the poignancy.

Tangiwai has certainly not been forgotten. A memorial was unveiled at Karori Cemetery, Wellington, in 1957, and another at Tangiwai itself in 1989. The disaster has been the subject of several paintings (including a rather inaccurate version by the Australian Phil Belbin, which appeared on the cover of *Reader's Digest*), folksongs (such as John Archer's 'Pillows of the Dead') and a sensationalist television documentary, *The Truth about Tangiwai* (2002). Several non-fiction accounts have traced its causes and aftermath, and there have been at least three publications aimed at children or young adults. It has also inspired a handful of novels, including Anne Marie Nicholson's *Weeping Waters* (2006), a romantic thriller 'about love, redemption and the secrets of family'. The daughter of a railway worker, Nicholson grew up in Masterton and Taumarunui and took many trips on the main trunk, recalling that

# The Long Train Journey

*The Tangiwai National Memorial at Karori Cemetery lists the names of all 151 victims and contains the graves of sixteen, including eight whose remains were never identified.*

Author's collection

as it approached Tangiwai the train would always 'slow to a crawl. Maybe out of standard procedure or maybe out of respect. But it was always spooky — always.'

For others, Tangiwai is a tale of what might have been, of the random hand of fate. Seventeen-year-old Barbara Mahy and her brother John, fifteen, were travelling on first-class tickets but could only find a seat in a second-class carriage (the second from the locomotive). After leaving Waiouru the guard found them first-class seats in the train's last car. Almost all the occupants of their original carriage were killed. Fifty years on from the tragedy, the broadcaster and publisher Christine Cole Catley recalled how she and her three small children had been booked to travel in a second-class car on the ill-fated train, before a last-minute change of work plans enabled them to go a day early. Ever since, she has wondered '[w]ho were the people who counted themselves lucky to get the last three seats, our seats, on Christmas Eve?'[17]

## Trainland

expatriate New Zealander Ngaio Marsh, along with Agatha Christie, Dorothy Sayers and Margery Allingham was one of the 'Queens of Crime' in 1930s Britain, and occasionally included railways in her mysteries, but their settings were European and their preoccupation with class typically English.

The *New Zealand Railways Magazine* briefly got in on the act that decade with its fourteen-part serial 'The Thirteenth Clue', a satirical mystery sparked by a murder in the Matamata signal box. A spin-off of the unpublished 'Murder by Eleven', collectively written by G.G. Stewart, Pat Lawlor, Alan Mulgan, O.N. Gillespie and seven other Wellington 'bookmen', this curiosity has recently been fictionalised in Maurice Gee's novel *The Scornful Moon*.[18]

In a rare railway thriller with a local setting, Ian Mackersey's *Long Night's Journey* (1974), a 'paranoid ex-farmer with a persecution complex' plots revenge on NZR for apparently asphyxiating his stock in the Porootarao tunnel on the North Island main trunk. He plants a bomb on the so-called 'Red Arrow' luxury night express, but it is defused (as usual) with seconds to spare. After shooting a policeman, he blows up a dam to sweep away a downstream rail bridge — shades of Tangiwai. Again, disaster is averted at the last minute.[19] But if New Zealand has produced little in the way of railway crime fiction, it does at least have one tale of real-life murder on the rails: the infamous case of Minnie Dean (see 'The Ballad of Minnie Dean' on page 206).

Railways have not featured prominently in New Zealand cinema or television, both of which have similarly been dominated by British and American imports. Several of the novels or real-life stories mentioned above have been turned into feature films, however, including *The Scarecrow* (1982), in which the sinister Salter (John Carradine) rides a rather curious mixed train through the Taranaki countryside; Frame's autobiographical *An Angel at My Table* (1990), with its brief early railway scenes; and *Bread and Roses* (1993), based on the life of one-time Nelson railway protester Sonja Davies (see page 217).

The most popular New Zealand films of the early 1980s, Geoff Murphy's *Goodbye Pork Pie* (1980) and Roger Donaldson's *Smash Palace* (1981), are both dominated by cars, but each includes memorable railway scenes. In the former, NZR cooperation allowed the filmmakers to shoot a spectacular sequence at Wellington railway station, where the yellow Mini swerves along platforms, barrels through pedestrian subways and makes a daredevil leap into a moving freight wagon. Filmed largely around National Park and Raurimu on the main trunk, *Smash Palace* was notable for its heart-stopping level-crossing scene, in which an oncoming freight train seems certain to crush the car carrying the fugitive Al Shaw (Bruno Lawrence) and his hostage, only to switch tracks at the last minute. Incidentally, Murphy and Donaldson both went on to direct Hollywood blockbusters — *Under Siege 2* and *Die Hard: With a Vengeance* respectively — that featured high-octane train crashes. Meanwhile, on the small screen, New Zealand's best-loved railway scene has been a long-running television commercial for Crunchie, a riot of gold rush, Wild West and war movie clichés filmed aboard the Kingston Flyer.

## Lines and Lyrics

In his 1938 *Railways Magazine* article, Gillespie devoted most of his attention to verse, which he considered a more promising field than prose for capturing the essence of rail. While conceding that this country's output had been modest, he made the startling claim that 'New Zealand has produced the best railway verse of any land'. Although George Gordon's 'The Driver' and John Maclennan's 'When the North Express Comes In' received honourable mentions, Gillespie's claim essentially rested on the work of one man, Will Lawson. The English-born Lawson spent most of his life flitting between New Zealand and Australia, and enjoyed '[m]any a night journey . . . in the cab of a hurtling train' and 'hours and hours in engine sheds and clattering workshops'. In 'Cattle Train', Lawson wrote how 'With thump and rattle of springs | And clatter of undergear | The long train rumbles and swings | Till the tail-lights twinkle clear'. In 'The Big Bull Yank' he celebrated the raw power of the Wellington and Manawatu Company's American Baldwins: 'And over the metals, hard and cold, | By Tokomaru Swamp, | She'll sing a song that is never old'. Gillespie's personal favourite was 'Drivin'':

> Now hear the words my engine speaks
> Slow, rhythmic yet not singin'
> As by the peaks and tumblin' creeks
> Her eighty tons goes ringin'.[20]

The 'best railway verse of any land'? Perhaps not. Nevertheless, from the late 1920s Lawson and Gillespie were both regular contributors to the Department's own *Railways Magazine*. When it was launched in 1926,

# Trainland

*'Limited Night Entertainments': as well as showcasing local verse, the* Railways Magazine *regularly published short stories by R. Marryat Jenkins and other writers.*

NZRM, Oct 1935

Minister Coates expressed a hope that the magazine would 'in self-expression, be racy of the soil to which we belong', and from 1933 it published a monthly column of 'New Zealand Verse'. Although much of its content was pure doggerel, the column did feature poems (not necessarily rail-related) by Denis Glover, Robin Hyde and Eve Langley.[21]

Ursula Bethell's childhood poem 'By the River Ashley' has been mentioned in Chapter 1, and Hone Tuwhare's description of the refreshment room 'scrum' in Chapter 4. Years later, in 'May Night', Bethell evoked the familiar sound of a night train: 'Even now up-beats the muffled tug of a freight-train | In travail beside the hidden seas; its repercussion | Taps and taps on fragile bowl of mountain quiet . . .'[22] One of New Zealand's best-known poets, Hone Tuwhare served an apprenticeship in the early 1940s at the Otahuhu railway workshops, where he became active in union and Communist Party circles. His rail-inspired works include 'Poet on a Night Train', in which the narrator gazes 'out again through reflective glass' at 'moving tree-groups in the mist', and the aforementioned 'Steam Loco on Siding', which begins with a muscular image of the black locomotive:

> Huffily, the southbound engine detaches itself, gleaming.
> The southbound engine sidles off to the water tower
> for a long drink. It is a black swimmer doing
> the sidestroke, huge steel arms pistoning.

The poem ends on a humorous note, as the narrator reads 'the writing on the end wall' of the station:

# The Long Train Journey

> New Zealand Government Railway
> warns, indeed expects, that no
> man pee, nor expectorate while
> the train is in motion.

More recent poems featuring local rail imagery or settings include Jenny Bornholdt's 'Raurimu Spiral' (1992) and Peter Olds' Baxter-influenced 'Disjointed on Wellington Railway Station' (selected for the collection *Best New Zealand Poems 2001*).[23]

Folk music has been another profitable field for railway culture. Our most celebrated rail song — and probably the best known of all New Zealand's folksongs — is Peter Cape's 'Taumarunui (on the Main Trunk Line)'. In this tale of unrequited love between 'an ordinary joker' and 'a sheila in Refreshments', Cape sings:

> You got cinders in your whiskers and a cinder in your eye
> So you hop off to Refreshments for a cupper tea and pie
> Taumarunui, Taumarunui
> Taumarunui on the Main Trunk Line

Another of Cape's ballads, the 'Okaihau Express', is set on a far more obscure railway, running between Okaihau and Otiria in Northland. The 'smallest train you've ever seen', consisting of an 'engine and a guard's van with a carriage in between', the 'Express' carries everything from 'puppies in an apple box' to 'pipis in a sack'; when '[s]he stops at Lake Omapere to take some water in . . . The fireman takes the bucket, the driver takes a swim'.[24] Barry Lineham's 'Wellington Express' and Rod Derrett's 'Kiwi Train', each of which evoke the refreshment room 'battle', have been mentioned in Chapter 4. 'The Fairlie Flyer' celebrates the long-lost heyday of the rural branch line: 'So firemen stoke the engine, steam down that railway track, | This train that's leaving Fairlie is never, never coming back'.

Other ballads were customised versions of overseas tunes. Railwayman Bruce Attwell, for example, recalled learning 'The Wreck of the Old 2-2-7', an adaptation of the popular 1930s American song 'The Wreck of the Old 97', at the Palmerston North locomotive depot in 1952. More curiously, in the 1960s steam locomotives became 'recording artists' in their own right, when the Kiwi record label (owned by publishers

Trainland

## The Ballad of Minnie Dean

*She dressed in black and she carried a hat*
*In a hatbox when early to the station she came*
*And on her way back she always wore the hat*
*Invercargill to Winton on the 5 o'clock train.*

'The Ballad of Minnie Dean' by Los Angeles-based singer-songwriter Helen Henderson captures the macabre fascination with the century-old case of the 'Winton baby farmer', who was hanged for infanticide in 1895. Dean's fate as the only woman ever executed in New Zealand has assured her lasting infamy; local legend even claims that no plants will grow on her grave. Henderson, who was born in Invercargill, recalled that 'Minnie was like the bogeyman of our town when I was a kid. If you were giving cheek to your mum or being naughty it was like, "You better watch out or I'll send you off to Minnie Dean's farm and you'll never be heard of again".' The story has also inspired other New Zealand songwriters, like the Celtic folk group Run the Cutter, who recorded a ballad called 'Minnie Dean' in 2000.

Dean's father had been an engine-driver in Scotland, and Southland's railways were central to the case. Her alleged crimes were uncovered by an eagle-eyed NZR guard, who noticed her board the Lumsden train on 2 May 1895 carrying a young

A.H. & A.W. Reed) issued several long-players of train sounds. To the surprise of some, they proved a hit with rail enthusiasts keen to listen to something different on their 'hi-fi' equipment.[26]

## Journey Through the Artland

From the earliest days of railways, European and American artists were drawn to the dramatic power of the steam locomotive in the landscape. J.M.W. Turner's atmospheric *Rain, Steam and Speed — The Great Western Railway* (1844) and Fanny Palmer's epic *Across the Continent: 'Westward the Course of Empire Takes*

baby and a hatbox, but disembark later with only the hatbox — which, as railway porters later testified, was suspiciously heavy. After a fruitless search along the tracks, police unearthed the recently buried bodies of two babies and the skeleton of an older boy in Dean's garden. An inquest determined that one of the babies had died of an overdose of the commonly used opiate laudanum. According to defence lawyer Alfred Hanlon:

> Sober, home-loving folk from end to end of the country shuddered . . . when the grim and ghastly story of Minnie Dean's infamy was narrated by the prosecution. Imagine a being with the name and appearance of a woman boldly using a public railway train for the destruction of her helpless victims, sitting serene and unperturbed in a carriage with one tiny corpse in a tin box at her feet and another enshrouded in a shawl and secured by travelling straps in the luggage rack at her head.

Despite Hanlon's impassioned defence that the baby's death was accidental, Dean was found guilty of murder and hanged on 12 August.[25]

*A scene from the music video for Helen Henderson's 'The Ballad of Minnie Dean', directed by Rose Bauer and filmed along the standard-gauge tracks of Pasadena, California.*

Courtesy of Helen Henderson

its Way' (1868), in which the smoke of the triumphant locomotive obliterates Native American onlookers, are among the most iconic of railway images. As Simon Schama has noted, 'Turner didn't need a whole new generation of writers to tell him that while once the river had been the favored metaphor for the flow of time, modern history was already being compared to the runaway force of the locomotive.'[27] Within two decades New Zealand was making its own tentative steps into the rail age, and by the late 1870s trains and stations were appearing in the work of local artists.

Like rail history itself, the story of railways art in New Zealand can be divided into three broad phases.[28]

In the first period, which coincided with the 'heroic' railmaking era, artists celebrated the colony's growing technological mastery over nature in works such as Charles Barraud's *Rimutaka Incline* (see page 34); others presented idealised images of the 'harmless' train at peace with the landscape — as in Alfred Sharpe's picturesque *Devonport and the Waitemata Harbour from the Domain* (1877) and Christopher Aubrey's *Upper Hutt With Railway Station* (1890), where grazing cows appear oblivious to the train's presence.

Another typical work of this era is *Mount Egmont with Train* (c.1880) by William Fox, the veteran politician

# The Long Train Journey

*William Fox's view of a train crossing a Taranaki bridge is a confident declaration of late-nineteenth-century colonial progress. In contrast to the smoke-obscured Native Americans in Fanny Palmer's epic* Across the Continent, *local Maori are nowhere to be seen.*

ATL, A-195-002

and former Premier who had overseen the introduction of Vogel's public works scheme in 1870. A determined champion of colonisation, Fox portrays the train and bridge as proud symbols of progress, delivering peace and prosperity to a region recently ravaged by war and land confiscation. While amateur artists like Fox had little interest in international art trends, in the early 1890s the Italian-trained Girolamo Nerli brought Impressionism to New Zealand with *A Wet Winter Day, 1893*, an atmospheric, rain-swept view of a railway platform that recalls Turner's *Rain, Steam and Speed* or Claude Monet's station paintings.

The first half of the twentieth century brought a new era of railways art. Rail's sights, sounds and smells were by now a familiar part of New Zealanders' lives. In this period many artists, both male and female, produced rail-related images, especially views of the ubiquitous station in its landscape setting. Given Canterbury's status as the birthplace of New Zealand railways, it is perhaps not surprising that 'Canterbury School' artists like Rata Lovell-Smith and Rita Angus led the way. Lovell-Smith's *Hawkins* (1933) and Angus' *Cass* (1936) each depict a lonely, almost empty station and rail sheds amidst towering physical landscapes. A distant train and single seated figure respectively are the only signs of movement or life. Other mid-century artists also focused on prosaic aspects of the railway world, such as the bustle of Louise Henderson's *Addington Workshop* (1930) — reproduced on page 36 — and studies of railway yards by May Smith (1944) and John Weeks (1946).

In most of these works, locomotives, passengers and railway workers are absent or incidental to the scene. In the field of realistic railway painting, one figure towers above all others — W.W. (Bill) Stewart, several of whose works have appeared earlier in this book. From the First World War until his death in 1976, he produced around 80 oil paintings, including dozens of careful studies of locomotives, royal trains, opening ceremonies

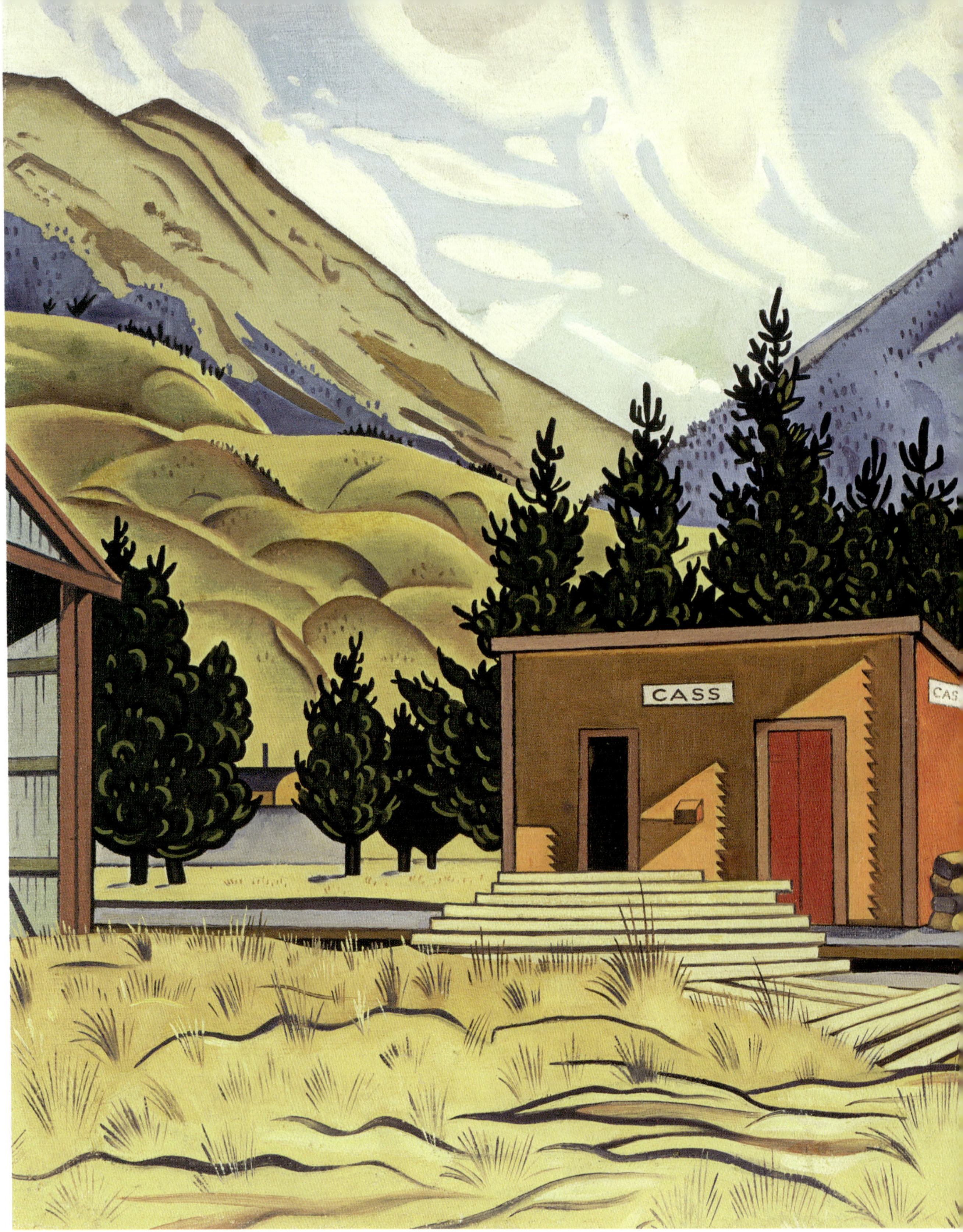
CASS
CAS

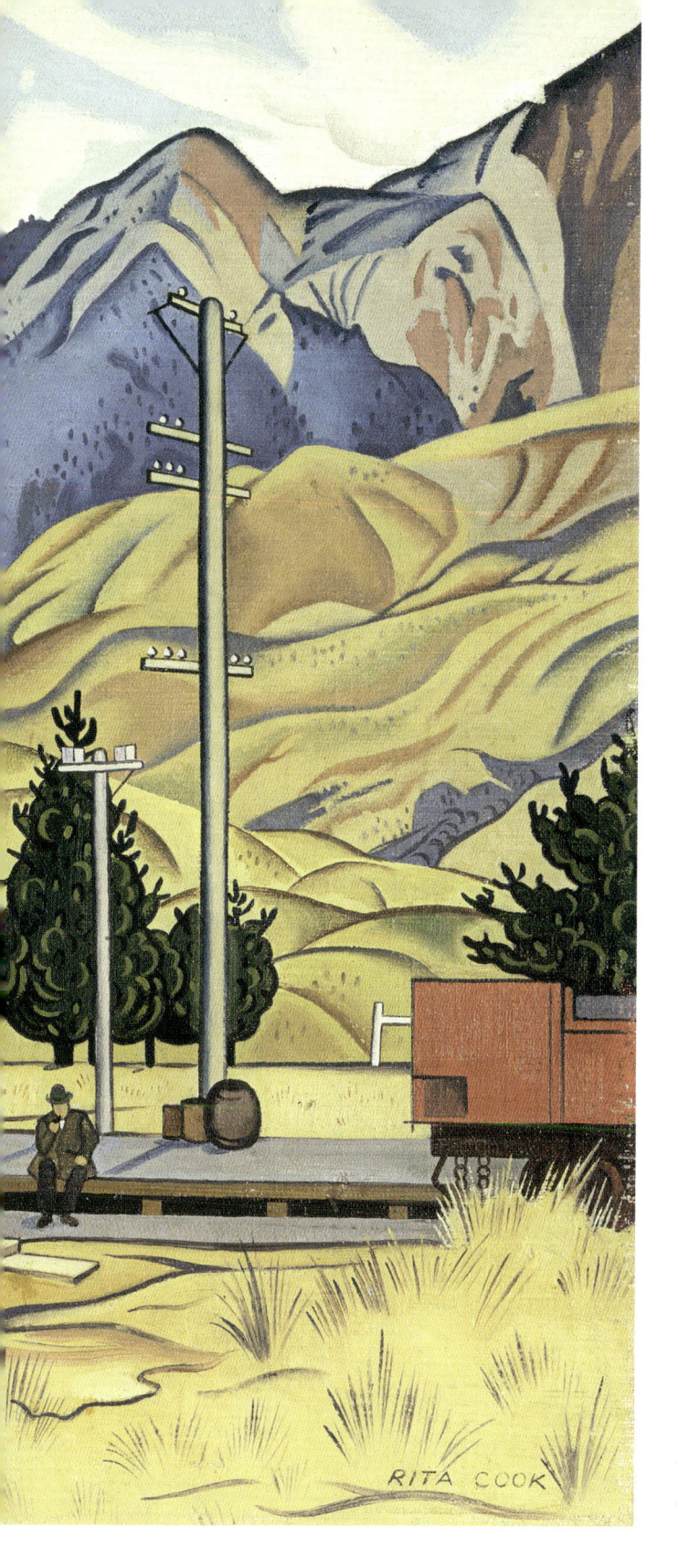

## The Long Train Journey

and other historical events. Stewart was also one of the country's leading rail photographers, and along with Albert Percy Godber (who worked at the Petone railway workshops), official NZR photographer John Le Cren and many other professional and amateur photographers he made a major contribution to the outstanding pictorial record of New Zealand railway history.[29]

In the early decades of the twentieth century images of trains even featured in Maori figurative art, notably in the Ruaihona meeting house at Te Teko (painted around 1910) and Puawairua at Whakatane (1920s). Curiously, while the former example represents a typical New Zealand locomotive and carriages, the latter clearly depicts an English-style Hornby toy train. Colin McCahon's dream-like *Trains and Boats and Planes* (1946), and more recently Jeff Thomson's giant corrugated-plastic sculpture *Train* (1985), also invite comparisons with the compact world of the toy train or model railway, and their strong associations with childhood.[30]

Since the 1960s, rail's perceived decline has been reflected in a new era of railway art. While skilful amateurs continue to produce realistic studies of

*Rita Angus' Cass (1936), with its red station buildings, lone seated figure and towering alpine backdrop, is probably New Zealand's best-known railway landscape painting.*

Collection Christchurch Art Gallery Te Puna o Waiwhetu (courtesy of the Estate of Rita Angus)

# Trainland

steam locomotives, others have captured vanishing rail landscapes or explored rail's complex role in this country's colonial past. The iconic railway station has remained popular, with Grahame Sydney immortalising the ghostly, disused Central Otago station or trackside shed in works such as *The Demolition at Waipiata* (1986). Robin White's *Mana Railway Station* (1971) and photographs by Robin Morrison have also focused on the familiar (and usually empty) station. Since the 1980s 'post-colonial' concerns have been evident in works such as George Baloghy's quirky *Fast Track* (1981), which juxtaposes a double-ended (two-faced?) Fairlie locomotive and Maori storehouse; Barry Brickell's ceramic *Stations of the Cross* series (1988); Paul Dibble's bronze sculpture *Journey through the Heartland* (2000); and recent paintings by John Horner, inspired in part by Te Kooti's railway prophecies. Here, the train is no longer the 'heroic' symbol of progress and prosperity, but an engine of colonisation and dispossession.[31]

RIGHT: *The three vertical panels of John Horner's* The Colonial Dream *(2002) — overwritten with excerpts from Te Kooti's 1883 prophecies, which warned of the coming of the Pakeha's 'whistling God' — symbolise the railway's complicity in European colonisation, shining heyday and perceived postwar decline.*

John Horner

## The Declining Years

Most railway enthusiasts have observed the transformation of the rail scene over the last half century with a sense of regret and loss. The slide in passenger numbers illustrated in the chart on page 215 highlights rail's flagging fortunes. In the four decades that followed the war-fuelled peak of 1944, total passenger journeys plunged dramatically, particularly considering the nation's population virtually doubled over the same period. Passenger numbers did rally strongly in the decade from 1952 to 1962 (when total journeys jumped from 21 to 26 million), but this growth was in suburban commuter services, notably in Wellington's burgeoning Hutt Valley and Porirua basin; over the same period long-distance journeys fell from 3.8 to 3 million. Smaller rebounds in the early and late 1970s, again almost exclusively confined to suburban lines, were spurred by rising petrol prices in the wake of the Middle East oil shocks.

Since the nadir of the early 1990s, when total journeys slumped to 10.4 million, around half their mid-1970s levels, the prospects for passenger rail have brightened somewhat. Commuter traffic rallied strongly in the early 2000s as road congestion and petrol price hikes (together with improvements to the Auckland network and the opening of the new Britomart station) lured more workers onto suburban trains. In the year to June 2006 Auckland's commuter network carried a record 5.66 million passengers (up from 3.2 million in

# The Long Train Journey

*Auckland's shiny new Britomart transport centre, opened in 2003, brought trains back to lower Queen Street for the first time in seven decades and contributed to a surge in rail commuter travel in the sprawling, car-dominated city.*

Jackson Perry

2002/03), while Wellington's Tranz Metro transported 11.1 million, almost a million more than in 2004/05.[32] The outlook for long-distance passenger services is less rosy. Patronage did climb in the 1990s, thanks largely to the success of the South Island's TranzAlpine service, but a string of inter-city passenger trains disappeared between 2001 and 2004. Despite the reprieve given to the Overlander in September 2006, the future of passenger services on the North Island main trunk remains far from certain.

# The Long Train Journey

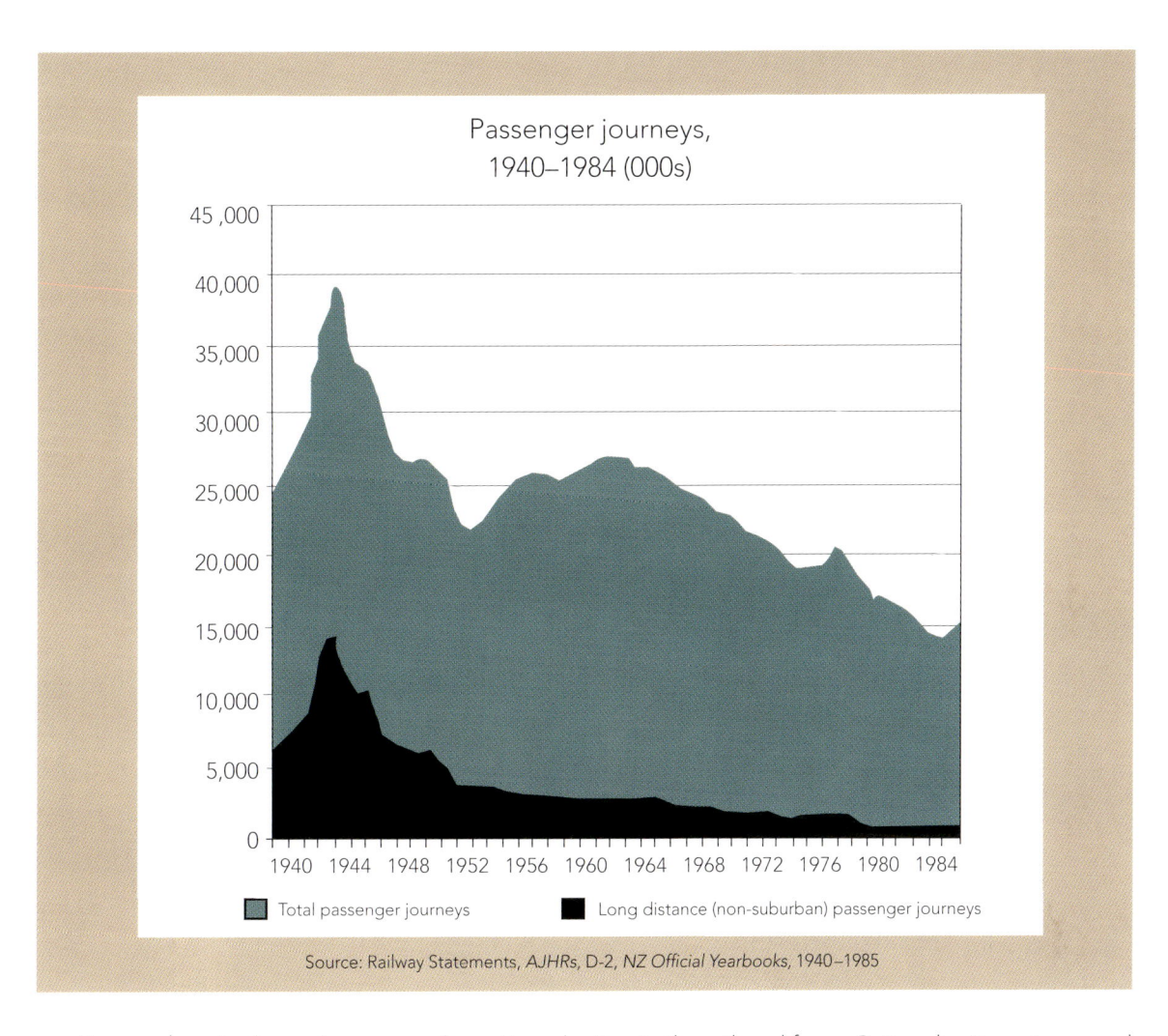

**Passenger journeys, 1940–1984 (000s)**

- Total passenger journeys
- Long distance (non-suburban) passenger journeys

Source: Railway Statements, *AJHRs*, D-2, *NZ Official Yearbooks*, 1940–1985

Recent decades have also seen a dramatic reduction in the rail workforce. Rationalisations, improved productivity, technological changes, mechanised freight handling, the withdrawal of passenger services, the sale of some operations and the trend towards contracting out, as well as intense competition in the transport sector, have all played their part. In 1982, when the old Railways Department became a corporation, it employed 21,834 workers; by 2001 the privatised Tranz Rail's workforce had shrunk to 4100. Today, Toll New Zealand directly employs about 3000 staff across its integrated rail and sea operations, Ontrack around 700 (mostly on track maintenance), and Auckland's commuter rail operator, Veolia Transport, 250.[33]

Similarly, the last half-century has seen the destruction of much of the physical fabric of New Zealand's

# Trainland

*New Zealand's rail network once boasted over 1350 stations, even if many were little more than weatherboard sheds — like this one at Aickens, near Otira, photographed in 2001. Today, fewer than a hundred stations survive.*

Paul Hamer

rail heritage. In the 1950s, 1350 railway stations dotted the landscape (even if many of them were only small shelter sheds); today fewer than a hundred survive, and only about 40 wooden stations remain on their original sites. The rationalisation of freight-handling facilities has been equally dramatic. In 1952, for example, 74 stations between Christchurch and Dunedin had sidings handling general freight, in addition to dozens of private sidings serving single users. Today there are four — Ashburton, Temuka, Timaru and Oamaru — plus a handful of industrial sidings. The closure of stations has been matched by the widespread removal of associated structures: goods sheds, signal boxes, stockyards, water tanks, trackmen's huts, loading banks and other railway 'furniture and fittings'.[34]

New Zealanders responded to the threats to their rail heritage in a variety of ways. When the first wave of branch closures swept the country in the years following the 1952 Royal Commission, some reacted with anger and dissent. Many small towns owed their very existence to the railway, symbolised by the prevalence of 'Railway Streets' and 'Railway Hotels'. The Department was often the biggest employer and landlord in town, and railway kids filled the school rolls. The prospect of losing precious local resources their forebears had fought to secure aroused the protective spirit of these communities, along with a sense of nostalgia for a simpler, gentler age. As Euan McQueen explains, 'the branch line and its train belonged; it was an institution, fought for, often abused, taken for granted, but in times of threats from outside, fiercely protected'.[35]

# The Long Train Journey

*Despite the efforts of museums and volunteers, over the last half-century much of the physical fabric of New Zealand's rail heritage has disappeared or deteriorated; this dilapidated ex-signals store wagon was photographed in 2005, awaiting restoration at Silver Stream.*

Paul Hamer

The most famous protest was the Nelson railway 'sit-in' of 1955. Although by the mid 1920s Nelson's lonely line snaked inland as far as Kawatiri on the upper Buller River, the long-promised link-up with the West Coast's Inangahua line remained agonisingly out of reach. In 1954 the National government decided to close and demolish the Nelson line, sparking a string of angry protest rallies, petitions and desperate pleas by the local Progress League. After a one-year 'stay of execution', the line's fate was sealed in September 1955. Amid further protests, a group of local women led by Ruth Page and the future union activist Sonja Davies drove to the tiny station at Kiwi and calmly sat on the track to block the demolition train. After attracting international media attention they were eventually arrested, convicted and fined. The line was removed.[36]

Although ultimately unsuccessful, theirs was a daring and dignified protest against what many saw as a blatant attempt to strip out local resources. Worse was to come. Another wave of rail cutbacks in the deregulated and privatised 1980s and nineties would have a devastating effect on many small communities, especially as they often coincided with the closure of post office and bank branches, schools, shops and local industries. Among the hardest hit were Maori, who by that time formed a significant proportion of the rail workforce.

Another product of rail's perceived decline has been a surge of nostalgia for an idealised past, especially among older generations. This sentiment is typically centred on the steam locomotive, and is at times

# Trainland

hostile to the modern machines that supplanted it. Many would agree that 'those wonderful old locomotives were the most human of man's inventions. They seemed to breathe as they thundered along, fed with coal and watered throughout their journey.' In contrast, 'the diesel engine is a ruthless, nerve-shattering machine, a mobile bucket of bolts'.[37] The notion that steam engines are somehow living creatures that 'breathe', and require regular feeding, watering and grooming like thoroughbred racehorses, is no doubt part of their enduring attraction. Compared to the 'invisible power' of diesel and electric locomotives, steam engines display a fascinating — and highly visible — complexity of movement, effort, noise, steam and smoke.

Of course, rail enthusiasts are not alone in their nostalgic longing for archaic technology. A direct comparison can be made with the maritime world, where

*Today, scenes like this 1957 line-up of locomotives outside the Dunedin sheds typically inspire nostalgic yearning for a lost golden age. But in the steam era itself, many people were less impressed by the clouds of choking smoke, soot, cinders, coal dust and noise produced by these machines.*

Otago Daily Times

# The Long Train Journey

**Compared to the 'invisible power' of diesel and electric locomotives, steam engines display a fascinating — and highly visible — complexity of movement, effort, noise, steam and smoke.**

for more than a century writers have lamented the passing of the sailing ship. Like steam locomotives, these great 'white-winged' craft were frequently imbued with animal or human characteristics and always referred to by the feminine pronoun. But there is an irony here: whereas the steam railway locomotive was the much-lamented victim of technological change, at sea steam was the villain, the soulless mechanical conqueror of the romantic sailing ship.

Meanwhile, industrious rail enthusiasts have been busy celebrating and saving what they can. As well as the Kingston Flyer, historic locomotives and rolling stock have been preserved or restored by a range of organisations including Auckland's Museum of Transport and Technology (MOTAT); Mainline Steam at Parnell, Plimmerton and Christchurch; the Glenbrook Vintage Railway; Steam Incorporated at Paekakariki; the Hutt Valley's Silver Stream Railway; North Canterbury's Weka Pass Railway; Christchurch's Ferrymead Historic Park; the Plains Railway near Ashburton; and Timaru's Pleasant Point Railway.

*The Silver Stream Railway is one of a number of museums and organisations dedicated to preserving and operating heritage locomotives and rolling stock. This photograph shows the shunting locomotive C 847, built at Hillside in 1930.*

Claire Taggart

Trainland

Stripped of their passenger services and often their tracks, lovingly restored stations have been reborn as cafés or restaurants, art galleries, museums, information centres, bed and breakfasts, garden centres, offices and even private homes.

220

# The Long Train Journey

LEFT: *Ormondville station in southern Hawke's Bay (built in 1880) is one of a handful of early wooden rail buildings that have been preserved thanks to community efforts. Since the demise in 2001 of the region's last passenger service, the Bay Express, part of the building has been converted into 'unique boutique accomodation'.*

Miriam Gibson

Equally strenuous efforts, led by the Rail Heritage Trust of New Zealand and countless community groups, have saved numerous stations and other structures from demolition. Stripped of their passenger services and often their tracks, lovingly restored stations have been reborn as cafés or restaurants, art galleries, museums, information centres, bed and breakfasts, garden centres, offices and even private homes. George Troup's stunning Dunedin station, with its soaring tower, stained glass windows, frieze of cherubs beneath the balcony and mosaic floor tiles, now houses a café, arts centre, the New Zealand Sports Hall of Fame, and offices for the Taieri Gorge Railway; its long platform has also been used as a runway for fashion shows. Auckland's grand beaux-arts station, opened in 1930, was sold to a private developer in the 1990s and now provides student accommodation under the name 'Railway Campus'. Notices warn any confused travellers that 'This is not the railway station'.[38]

Physical preservation efforts have been matched by a flourishing of rail history writing. A bibliography published in 2000 listed more than 500 works on New Zealand railways (of which the industrious New Zealand Railway and Locomotive Society had alone published 129), not counting the thousands of articles in magazines like *Rails* and the six-decade-old *New Zealand Railway Observer*. Like their many overseas equivalents, New Zealand's modern rail histories dutifully salute and lament the rise and fall of a once-great enterprise, but often end on a rousing, optimistic note, confident that a new, leaner, different railway has a positive future.[39]

Some commentators argue that reports of rail's demise have been exaggerated, highlighting Toll's record freight hauls in recent years, the revival of Auckland's suburban traffic, and the popularity of special trains to events like the Martinborough wine festival and Auckland's Big Day Out concert. Environmental activists maintain that the looming threat of climate change and the spectre of 'peak oil' demand renewed state investment in rail infrastructure. Meanwhile, many motorists see rail as a key ally in reducing the number of giant trucks on the country's congested roads. Time alone will tell whether a glorious rail renaissance is lurking just around the corner.

## Trainland

# End of the Line?

Where the railway was once the epitome of shining modernity, it is now more often a symbol of the past. Of course, rail's historic pre-eminence has left its imprint on our language, where people try to stay 'on track', see 'the light at the end of the tunnel', climb aboard 'the gravy train', and avoid going 'off the rails', 'running out of steam' or growing up 'on the wrong side of the tracks'. Similarly, rail holds a place in the Anglo-American popular culture that saturates New Zealand society with imported creations like Thomas the Tank Engine, *Harry Potter*'s Hogwarts Express and the 2004 movie *The Polar Express*. But these inevitably portray the train as history, an evocation of the way we were or a magical alternative reality. Railways are not alone in this regard — the deep-sea passenger ship has suffered the same fate. Just as the Boeing 747 has supplanted the 'Home boat', the 737 and the Toyota Corolla have replaced the mixed train and Night Limited as New Zealanders' favoured modes of domestic travel. Commuter and tourist trains survive (as do ferries and cruise ships), but for everyday travel the private car offers a flexibility that rail cannot match — or at least, not while relatively cheap petrol continues to flow.

Rail's rise and fall can also be compared to the fate of another great nineteenth-century innovation, the cinema. In the later twentieth century these once-revolutionary forms of mass public transportation and entertainment were each supplanted by private, domestic rivals: the family automobile and the television set.

> **It is not merely in scale or dimension that the machines in question are reduced when they move from the public sphere into domestic use — cars are smaller than locomotives, television sets smaller than movie screens — but the essential character of things is also diminished; the heroic aspect is lost, so to speak. In comparison with their tiny successors the railroad and cinema are powerful instruments that excite the imagination, inviting near mythic associations.[40]**

Of course, just as cinema has adapted to survival in a world of television, DVDs and the Internet,

RIGHT: *Des Somers (left) and Brett Green prepare Glenbrook Vintage Railway locomotives for a Thomas the Tank Engine weekend in November 2005. Although their English-style locomotives and settings bear little resemblance to New Zealand railways, Thomas and his friends are today probably better known than any of this country's real locomotives, especially among children.*

New Zealand Herald / APN

# The Long Train Journey

the railway is far from finished. Tens of millions travel on urban underground trains every day; rail freight flourishes in the United States, Russia, China and elsewhere; Europe's TGVs and AVEs, Japan's *Sinkansen* and Shanghai's German-built Magnetic Levitation train (capable of 501 km per hour) remain on the cutting edge of technological innovation. But no space-age MagLev will recapture the romance of rail's glory days, 'stir the emotions or befuddle the senses of otherwise normal and rational adults' in the way the steam railway can.

It is this 'heroic aspect', and rail's 'near mythic associations', that help us answer the *Star*'s 1959 question, 'What is it about railways?' Memories of rail's heyday are entangled with a wider sense of nostalgia for the more secure, intimate world the people's railway inhabited. Just as the 'old NZR' has vanished, in recent

## Trainland

decades 'old New Zealand', with its modest culture of social cohesion and state paternalism, has been supplanted by an increasingly individualistic, commercialised and globalised culture. For many, the transition has been painful, and the results unwelcome. The steam railway, therefore, symbolises an idealised, rural and small-town society of cohesive communities and simple certainties — a world many older New Zealanders associate with the 'golden weather' of their own childhood. Every gleaming steam locomotive, restored station, local rail museum and recollection of the 'good old days' provides a link to that past. So too do the compact little landscapes lovingly created by rail modellers, where even derailed trains can be put 'back on track' by a giant hand from above.

Nostalgia, however, always relies on the selective sifting of memory. The drunken sports teams, vandalism, railway-cup throwing, refreshment room stampedes and sundry irritations mentioned earlier in this book are the darker side of this idealised railway past. The old NZR was of course far from perfect; it was, after all, a rough mirror of the society that produced it. Ultimately, 'Trainland' was not a creation of steel, coal and timber, buildings, tunnels and viaducts — although naturally those elements were hugely important. Rather, it was made up of people, the thousands of ordinary New Zealanders who ran the railways, journeyed on them, used them, abused them, and made them their own. The future of railways, especially as a form of passenger travel, today stands at a crossroads in this country. But as long as rail retains its mythic power to fire the imagination, our 'long train journey' will continue rolling on.

*Rail heritage continues to fascinate many New Zealanders and draw large crowds to events like Dunedin station's 2006 centenary celebrations, which featured this cavalcade of restored steam locomotives. Nearest to the camera is the Plains Railway's Rogers K 88 Washington, followed by D 140 from Ferrymead, Mainline Steam's A$^B$ 663, W$^{AB}$ 794 from Feilding and J$^A$ 1271 from Steam Incorporated at Paekakariki.*

*Otago Daily Times*

# The Long Train Journey

The future of railways, especially as a form of passenger travel, today stands at a crossroads in this country. But as long as rail retains its mythic power to fire the imagination, our 'long train journey' will continue rolling on.

# Notes

## Introduction

1. *New Zealand Railway Observer (NZRO)*, Issue 280 (Dec 2006–Jan 2007), pp. 149, 159–66, 176; 'Dunedin station ranked one of "wonders of the world"', *Stuff: NZ's Leading News and Information Website*, 7 Aug 2006, URL: http://www.stuff.co.nz.
2. William R. Everdell, *The First Moderns*, University of California Press, Berkeley, 1997, p. 4, cited in Ian Carter, *Railways and Culture in Britain: The Epitome of Modernity*, University of Manchester Press, Manchester, 2001, p. 4.
3. Carter, *Railways and Culture in Britain*, pp. 8–9; E.P. Thompson, 'Time, Work Discipline, and Industrial Capitalism', *Past and Present*, Vol. 38, No. 1 (1967), pp. 56–97.
4. See Robin Law, 'On the Streets of Southern Dunedin: Gender in Transport', in Barbara Brookes, Annabel Cooper & Robin Law (eds), *Sites of Gender: Women, Men and Modernity in Southern Dunedin, 1890–1939*, p. 266; Erik Olssen, *Building the New World*, Auckland University Press, Auckland, 1985, Ch. 6 ('The Hillside Workshops'); and Carter, *Railways and Culture in Britain*, pp. 11, 39 (Note 61).
5. For a general overview of New Zealand railway history, see Geoffrey B. Churchman & Tony Hurst, *The Railways of New Zealand: A Journey through History*, 2nd edn, Transpress, Wellington, 2001; David B. Leitch, *Railways of New Zealand*, Leonard Fullerton / David & Charles, Newton Abbot (UK), 1972; David Leitch & Bob Stott, *New Zealand Railways: The First 125 Years*, Heinemann Reed, Auckland, 1988; and Gordon Troup (ed.), *Steel Roads of New Zealand: An Illustrated Survey*, 2nd edn, A.H. & A.W. Reed, Wellington, 1974. Other useful recent works include Robin Bromby, *Rails that Built a Nation: An Encyclopedia of New Zealand Railways*, Grantham House, Wellington, 2003; Euan McQueen, *Rails in the Hinterland: New Zealand's Vanishing Railway Landscape*, Grantham House, Wellington, 2005; Roy Sinclair, *Journeying with Railways in New Zealand*, Random House, Auckland, 1997; James Watson, *Links: A History of Transport and New Zealand Society*, GP Publications / Ministry of Transport, Wellington, 1996; and Matthew Wright, *Rails Across New Zealand: A History of Rail Travel*, Whitcoulls, Auckland, 2003.
6. See, for example, *New Zealand Railways Magazine* (*NZRM*), Vol. 13, No. 2 (May 1938), p. 4.
7. The quote is from the *Wanganui Chronicle*, 5 Sep 1885.

## Chapter 1: The Railmaking State

1. *New Zealand Parliamentary Debates* (*NZPD*), Vol. 5, 1869, p. 522.
2. W. David McIntyre (ed.), *The Journal of Henry Sewell 1853–7*, Whitcoulls, Christchurch, 1980, Vol. I, pp. 356, 510, Vol. II, pp. 12–20; John E. Martin, *The House: New Zealand's House of Representatives 1854–2004*, Dunmore Press, Palmerston North, 2004, p. 14.
3. Judith Binney, *Redemption Songs: A Life of Te Kooti Arikirangi Te Turuki*, Auckland University Press / Bridget Williams Books, Auckland, 1997, p. 278. See also Alan Ward, *An Unsettled History: Treaty Claims in New Zealand Today*, Bridget Williams Books, Wellington, 1999, p. 141.
4. *The Journal of Henry Sewell*, Vol. I, p. 481.
5. See W.A. Pierre, *Canterbury Provincial Railways*, New Zealand Railway & Locomotive Society (NZRLS), Wellington, 1964.
6. T.A. McGavin (ed.), *New Zealand Railways to 1900: Being an Adaptation of Three Articles Contributed to the Railway Magazine (England) in December 1899 and January and February 1900, by Charles Rous-Marten*, NZRLS, Wellington, 1985, p. 8. See also J.O.P. Watt, *Southland's Pioneer Railways, 1864–1878*, NZRLS, Wellington, 1965.
7. This and subsequent mileage figures, together with railway opening dates, are drawn from the *New Zealand Railways Geographical Mileage Table 1957* (NZR, Wellington, 1958) and the *New Zealand Railway and Tramway Atlas* (4th edn, Quail Map Company, Exeter, UK / Southern Press, Porirua, 1993).
8. *NZPD*, Vol. 7, 1870, p. 103.
9. Ibid, p. 115; Raewyn Dalziel, *Julius Vogel: Business Politician*, Auckland University Press, Auckland, 1986, pp. 107–08.
10. *Wellington Independent*, 25 Aug 1870; the Pollen quote is cited in Dalziel, *Julius Vogel*, pp. 108–09.
11. W.P. Reeves, *The Long White Cloud (Ao tea roa)*, 3rd rev. edn, Allen & Unwin, London, 1924, p. 237.
12. The Fox quote is from *NZPD*, Vol. 7, 1870, p. 395; the Vogel quote is from an 1893 lecture in London, cited in Dalziel, *Julius Vogel*, p. 106.
13. Immigration to New Zealand, *Appendix to the Journals of the House of Representatives* (*AJHR*), 1873, D-2D, pp. 29–31; Rollo Arnold, *The Farthest Promised Land: English Villagers, New Zealand Immigrants of the 1870s*, Victoria University Press, Wellington, 1981, pp. 2–6.

# Trainland

14. Troup, *Steel Roads*, p. 9.
15. *Appendix to the Journals of the Legislative Council*, No. 12, 1873, p. 40; Arnold, *Farthest Promised Land*, pp. 13–14.
16. Dalziel, *Julius Vogel*, pp. 161–3.
17. 'By the River Ashley', in Vincent O'Sullivan (ed.), *Ursula Bethell: Collected Poems*, 2nd edn, Victoria University Press, Wellington, 1997, p. 85.
18. Herman Foston, *At the Front: A Story of Pluck and Heroism in the Railway Construction Camps in the Dominion of New Zealand*, Arthur H. Stockwell, London, 1921, p. 47.
19. *Southland Times*, 23 Jan 1879; Leitch, *Railways of New Zealand*, pp. 33–7. For an entertaining account of the Liverpool and Manchester Railway and Huskisson's sad demise, see Simon Garfield, *The Last Journey of William Huskisson*, Faber & Faber, London, 2002.
20. *Southern Cross*, 22 & 25 Dec 1873.
21. *Auckland Weekly News*, 30 Oct 1875; Deborah Dunsford, *Doing It Themselves: The Story of Kumeu, Huapai and Taupaki*, Kumeu District History Project, Albany, 2002, pp. 29–35.
22. See W.N. Cameron, *A Line of Railway: The Railway Conquest of the Rimutakas*, NZRLS, Wellington, 1976.
23. Report of the Department of Labour, *AJHR*, 1901, H-11, pp. 16–18. See also Troup, *Steel Roads*, Ch. 8; Jack McClare, *Auckland's Railway Workshops*, NZRLS, Wellington, 1998; and Olssen, *Building the New World*, Ch. 6.
24. *Otago Daily Times* (*ODT*), 14 Sep 1870.
25. Public Works Statement, *AJHR*, 1880, E-1, pp. vi, 96, 113.
26. Ibid, pp. vi, 105.
27. Report of the Royal Commission Appointed to Inquire and Report Upon the Civil Service of New Zealand, *AJHR*, 1880, H-2, p. 3; Public Works Statement, *AJHR*, 1880, E-1, pp. iii–v; Report of Railway Commission, *AJHR*, 1880, E-3, pp. iv, xvii.
28. *Yeoman* (Wanganui), 27 Apr 1889, p. 11.
29. Rollo Arnold, *New Zealand's Burning: The Settlers' World in the Mid 1880s*, Victoria University Press, Wellington, 1994, pp. 140–3.
30. *Evening Post*, 4 Nov 1886; D.G. Hoy, *West of the Tararuas: An Illustrated History of the Wellington and Manawatu Railway Company*, Southern Press, Wellington, 1972; T.A. McGavin, *The Manawatu Line: A Commemoration of the Wellington and Manawatu Railway Company*, 2nd edn, NZRLS, Wellington, 1982; Geoffrey B. Churchman, *The Midland Line: New Zealand's Trans-Alpine Railway*, 4th edn, IPL Books, Wellington, 1995.
31. Manuka Henare, 'Wahanui Huatare (?–1897)', Chris Koroheke, 'Te Mahuki (?–1899)', and John Pollard, 'Rochfort, John (1832–1893)', in *Dictionary of New Zealand Biography*, updated 7 April 2006, URL: http://www.dnzb.govt.nz; Alan Ward, *A Show of Justice: Racial 'Amalgamation' in Nineteenth Century New Zealand*, Auckland University Press, Auckland, 1995, pp. 287–8, 296.
32. *Waikato Times*, 16 Apr 1908; North Island Main Trunk Railway — Report on the Ceremony of Turning the First Sod of, at Puniu, *AJHR*, 1885, D-6, p. 5.
33. Plunket is quoted from P.S. O'Connor, *Richard John Seddon*, A.H. & A.W. Reed, Wellington, 1968, pp. 28–30; the school question is cited in J.B. Condliffe, *New Zealand in the Making*, 2nd edn, Allen & Unwin, London, 1958, p. 222; the Hall-Jones quote is from *Weekly Graphic*, 7 Oct 1908, p. 3.
34. Railway Statements, *AJHR*, 1891, p. 33, and 1912, D-2, p. 48. See also '100 Years Old', *New Zealand Railway Review: Special Centenary Supplement*, ASRS, Wellington, 1986; and Neill Atkinson, *Rewarding Service: A History of the Government Superannuation Fund*, Otago University Press, Dunedin, 2002, pp. 17–18.
35. P.J. Gibbons, 'Some New Zealand Navvies: Co-operative Workers, 1891–1912', *New Zealand Journal of History*, Vol. 11, No. 1 (Apr 1977), pp. 54–75.
36. Quoted in Gibbons, 'Some New Zealand Navvies', p. 57.
37. G.G. Stewart, *The Romance of New Zealand Railways*, A.H. & A.W. Reed, Wellington, 1951, p. 38; Peter Keller, 'Early Days on Railway Construction', p. 17, MS-Papers-1073, Alexander Turnbull Library (ATL); Bill Pierre, *The North Island Main Trunk: An Illustrated History*, A.H. & A.W. Reed, Wellington, 1981, p. 272.
38. Keller, 'Early Days on Railway Construction', p. 2; *Waikato Times*, 20 Jun 1904.
39. *Census of the Colony of New Zealand*, 1906, Government Printer, Wellington, 1907, p. 51; *Manawatu Evening Standard*, 3 Jan 1908; Foston, *At the Front*, p. 67.
40. *Evening Post*, 8 & 10 Aug, 9 Nov 1908. See also Malcolm McKinnon (ed.), *New Zealand Historical Atlas*, David Bateman / Department of Internal Affairs, Auckland, 1997, plate 84.
41. See House Factory at Frankton Junction, Railways (R), Series 3, Acc W2278, box 234, 1911/1981/13, part 1, 1920–44, Archives New Zealand (ANZ); Railways Statements, *AJHR*, 1920, D-2, p. viii; 1923, D-2, pp. v, xi; Report of the Railway Commission, *AJHR*, D-4, 1930, p. 19; *Heritage Hamilton: A Celebration of the City's Historic Buildings*, Wintec, Hamilton, 2006, p. 86.
42. Railways Statement, *AJHR*, 1914, D-2, pp. 6–7. These passenger figures are for 'ordinary' tickets only, and do not include season ticket holders — a significant majority of whom

were also in the North Island.

43. NZR General Manager (GM) to Manager, Trade Auxiliary Co., 12 May 1950, Tourist Traffic and Resorts, R 18, W2854, PUB 51, part 1, 1929–58, ANZ.
44. Public Works Statement, *AJHR*, 1929, D-1, Table No. 1, p. 2.

## Chapter 2: Business and Pleasure

1. H.C.D. Somerset, *Littledene: Patterns of Change*, enl. edn, New Zealand Council for Educational Research, Wellington, 1974, p. 149.
2. Railways Statement, *AJHR*, 1923, D-2, pp. i–ii.
3. The 'Big Four' were the London, Midland & Scottish Railway (LMS), which was Britain's largest; the London & North Eastern Railway (LNER); the Great Western Railway, and the Southern Railway. See Colin Divall, 'What happens if we think about railways as a kind of consumption? Towards a new historiography of transport and citizenship in early-twentieth-century Britain', Institute of Railways Studies & Transport History, York, UK, URL: http://www.york.ac.uk/inst/irs.
4. *AJHR*, 1923, D-2, p. xvii.
5. Ibid, p. ii.
6. *New Zealand Gazette* (*NZG*), 1877, pp. 591–7.
7. McKinnon, *NZ Historical Atlas*, plate 46.
8. Watson, *Links*, p. 154; *New Zealand Official Year-book, 1924*, Government Printer, Wellington, 1923, p. 344.
9. Somerset, *Littledene*, p. 149. For a useful study of rural railways and their demise over the last half century, see McQueen's *Rails in the Hinterland*.
10. See, for example, Yuilleen White, *Life Along the Steel Road: A Story of the Midland Railway*, Y. White, Renwick, 1988, pp. 24, 86.
11. Janet Frame, *An Angel at My Table: An Autobiography: Volume Two*, 2nd edn, Century Hutchinson, Auckland, 1985, pp. 14, 77.
12. Somerset, *Littledene*, p. 149.
13. A.H. McLintock (ed.), *An Encyclopaedia of New Zealand*, Government Printer, Wellington, 1966, Vol. I, pp. 16–17; Rates on Stock, Implements, Dogs, Poultry, Produce, etc, Exhibited at Shows, R 4, box 122, 1899/1572, 1884–1902; Rates for Stock Exhibitors, R 4, box 129, 1899/2247, part 1, 1897–1933; Excursion Fares for Exhibitors and Stock Attendants Attending Agricultural Shows, R 4, box 129, 1899/2247, part 1, 1935–75, ANZ; Peter Reaves (ed.), *The Kaipara Line*, Rodney Community Tourist & Development Trust, Helensville, 2000, p. 49; Toss Woollaston, *Sage Tea: An Autobiography*, Te Papa Press, Wellington, 2001, p. 157.
14. Free Carriage of Ploughs, New Zealand Rail Ltd Corporate Support Services Group (ABJP), W4908, box 42, 06/2558, part 1, 1900–87, ANZ.
15. Further representations from the New Zealand Federation of Cage Bird Clubs were ultimately successful in securing concession rates in 1936. See GM to Minister, 6 Jul 1937, Rate on Dogs to Dog Trials, R 4, box 120, 1899/1245, 1899–1951; GM to A.M. Bartley, 25 Jun 1934, GM to all Station Masters (SMs) and District Traffic Managers (DTMs), 20 May 1936, in Exhibits Forwarded to Pigeon, Canary, Cagebird or Similar Shows, New Zealand Government Railways Department General Manager's Office (AAEB), W3293, box 127, 16/2302/1, part 1, 1934–76, ANZ.
16. J.M. Grainger, *On and Off the Rails: A Railwayman's Story*, Whitcombe & Tombs, Christchurch, 1964, pp. 93–4.
17. Albert B. Johnston & Robin M. Startup, *Mails by Rail in New Zealand: The Story of the Railway Travelling Post Offices of New Zealand*, Royal Philatelic Society of New Zealand, Wellington, 2001, pp. xi, 5, 8, 30; Bromby, *Rails that Built a Nation*, p. 119.
18. Watson, *Links*, pp. 115–16; NZG, 1882, p. 1671; Commercial Travellers Season Tickets, R 4, box 40, 1895/5724, 1895–1938, ANZ; *Southland Times*, 1 Jul 1962.
19. *NZG*, 1877, pp. 591–2, 1065; 1878, pp. 80, 1711–12; 1879, pp. 17–19; 1880, p. 351; 1881, p. 592; 1884, pp. 1056–7; 1885, p. 1137; 1887, p. 1177; 1889, p. 573; 1894, pp. 1794–9; 1899, pp. 1633–42; NZR Circular No. 85/73 (26 Nov 1885), Concession Fares for Sporting Teams, R 4, box 91, 1898/3596, 1885–1900, ANZ; Railways Statement, *AJHR*, 1895, D-2, p. 3.
20. *NZG*, 1882, pp. 1669–71; Janet Frame, *To the Is-land: An Autobiography: Volume One*, Century Hutchinson, Auckland, 1983, pp. 147, 253; Free Conveyance of Corpse of Employees, their Wives and Children, AAEB, W3293, box 167, 17/4198, part 3, 1946–81, ANZ.
21. Railway Concessions, *AJHR*, 1900, D-8, p. 1.
22. *NZG*, 1885, p. 1134; 1894, p. 1799; 1899, pp. 1635–6, 1644, 1646; *AJHR*, 1900, D-8, p. 1; 1914, D-2, p. 12.
23. *Waikato Times*, 6 Aug 1881; Lawrence Nathan to Joseph Ward, 29 May 1900, Weekend Excursion Tickets to Rotorua and Te Aroha, R 3, W2381, 1915/973/1, part 1, 1892–1917, ANZ; Frank Sargeson, *Never Enough!*, Reed, Wellington, 1977, pp. 16–17; Mrs Martin to Minister, 14 Nov 1924, Persons Suffering from Infectious Diseases Travelling by Rail, ABJP, W4098, box 29, 04/2824, part 1, 1899–1982, ANZ; Hector Bolitho, *Ratana: The Maori Miracle Man*, Geddis & Blomfeld, Auckland, 1921, pp.

# Trainland

6–7, 8, 22; Fares and Carriage of Livestock and Provisions for Maori Attending Official Functions at Marae, ABJP, W4098, box 28, 04/2340/3, 1937–85, ANZ.

24. *NZG*, 1877, p. 592; 1878, p. 80; 1879, p. 17; 1882, p. 1056; 1885, p. 1133; 1889, p. 573; *NZPD*, Vol. 48, 1884, p. 274 (Buchanan); Return Showing Number of School Tickets Issued to 31 Mar 1895, Free School Tickets, R 4, box 104, 1898/4837, 1894–1900, ANZ; *AJHR*, 1900, D-8, p. 28; Education: Annual Report of the Minister, *AJHR*, E-1, p. xiv.

25. Seddon to GM, 12 Feb 1895, GM to Seddon, 18 Feb 1895, Free School Tickets, R 4, box 104, 1898/4837; *NZG*, 1898, p. 694; 1909, pp. 209–10; *AJHR*, 1915, D-2, p. 12.

26. Railways Statement, *AJHR*, 1896, D-2, p. 38; Secretary, New Zealand Sheepowners' Acknowledgement of Debt to British Seamen Fund, to GM, 27 May 1926, GM to William Riddet (Massey Agricultural College), 27 Apr 1929, Concession Fares, R 3, W2476, 1920/4881, part 1, 1920–72, ANZ; *Oamaru Mail*, 30 Mar 1936.

27. *NZPD*, Vol. 54, 1886, p. 137 (Kerr); Frank S. Anthony, *Follow the Call*, ed. Terry Sturm, Auckland University Press, Auckland, 1975, p. xvii; F.H.E. King, 'Railway Recollections', *NZRO*, Issue 196 (Summer 1988–9), pp. 141–2.

28. *AJHR*, 1895, D-2, p. 2; Robin Hyde, *The Godwits Fly*, Auckland University Press, Auckland, 1970, pp. 33–4.

29. *New Zealand Times*, 16 Mar 1898; DTM Invercargill to GM, 3 Feb 1898; GM to DTM Invercargill, 2 Mar 1898, Excursion Fares for School Parties and Friendly Societies, R 4, box 73, 1898/1328, 1897–1900, ANZ.

30. Sorrel Hoskin, 'Rail Relief: New Plymouth's First Railway', *Puke Ariki: Taranaki Stories*, URL: http://www.pukeariki.com/en/; 'Those Oamaru Excursion Trains of 1876', *NZRO*, Issue 191 (Spring 1987), pp. 120–1; Bromby, *Rails that Built a Nation*, p. 116.

31. *NZG*, 1877, p. 591; 1882, p. 1671; Holiday Excursion Tickets, R 4, box 132, 1899/2927, 1885–1900, ANZ.

32. Public Works Statement, *AJHR*, 1885, D-1, p. 13; Troup, *Steel Roads*, p. 25; Free Picnic Trains for Inmates of Asylums, R 4, box 41, 1896/525, 1882–96, ANZ.

33. *Lyttelton Times*, 1 Nov 1888; NZR Circulars No. 88/36 (11 Sep 1888), No. 95/74 (6 Sep 1895), No. 95/7276 (10 Oct 1895), GM to Minister, 5 Jul 1895 & 17 Dec 1902, in Holiday Excursion Tickets, R 4, box 132, 1899/2927; *AJHR*, 1895, D-2, p. 3.

34. *ODT*, 5 Apr 1904.

35. *ODT*, 13 Oct 1904 & 3 Jan 1906; *NZPD*, 1906, Vol. 138, p. 306.

36. Paul Mahoney, *From the Station Platform: An Historical Account of Ormondville Station and District from a Railway Perspective*, Ormondville Rail Preservation Group, Wellington, 2000, p. 24; Reaves, *Kaipara Line*, p. 50; Holiday Excursion Tickets, R 4, box 132, 1899/2927; Railways Statement, *AJHR*, 1907, D-2, p. viii.

37. R.S. Gormack, *The Circus: A Reminiscence in Story Form*, Nag's Head Press, Christchurch, 1997, pp. 9–10, 32; *NZRM*, Vol. 10, No. 11 (Feb 1936), p. 53; Rex Hercock, *More Footplate Memories: Some More Recollections*, comp. by Don Rudd, NZRLS, Wellington, 2005, p. 24; Rex Kerr, *Otaki Railway: A Station and its People Since 1886*, Otaki Railway Station Community Trust, Otaki, 2001, pp. 91–2.

38. *NZG*, 1887, p. 1177; Concession Fares for Sporting Teams, R 4, box 91, 1898/3596.

39. *Southern Cross*, 27 Dec 1873; Bromby, *Rails That Built a Nation*, pp. 121–2; *AJHR*, 1900, D-8, p. 1; Excursion Tickets for Trainers and Jockeys Going to Race Meetings with Horses, R 3, W2381, 1916/5449, part 1, 1902–28; Conveyance of Racehorses Central, AAEB, W3293, box 144, 16/4016, 1921–68, ANZ.

40. Return of Excursion Bookings to Races and Shows, AAEB, W3293, 114, 16/918, part 1, 1914–79, ANZ.

41. Lance Waters, *Mostly a Farmer: Eighty Years of Living*, Cape Catley, Whatamongo Bay, 1976, pp. 30–1.

42. Eris Parker, *110 Years of Cambridge Rail*, E. Parker, Cambridge, 1995, p. 8.

43. Railways Statements, *AJHR*, 1915, D-2, p. x; 1916, D-2, p. viii; 1919, D-2, pp. xix–xxxviii; 1920, D-2, p. xviii.

44. Railways Statement, *AJHR*, 1918, D-2, pp. v, viii–ix; 'Railway Dining Cars in New Zealand, 1887–1917' (Publicity & Advertising Branch, 1962), in Dining Cars, R 3, W2478, 1901/128, 1895–1962, ANZ.

45. See Railways Statement, *AJHR*, 1920, D-2, p. vi; and Ian Bullock, 'The 1919 Coal Crisis', *NZRO*, Issue 276 (Apr–May 2006), pp. 26–9.

46. *AJHR*, 1923, D-2, pp. iii–iv.

## Chapter 3: Exploring New Zealand

1. Advertisement, Commercial Manager (CM) to Officer-in-Charge Advertising Branch (OCAB), 29 May 1925, Hoardings General, R 19, W2497, box 583, part 1, 1917–28, ANZ.

2. Railways Statement, *AJHR*, 1923, D-2, pp. vi, xi, xxiii, 7, 13, 24; *NZ Official Year-book, 1924*, Government Printer, Wellington, 1923, pp. 341–6.

3. See Railway Statements and Reports of the Government

# Notes

Railways Board, *AJHR*, 1921–33, D-2/3.

4. *NZ Official Year-book, 1926*, Government Printer, Wellington, 1925, p. 835; *NZ Official Year-book, 1931*, Government Printer, Wellington, 1930, pp. 353, 383–5.
5. Railways Statement, *AJHR*, 1929, D-2, p. xv.
6. See Report of the Railways Commission, *AJHR*, 1925, D-2A; and Pierre, *North Island Main Trunk*, Ch. 31.
7. DTM Auckland to Railway Commissioners, 2 Dec 1892, Weekend Excursion Tickets to Rotorua and Te Aroha, R 3, W2381, 1915/973/1, part 1; J.D. Mahoney, *Kings of the Iron Road: Steam Passenger Trains of New Zealand*, Dunmore Press, Palmerston North, 1982, p. 41.
8. *The Cyclopedia of New Zealand*, Vol. I, Cyclopedia Company, Wellington, 1897, p. 346; Margaret McClure, *The Wonder Country: The Making of New Zealand Tourism*, Auckland University Press, Auckland, 2004, pp. 25–7.
9. Nathan to Ward, 27 Jun 1900, Weekend Excursion Tickets to Rotorua and Te Aroha, R 3, W2381, 1915/973/1, part 1; McClure, *Wonder Country*, pp. 58–9, 63; Mahoney, *Kings of the Iron Road*, p. 41.
10. See Bronwyn Dalley & Gavin McLean (eds), *Frontier of Dreams: The Story of New Zealand*, Hachette Livre, Auckland, 2005, pp. 259–67; and Angela M. Verry, '"I'm Going to See New Zealand Too!": The New Zealand Railways Publicity Branch and Family Holidays During the Interwar Period', BA (Hons) research essay, University of Otago, 2004.
11. Hamish Thompson, *Paste Up: A Century of New Zealand Poster Art*, Godwit, Auckland, 2003, pp. 8–9. Thompson is currently working on an illustrated history of the Railways Studios.
12. The quotes are from 'Tour of His Royal Highness the Prince of Wales', report by Comptroller Refreshment Branch (CRB) to GM, 6 Jun 1921, in Royal Visit 1920, R 3, W2476, 1920/954/65, ANZ. See also Royal Visit 1901, R 3, W2278, 1901/400, part 1; Railways Statement, *AJHR*, 1927, D-2, p. ii; Bromby, *Rails that Built a Nation*, pp. 125–6; Jock Phillips, *Royal Summer: The Visit of Queen Elizabeth II and Prince Philip to New Zealand 1953–54*, Daphne Brasell / Department of Internal Affairs, Wellington, 1993; and Gavin McLean, *The Governors: New Zealand's Governors and Governors-General*, Otago University Press, Dunedin, 2006, pp. 229, 257.
13. *AJHR*, 1923, D-2, pp. x–xi.
14. Advertising the Tourist Attractions of New Zealand, R 3, W2381, 1914/4857/1, part 2, 1921–25, ANZ; Railways Statements, *AJHR*, 1924, D-2, pp. xvi–xvii; 1931, D-2, p. xxvi.
15. Railways Statements, *AJHR*, 1926, D-2, p. xxxviii; 1928, D-2, pp. xxiii, 6–7; J.D. Mahoney, *Down at the Station: A Study of the New Zealand Railway Station*, Dunmore Press, Palmerston North, 1987, p. 18; McClure, *Wonder Country*, p. 98.
16. The quotations are from Grace Adams, *Jack's Hut*, Reed, Wellington, 1968, pp. 96–7. In general, see McClure, *Wonder Country*, pp. 93–6, and White, *Life Along the Steel Road*, p. 18.
17. See *Evening Post*, 27 Dec 1934; *Dominion*, 8 Jan 1937 & 27 Dec 1938; Mahoney, *Kings of the Iron Road*, pp. 26–9; and Pierre, *North Island Main Trunk*, pp. 156–61.
18. *AJHR*, 1928, D-2, pp. 6–7.
19. On British railway company publicity, see Ralph Harrington, 'Beyond the Bathing Belle: Images of Women in Inter-war Railway Publicity', *Journal of Transport History*, Vol. 25, No. 1 (Mar 2004), pp. 22–45.
20. *NZ Official Year-book, 1930*, Government Printer, Wellington, 1929, p. 163.
21. *Press*, 12 Feb 1924, 15 Apr 1926 & 9 Jul 1928; *Sun* (Christchurch), 14 Nov 1925 & 4 Jul 1928; T. Harkness (ganger) to Inspector of Permanent Way, Middlemarch, 8 Jun 1930, Malicious Treatment of and Interference to Advertisements and Structures, R 19, W2497, box 1272, part 1, 1922–39, ANZ; *Dominion*, 18 Sep 1930; *ODT*, 18 Oct 1930.
22. Title page, *NZRM*, Vol. 1, No. 1 (May 1926), p. 1; see also 'To the Staff of the Railways: A Talk with our Minister about our Magazine', p. 4.
23. *NZRM*, Vol. 2, No. 2 (Jun 1927), p. 3.
24. See Stephen Hamilton, 'New Zealand English Language Periodicals of Literary Interest Active 1920s–1960s', PhD thesis, University of Auckland, 1995, Chs 9.1 & 9.2; and Chris Hilliard, *The Bookmen's Dominion: Cultural Life in New Zealand 1920–1950*, Auckland University Press, Auckland, 2006, pp. 91, 100.
25. See *NZ Official Year-book, 1935*, Government Printer, Wellington, 1934, pp. 258–62; and Railways Statements/Reports of the Government Railways Board, *AJHR*, 1930–3, D-2/3. On branch closures, see *NZR Geographical Mileage Table 1957*, p. 31; and Report of the Railways Royal Commission, *AJHR*, 1930, D-4.
26. *AJHR*, 1930, D-2, p. xxxiv.
27. See *AJHR*, 1930, D-4; Report of the Government Railways Board, *AJHR*, 1931, D-3; and Transport Licensing Act 1931, *Statutes of New Zealand, 1931*, p. 413.
28. *AJHR*, 1931, D-2, p. xxvi; 1932, D-2, p. xxiv; *Evening Post*, 29 Dec 1933.
29. *NZRM*, Vol. 13, No. 4 (July 1938), p. 56; Railways Statements,

*AJHR*, 1936, D-2, pp. i–ii; 1937, D-2, p. ii.

30. *AJHR*, 1936, D-2, p. 2; Transport Licensing Amendment Act 1936, *Statutes of New Zealand, 1936*, p. 102.
31. 'A Great Railway Event: Inauguration of the Wellington-Johnsonville Electric Train Service', *NZRM*, Vol. 13, No. 5 (Aug 1938), pp. 17–23; Railways Statements, *AJHR*, 1938, D-2, p. ii (and colour plates); 1939, D-2, pp. v–vi.
32. See *AJHR*, 1938, D-2, p. i (and colour plates); 1939, D-2, p. v; Bromby, *Rails that Built a Nation*, pp. 122–4.
33. *AJHR*, 1939, D-2, pp. viii, xxiii–xxvi; Leitch & Stott, *New Zealand Railways*, pp. 84–5; *NZ Official Yearbook, 1966*, Government Printer, Wellington, 1966, pp. 318–19; Toll NZ website, http://www.tollnz.co.nz.
34. *Evening Post*, 15 Apr 1936; *Dominion*, 8 Jan & 27 Dec 1938; *New Zealand Herald*, 24 Dec 1935.
35. 'Christchurch to Queenstown', *NZRM*, Vol. 10, No. 3 (Jun 1935), p. 51; *AJHR*, 1936, D-2, p. xxvi; 1937, D-2, p. xxxii; W.J. Cowan, 'The 1937 Lawrence Daffodil Excursions', *NZRO*, Issue 195 (Spring 1988), pp. 94–6.
36. *AJHR*, 1938, D-2, p. xxxvii; Press, 8 Aug 1939; Booking Holiday Tours to Various Tourism Resorts, AAEB, W3293, box 212, 15/3690/7, part 1, 1937–45, ANZ; 'Broadcasting by the Way', *NZRM*, Vol. 13, No. 12 (Mar 1939), p. 7.
37. *AJHR*, 1939, D-2, pp. x, xiv; *NZ Official Year-book, 1940*, Government Printer, Wellington, 1939, p. 323.
38. See Brendon Judd, *The Desert Railway: The New Zealand Railway Group in North Africa and the Middle East During the Second World War*, Penguin, Auckland, 2004; J.V.T. Baker, *War Economy*, Historical Publications Branch, Wellington, 1965, pp. 406–7; Kathleen Ross, 'Are They 80% Efficient?', *Public Service Journal*, Dec 1944, p. 505; and Railways Statements, *AJHR*, 1942, D-2, pp. 1–2; 1943, D-2, p. 2.
39. Railways Statements, *AJHR*, 1940, D-2, p. 28; 1944, D-2, p. 2.
40. Geoff Conly & Graham Stewart, *Tragedy on the Track: Tangiwai and Other New Zealand Railway Accidents*, Grantham House, Wellington, 1986, pp. 103–8.
41. *Mercantile Gazette of New Zealand*, 6 Oct 1948. See also Publicity & Advertising Manager to editor, *Evening Post*, 20 Apr 1949, and GM to Manager, Trade Auxiliary Co., 12 May 1950, Tourist Traffic and Resorts, R 18, W2854, PUB 51, part 1, ANZ.
42. Peter Kitchin, 'Riding the rails in a style that couldn't last', *Dominion Post*, 2 Sep 2006, p. E9.
43. Peter Aimer, 'Aviation', *Te Ara: The Encyclopedia of New Zealand*, updated 9 Jun 2006, URL: http://www.TeAra.govt.nz/EarthSeaAndSky/SeaAndAirTransport/Aviation/en.
44. *NZ Official Yearbook 1994*, Statistics NZ, Wellington, 1994, pp. 440–1; *NZ Official Yearbook 2002*, Statistics NZ / David Bateman, Auckland, 2002, pp. 499–500.
45. Sally Blundell, 'End of the Line?', *New Zealand Listener*, Vol. 205, No. 3460 (2 Sep 2006), pp. 28–30; 'Government rejects Overlander rescue bid', *Dominion Post*, 26 Sep 2006, p. A1; 'Overlander stays on track for weekends', *NZ Herald*, 28 Sep 2006, p. A5.

## Chapter 4: Citizens of Trainland

1. 'On the Road to Anywhere: Adventures of a Train Tramp', *NZRM*, Vol. 10, No. 1 (Apr 1935), p. 30.
2. Hyde, *NZRM*, Apr 1935, p. 30; Janet Frame, *Owls Do Cry*, Sun Books, Melbourne, 1981, p. 166.
3. Quoted in Leitch, *Railways of New Zealand*, p. 197.
4. *Evening Post*, 22 May 1937; *Auckland Star*, 18 Oct 1939. On passenger cars in general see Pierre, *North Island Main Trunk*, pp. 112–13, 119–22, 158–9, 169–74; Leitch, *Railways of New Zealand*, pp. 196–200; Mahoney, *Kings of the Iron Road*, pp. 29, 33–4; and Churchman & Hurst, *The Railways of New Zealand*, pp. 72–7.
5. Frame, *An Angel at My Table*, p. 28; Hyde, *NZRM*, Apr 1935, p. 30.
6. *NZRM*, Apr 1935, p. 31; Mahoney, *Kings of the Iron Road*, p. 25. For the pillow-hire service — which issued 38,519 pillows in its first year — see *AJHR*, 1926, D-2, p. xli.
7. See Conly & Stewart, *Tragedy on the Track*; and Stewart's updated *Tangiwai: A Christmas Eve Tragedy*, Grantham House, Wellington, 2003.
8. WCTU to Minister, 5 Feb 1910, GM to Mrs Bardsley, 24 Mar 1910, Minister to GM, 24 Jul 1914, GM to A.G. Warburton, 19 Apr 1915, in Ladies Cars, R 3, W2278, 1903/2569/1, part 1, 1900–39, ANZ.
9. Chief Mechanical Engineer to GM, 27 Aug 1917, GM to DTM Wellington, 6 Dec 1917, GM to Chief Traffic Manager (CTM), 3 Nov 1919, in Ladies Cars, R 3, W2278, 1903/2569/1, part 1; *Auckland Star*, 15 Aug 1922; CRB to GM, 11 Mar 1932, GM to CRB, 24 Jul 1933, Transportation Superintendent to DTMs, 17 Oct 1938, in Ladies Cars, R 3, W2278, 1903/2569/1, part 3, 1932–9, ANZ. See also part 2 (R 3, W2278, 1922–31) and part 4 (AAEB, W3199, 1938–78) of the same file series.
10. *Dominion*, 18 Nov 1912; CM to GM, 25 Jan 1929, Car Accommodation on Mixed Trains — Proportion of Smoking

# Notes

to Non Smoking Cars on All Services, AAEB, W3199, box 108, 07/117, part 1, 1907–59, ANZ. See also Number and Position of Smoking Carriages on Trains, New Zealand Railways Corporation Railways Freight System Regional Administration, Christchurch (CAHV), CH77, 13/2124, part 1, 1913–60; Smoking in Non-Smoking Carriages, CAHV, CH77, 19/866, part 1, 1954–75, ANZ (Christchurch); and Pierre, *North Island Main Trunk*, pp. 114–15, 163.

11. 'Railway Dining Cars in New Zealand, 1887–1917', p. 1, in Dining Cars, R 3, W2478, 1901/128.
12. The Department's first Supervisor of Refreshment Cars was the former Chief Steward of the government steamer *Tutanekai*. See 'Railway Dining Cars', pp. 2–5, 9–12; Menu Cards, R 3, W2381, 1915/4358, part 1, 1902–29; Uniforms — Refreshment Branch, R 3, W2381, 1915/4361, part 1, 1904–61, ANZ; Pierre, *North Island Main Trunk*, pp. 121–4.
13. 'Railway Dining Cars', pp. 6–7, 14–18; Pierre, *North Island Main Trunk*, pp. 123–6.
14. *ODT*, 9 Nov 1905; Waters, *Mostly a Farmer*, pp. 30–1; DTM Auckland to GM, 28 Aug 1929, Drinking on Trains, R 3, W2334, box 303, 1913/5209/1, part 1, 1899–1919, ANZ; Hyde, 'On the Road to Anywhere: Acquaintance with the Glow-worms', *NZRM*, Vol. 10, No. 12 (Mar 1936), p. 41.
15. *Lyttelton Times*, 11 Nov 1911; *Manawatu Daily Times*, 11 & 12 Jan 1912; R.H.W. Bligh to GM, 2 Mar 1908, Indecent Literature, ABJP, W4098, box 49, 08/1545, part 1, 1906–82, ANZ.
16. Rev. Herbert Daniel to Minister, 23 Feb 1912, DTM Wanganui to GM, 2 Apr 1912, and DTM Wellington to GM, 3 Apr 1912, Indecent Literature, ABJP, W4098, box 49, 08/1545, part 1.
17. Alexander Moller to Minister, 28 Dec 1926, DTM to Railways Board, 14 Jan 1927, and Publicity Manager to GM, 12 Mar 1931, Indecent Literature, ABJP, W4098, box 49, 08/1545, part 1.
18. *NZRM*, Apr 1935, p. 31.
19. William Herries (Minister of Railways) to William Russell (Minister of Internal Affairs), 8 May 1916, Drinking on Trains, R 3, W2334, box 303, 1913/5209/1, part 1.
20. *NZ Times*, 6 Apr 1904; George Smith (Secretary, Otago Rugby Football Union) to DTM Christchurch, 7 Apr 1904, DTM to Smith, 16 Apr 1904, in Drinking on Trains, R 3, W2334, box 303, 1913/5209/1, part 1; *ODT*, 26 Apr & 11 May 1904.
21. *ODT*, 19 Aug 1904; Ian Church, *Port Chalmers Hotel: 150 Years of Southern Hospitality, 1846–1996*, Fred Morgan, Port Chalmers, 1999, p. 11; 'Sale of Alcoholic Liquor on Railway Premises', R. Kearney (Legal Division) to Chief Advertising Officer, 6 Jan 1959, Question of Sale of Liquor at Refreshment Rooms, AAEB, W3199, box 31, 03/4214, part 1, 1894–1968, ANZ.
22. CTM to GM, 22 Feb 1906, SM Invercargill to Under-Secretary for Justice, 11 Mar 1904, and SM Paeroa to DTM Auckland, 2 Aug 1909, Drinking on Trains, R 3, W2334, box 303, 1913/5209/1, part 1; *Thames Star*, 2 Aug 1909; *Westport Times & Star*, 21 Jul 1910.
23. Letter to GM, 28 Jan 1907, and Guard to SM Taumarunui, 15 Feb 1907, Drinking on Trains, R 3, W2334, box 303, 1913/5209/1, part 1.
24. *NZG*, 1922, p. 1614.
25. Grainger, *On and Off the Rails*, pp. 88–90.
26. Guard to SM Christchurch, 10 Mar 1908, DTM Christchurch to Inspector of Police, 23 Mar 1908, and Guard to SM Christchurch, 19 Jun 1931, Indecent Acts, CAHV, CH77, 8/724, part 1, 1908–75, ANZ (C).
27. Crossing-keeper (Montreal Street) to DTM Christchurch, 22 Feb 1926, and Guard to DTM Christchurch, 7 Oct 1953, Indecent Acts, CAHV, CH77, 8/724, part 1; *Christchurch Star-Sun*, 28 Feb & 7 Mar 1938; *Press*, 16 May 1955; *Greymouth Evening Star*, 28 Jan & 18 Feb 1972.
28. Redmer Yska, *All Shook Up: The Flash Bodgie and the Rise of the New Zealand Teenager in the Fifties*, Penguin, Auckland, 1993, pp. 208–9; *Press*, 5 & 6 Aug 1957; *Christchurch Star*, 14 Jul 1959; Miss Clarke to DTM Christchurch, 5 Aug 1957, and DTM to Chief SM Christchurch, 22 Aug 1957, in Misbehaviour on Railway Premises, CAHV, CH77, 23/562, part 1, 1957–67, ANZ (C).
29. C.E.J. Lewin to Commissioner of Police, 19 Jul 1968, and DTM Wellington to Transport Superintendent, 12 Aug 1968, Passengers Loitering in Vicinity of Carriages and Creating Nuisances in Carriages, AAEB, W3199, box 55, 04/2527/2, part 1, 1897–1970, ANZ.
30. Hyde, 'On the Road to Anywhere: A Matter of Pipis and Kowhai', *NZRM*, Vol. 10, No. 10 (Jan 1936), p. 35. See also Denis Robertson, *Give Me Taihape on a Saturday Night*, Heritage Press, Waikanae, 1995.
31. Lee, *Children of the Poor*, Whitcombe & Tombs, Christchurch, 1973, p. 24; *Gisborne Herald*, 25 Mar 1959, cited in McQueen, *Rails in the Hinterland*, p. 56.
32. Quoted in Mahoney, *Kings of the Iron Road*, pp. 59–61.
33. Grainger, *On and Off the Rails*, p. 95.
34. Jane Moodie, 'Hill, Catherine (1893–1983)', *Dictionary of New Zealand Biography*, updated 7 April 2006, URL: http://www.dnzb.govt.nz; Paul Mahoney, *From the Station Platform*, p. 19.
35. GM to Minister, 19 May 1909, Question of Sale of Liquor at

## Trainland

Refreshment Rooms, AAEB, W3199, box 31, 03/4214, part 1; *Dominion*, 18 Nov 1912; Drinking on Trains, R 3, W2334, box 303, 1913/5209/1, part 2, 1919–32, ANZ.

36. See Bronwyn Dalley, *Living in the 20th Century: New Zealand History in Photographs*, 1900–1980, Bridget Williams Books, Wellington, 2000, p. 133; Clem Sole to Minister of Maori Affairs, 31 Jul 1952, and Under-Secretary of Maori Affairs to Commissioner of Police, 22 Aug 1952, in Frankton Railway Huts — Conduct of Maori Girls, Maori Affairs (MA), W2490, box 69, 36/1/8, 1952–3, ANZ.

37. R.H.W. Bligh to GM, 18 Mar 1908 & 15 Aug 1918, Indecent Writing on Railway Premises, ABJP, W4098, box 48, 08/1245, part 1, 1908–85; OCAB to GM, 25 Aug 1928, OCAB to Superintendent of Police, Christchurch, 19 Dec 1928, and OCAB to Commissioner of Police, 26 Feb 1929, in Malicious Treatment of and Interference to Advertisements and Structures, R 19, W2497, box 1272, part 1, 1922–39, ANZ.

38. Clerk in Charge (CC), Opawa, to DTM Christchurch, 24 Feb 1914, CC Opawa to SM Christchurch, 9 Jun 1915, Relief Clerk, Opawa, to Police Constable, 9 Sep 1924, DTM Christchurch to Inspector of Police, 24 Aug 1928, Inspector of Police to DTM Christchurch, 13 Dec 1937, and CC Opawa to DTM Christchurch, 16 Dec 1938, all in Misconduct and Behaviour of Children in Waiting Rooms — Indecent Writing, CAHV, CH77, 14/597, part 1, 1914–60; Superintendent of Police to DTM Christchurch, 13 Mar 1956, Missiles Thrown From and At Trains, CAHV, CH77, 16/718 part 1, 1956–61, ANZ (C).

39. Quoted in G.W. Turner, *The English Language in Australia and New Zealand*, Longman, London, 1966, p. 156.

40. Frame, *Owls Do Cry*, p. 158; Claridge, *The Iron Horse: My Trip on the 'Limited' Auckland to Wellington*, Thrift Print, Auckland, 1936, p. 5; Fairburn, 'Note on N.Z.R.', quoted in Harry Orsman & Jan Moore (eds), *Heinemann Dictionary of New Zealand Quotations*, Heinemann, Auckland, 1988, p. 257; 'Steam Loco on Siding', Hone Tuwhare, *Deep River Talk: Collected Poems*, Godwit, Auckland, 1993, p. 138.

41. During the Depression (1933) refreshment room charges were cut by 25 per cent, with coffee, tea and sandwiches reduced from 4d to 3d; as patronage revived in the late 1930s, prices were restored to previous levels.

42. Dates for the takeover of rooms by the Department are taken from files on each room in the R 3 and AAEB series at ANZ. See also *Hawke's Bay Herald*, 6 Aug 1925; *NZ Herald*, 25 Jan 1929 & 7 Jan 1946; and 'The Happy Travellers', *NZRM*, Vol. 10, No. 7 (Oct 1935), p. 9.

43. The quotes are from *Oamaru Mail*, 31 Jan 1925; *Northlander*, 21 Nov 1923; and *ODT*, 19 Apr 1928. See also *ODT*, 22 Apr 1926; Complaints from Public re Railway Refreshment Rooms, R 3, W2476, 1917/4335, part 2, 1923–42; Refreshment Rooms — Time for Meals, R 3, W2476, 1917/2844/1, part 1, 1896–1930, ANZ; and Report of Royal Commission to Inquire into and Report upon the New Zealand Government Railways, *AJHR*, 1952, D-3, pp. 20–1.

44. *Wanganui Herald*, 13 Apr 1928; *Press*, 14 Mar 1946 & 15 Oct 1950; *Evening Post*, 30 Jul 1947.

45. Letter to editor, *NZ Times*, 25 Mar 1920; CRB to GM, 23 Feb 1949, Railway Refreshment Rooms, AAEB, W3199, box 182, 11/5883, part 1, 1912–73, ANZ; McClure, *Wonder Country*, p. 178; CRB to GM, 8 May 1945, Complaints from Public re Railway Refreshment Rooms, R 3, W2476, 1917/4335, part 3, 1942–65. See also Railway Refreshment Rooms Menu, ABJP, W4098, box 115, 15/4358, part 2, 1930–83, ANZ.

46. Dalley, *Living in the 20th Century*, p. 235; George Smith to Minister, 6 Sep 1943, General File re Congestion at Railway Refreshment Rooms, R 3, 1925/339, part 1, 1922–54, ANZ; *New Zealand Farmer*, 21 Aug 1947; 'A Woman', letter to editor, *Christchurch Star*, 11 Dec 1934; *Dominion*, 10 Feb 1949.

47. There is a copy of 'Wellington Express' (Nixa Records, 1959) in Refreshment Room Account/Scrapbook, AAEB, W3734, box 42, 1921, ANZ.

48. CRB to Railways Board, 6 Apr 1927, Acting CRB to Board, 4 Jun 1927, CRB to Board, 5 Dec 1927, and GM to CRB, 12 Nov 1931, in Mr J. Pickard's and Others Observations on Railway Refreshment Rooms and Dining Cars Services Overseas, R 3, 1926/1454, 1917–68, ANZ. See also Railways Refreshment Rooms and Services, CAHV, CH21, 1926/823/1,1926–41, ANZ (C); and General File re Congestion at Railway Refreshment Rooms, R 3, 1925/339, part 1.

49. Quoted in Roy Sinclair, *Journeying with Railways in New Zealand*, pp. 163–4.

50. CRB to GM, 10 Feb 1920, Complaints from Public re Railway Refreshment Rooms, R 3 W2476, 1917/4335, part 1, 1917–23, ANZ; *NZ Herald*, 24 Oct 1949.

51. 'Family Knows How to Bake Pies', *NZ Herald*, 8 Aug 1967, Section 2, p. 2; Sinclair, *Journeying with Railways in New Zealand*, p. 169.

52. CRB to GM, 26 Jun 1942 & 4 Apr 1950, Crockery for Railway Refreshment Rooms, R 3, W2476, 1917/4598/4, part 1, 1924–51; CRB to GM, 28 Aug 1928, Misuse of Refreshment Branch Crockery, R 3, W2476, 1917/4598/2, part 1,1917–30; GM to

CRB, 7 Jun 1939, GM to Army Secretary, 1 Feb 1940, and NZR Circular No. 98 (21 Nov 1946), in Misuse of Refreshment Branch Crockery, R 3, W2476, 1917/4598/2, part 2, 1931–54; CRB to GM, 27 Nov 1951, Crockery for Railway Refreshment Branch, AAEB, W3293, box 170, 17/4598/4, part 2, 1951–82, ANZ; *Dominion*, 9 Oct 1934 & 28 Mar 1942; *Evening Post*, 9 Feb 1946; *Press*, 26 Nov 1952. Derrett's 'Kiwi Train' appears on the *New Zealand Folksong* website, URL: http://folksong.org.nz/kiwitrain/index.html. For more on NZR's Crown Lynn cups, see Valerie Monk, *Crown Lynn: A New Zealand Icon*, Penguin Books, Auckland, 2006, pp. 17–19.

53. Closing dates are from files on individual rooms in the R 3 and AAEB series, ANZ. The quotes are from *Auckland Star*, 19 Oct 1956, and *Waikato Times*, 19 Jul 1975.

54. A.W. Essex (Canadian Pacific) to CRB, 14 Dec 1948, Buffet Cars General, AAVK, W3185, box 2, 187/1, 1935–67, ANZ; W. Elsom (CRB), 'Meals on Wheels', *NZRO*, Vol. 7, No. 43 (Jan–Feb 1951), pp. 5–8; 'Buffet Cars on New Zealand Railways', *New Zealand Railway Review* (ASRS), Vol. 65, No. 3 (27 Mar 1951), p. 1; GM, press release, 17 Dec 1968, Sale of Liquor at Refreshment Rooms, AAEB, W3199, box 31, 03/4214, part 1, ANZ; *NZ Herald*, 20 Sep 1968.

55. *Dominion*, 31 Jan 1985; 'We hope you have had a pleasant journey', Radio New Zealand Spectrum programme, SP1433, broadcast 1 Oct 2006.

56. Anne Beston, 'Down the line, towns mourn train's end', *Weekend Herald*, 5 Aug 2006, p. A7.

## Chapter 5: The Long Train Journey

1. Janet Frame, *To the Is-Land*, p. 51.
2. *Auckland Star*, 15 Apr 1959.
3. For example, there are virtually no references to railways in *The Oxford History of New Zealand Literature in English* (ed. Terry Sturm, 2nd edn, Oxford University Press, Auckland, 1998), *The Oxford Companion to New Zealand Literature* (eds Roger Robinson & Nelson Wattie, OUP, Auckland, 1998), or in standard surveys of New Zealand music, painting and film. On the British experience, see Carter, *Railways and Culture in Britain*, pp. 6–7, in which the author argues that if the scope of searching is widened 'beyond the canon' to embrace 'disdained literary genres' like crime stories and comic fiction, the contribution of railways to British literature and culture is far more impressive.
4. *NZRM*, Vol. 13, No. 1 (Apr 1938), p. 9.
5. Miles Fairburn has explored the impact of British, American and Australian cultural influences, especially in areas such as cinema, language and popular literature, in 'Is There a Good Case for New Zealand Exceptionalism?', in Tony Ballantyne & Brian Moloughney (eds), *Disputed Histories: Imagining New Zealand's Past*, Otago University Press, Dunedin, 2006, pp. 143–68.
6. Michael King, *Wrestling with the Angel: A Life of Janet Frame*, Penguin, Auckland, 2000, pp. 14, 36, 45; Frame, *To the Is-land*, p. 119; *An Angel at My Table*, p. 159.
7. *To the Is-land*, pp. 31, 51; *Scented Gardens for the Blind*, Women's Press, London, 1991, p. 22; *An Angel at My Table*, p. 159.
8. *An Angel at My Table*, p. 172.
9. *Scented Gardens for the Blind*, pp. 213–4; *A State of Siege*, Braziller, New York, 1966, p. 32.
10. Hyde, *The Godwits Fly*, pp. 129, 143.
11. Mulgan, *Man Alone*, Paul's Book Arcade, Hamilton, 1960, p. 65; Pearson, *Coal Flat*, Paul's Book Arcade, Auckland, 1963, pp. 51, 96; Morrieson, *The Scarecrow*, Angus & Robertson, Sydney, 1963, pp. 22–3, 26–8.
12. Gee, *Plumb*, Penguin, Auckland, 2000 (1st pub. 1978), p. 84; *Going West*, Faber & Faber, London, 1992, pp. 2–4.
13. Grace, *Cousins*, Penguin, Auckland, 1992, pp. 109–11; *Tu: A Novel*, Penguin, Auckland, 2004, p. 72.
14. Mansfield, *The Letters and Journals of Katherine Mansfield: A Selection*, ed. C.K. Stead, Penguin, Harmondsworth, 1977, pp. 27–8; *The Urewera Notebook*, ed. by Ian A. Gordon, Oxford University Press, Oxford, 1978, pp. 38–9.
15. Sargeson, *Never Enough!*, pp. 16, 21; Michael King, *Frank Sargeson: A Life*, Viking, Auckland, 1995, pp. 50, 397.17.
16. *Your Own Railway*, Publicity Branch, NZR, Wellington, 1938; *The Steel Road*, School Publications Branch, NZ Education Department, 1950; Peter Walsh & W.M. Papas, *Freddy the Fell Engine*, Oxford University Press, Oxford, 1966.
17. On Nicholson's *Weeping Waters*, see Nathan Crombie, 'Novel rises from the tragedy of the Tangiwai rail disaster', *Wairarapa Times-Age*, 7 Jun 2006, URL: http://www.times-age.co.nz. For the song 'Pillows of the Dead' see the *NZ Folksong* website, URL: http://folksong.org.nz. The Cole Catley story is told in 'Another Day at the Beach', *New Zealand Listener*, Vol. 191, No. 3320 (27 Dec 2003–2 Jan 2004), pp. 32–4. Other relevant works include Kevin Boon's *The Tangiwai Rail Disaster*, Kotuku, Wellington, 1999; Conly & Stewart's *Tragedy on the Track* (and Stewart's updated *Tangiwai*); Ruth Dawson's *The Tangiwai*

# Trainland

*Railway Disaster*, Department of Education, Wellington, 1979; David Hill's *Journey to Tangiwai: The Diary of Peter Cotterill, Napier, 1953*, Scholastic New Zealand, Auckland, 2003; and Trish Gray's *Tangiwai (Weeping Waters): New Zealand's Greatest Railway Disaster and its Impact on One Family*, T. Gray, Upper Hutt, 2003.

18. Hilliard, *The Bookmen's Dominion*, pp. 37–46; Hamilton, 'New Zealand English Language Periodicals', pp. 545–7; Gee, *The Scornful Moon: A Moralist's Tale*, Penguin, Auckland, 2003. For a detailed discussion of British 'Crime on the Line', see Carter, *Railways and Culture in Britain*, Chs 7–8.
19. Ian Mackersey, *Long Night's Journey*, Robert Hale & Co, London, 1974.
20. *NZRM*, Apr 1938, pp. 9, 11; Leitch, *Railways of New Zealand*, p. 150.
21. Coates, 'To the Staff of the Railways', *NZRM*, May 1926, p. 4. Eve Langley also contributed three pieces of imaginative prose to the *Railways Magazine*, including 'Locomotivo: A Fantasy', in which she likened a steam locomotive to a medieval charger, and 'The Iron Common-wheel', which described fellow passengers on a night train. See Hamilton, 'New Zealand English Language Periodicals', pp. 549–50.
22. Bethell, *Time and Place*, Caxton Press, Christchurch, 1936, p. 35.
23. Tuwhare, *Deep River Talk*, pp. 121, 138–9; Bornholdt, 'Raurimu Spiral', *Sport 9* (Spring 1992), pp. 10–11; Olds, 'Disjointed on Wellington Railway Station', *Southern Ocean Review*, 19th Issue (12 Apr 2001), URL: http://www.book.co.nz/olds.htm.
24. Roger Steele (ed.), *Ordinary Joker: The Life and Songs of Peter Cape*, Steele Roberts, Wellington, 2001, pp. 44–5, 62–3.
25. 'The Ballad of Minnie Dean', written by Henderson and Doug Hamblin, appeared on Henderson's CD *The Sonora Sessions* (2000). See her website, URL: http://www.helenhenderson.net; *NZ Folksong*, URL: http://folksong.org.nz/minniedean/index.html; Alfred Hanlon, *Random Recollections: Notes on a Lifetime at the Bar*, ODT/Witness, Dunedin, 1939, p. 169; and Lynley Hood, *Minnie Dean: Her Life and Crimes*, Penguin, Auckland, 1994.
26. 'The Kiwi Train', 'The Wreck of the Old 2-2-7' and 'The Fairlie Flyer' appear on *NZ Folksong*, URL: http://folksong.org.nz. On the Kiwi train recordings, see Gavin McLean, *Whare Raupo: The Reed Books Story*, Reed, Auckland, 2007, p. 98.
27. Schama, *Landscape and Memory*, Harper Collins, London, 1995, p. 362.
28. I am indebted to John Horner for lending me his Master of Fine Arts dissertation, 'Railway Art in New Zealand' (Whitecliffe College of Arts and Design, Auckland, 2003), on which much of this section is based. See also Richard Wolfe, 'Trains and Boats and Planes', *Art New Zealand*, Issue 89 (Summer 1998–9), pp. 70–5.
29. Euan McQueen, *W.W. Stewart: 20th Century Railway Painter*, Grantham House, Wellington, 1998; W.W. Stewart, *When Steam was King*, Reed, Wellington, 1970.
30. See Horner, 'Railway Art in New Zealand', Ch. 2; and Roger Neich, *Painted Histories: Early Maori Figurative Painting*, Auckland University Press, Auckland, 1994, pp. 260–1, 264 & Plates 42–3.
31. See Horner, 'Railway Art in New Zealand', Chs 3–4.
32. *NZRO*, Dec 2006–Jan 2007, pp. 173–4; Toll NZ Ltd Annual Report 2006, p. 8, Toll NZ website, URL: http://www.tollnz.co.nz.
33. Report of the Railways Department, *AJHR*, 1983, F-7, p. 13; *NZ Official Yearbook 2002*, David Bateman, Auckland, 2002, p. 498; and information provided by Euan McQueen.
34. Penelope Carroll, 'Stations on the Move', *Heritage New Zealand*, Issue 89 (Winter 2003), p. 19; McQueen, *Rails in the Hinterland*, pp. 9–10 & Ch. 5.
35. McQueen, *Rails in the Hinterland*, p. 56.
36. On the Nelson protest see Lois Voller, *Rails to Nowhere: The History of the Nelson Railway*, Nikau Press, Nelson, 1991; Barry O'Donnell, *When Nelson had a Railway*, Schematics, Wellington, 2005; and Carol Markwell, 'Page, Ruth Allan (1905–1992)', *Dictionary of New Zealand Biography*, updated 7 Apr 2006, URL: http://www.dnzb.govt.nz.
37. White, *Life Along the Steel Road*, p. 17; M. Hodgkins, letter to *NZ Herald*, 27 Oct 1965.
38. Carroll, 'Stations on the Move', *Heritage NZ*, Winter 2003, pp. 17–19. See also Paul Titus' feature article, 'Fight to Keep Rail Heritage on Track', in the same issue, pp. 10–14.
39. Sean Millar, *New Zealand Railway, Tramway and Bus Bibliography*, S. Millar, Auckland, 2000. For New Zealand examples of the hopeful, future-oriented final flourish, see John L. Stichbury's 'The Vital Railway', in Troup, *Steel Roads*, pp. 275–8, and the concluding pages of Leitch & Stott's *New Zealand Railways*, pp. 169–70. For a discussion of British rail histories, see Carter, *Railways and Culture in Britain*, pp. 302–3.
40. Wolfgang Schivelbusch, quoted in Carter, *Railways and Culture in Britain*, p. 305.

# Select Bibliography

## Manuscripts and Archives

**Archives New Zealand (ANZ)**

*Head Office, Wellington*

AAEB New Zealand Government Railways Department, General Manager's Office

AAVK New Zealand Railways Corporation, Corporate Services, Head Office

ABIN New Zealand Railways Corporation, Lower Hutt Office

ABIW New Zealand Railways Corporation, Passenger Business Group

ABJP New Zealand Rail Ltd, Corporate Support Services Group

ABJQ New Zealand Railways Corporation, Head Office

ADQD New Zealand Railways Record Group (R)

    Series 3–5, General Manager's Office registered files

    Series 18–19, Publicity and Advertising Branch registered files

ADRM New Zealand Railways District Office, Wellington

*Christchurch Regional Office*

CAHV New Zealand Railways Corporation, Railways Freight System Regional Administration, Christchurch

**Alexander Turnbull Library, Wellington (ATL)**

Andrews, Reginald Percy, Memories, 1931–1970, MS-Papers 3836

Keller, Peter, Early Days on Railway Construction, 1903–1911, 1970, MS-Papers 1073

Ray, Lena Marie (Williams), Living on the Line, 1909–1914, 1968, 1970, MS-Papers-1898

## Official Publications

*Appendix to the Journals of the House of Representatives (AJHR)*

*New Zealand Gazette (NZG)*

# Trainland

*New Zealand Official Yearbook*

*New Zealand Parliamentary Debates (NZPD)*

*New Zealand Railways Geographical Mileage Table 1957*, New Zealand Railways, Wellington, 1958

## Newspapers and Periodicals

*Dominion*

*Evening Post*

*New Zealand Herald*

*New Zealand Railways Magazine (NZRM)*

*New Zealand Railway Observer (NZRO)*

*New Zealand Times*

*Otago Daily Times (ODT)*

*Waikato Times*

## Books

Bromby, Robin, *Rails that Built a Nation: An Encyclopedia of New Zealand Railways*, Grantham House, Wellington, 2003

Churchman, Geoffrey B. & Tony Hurst, *The Railways of New Zealand: A Journey Through History*, 2nd edn, Transpress, Wellington, 2001

Conly, Geoff & Graham Stewart, *Tragedy on the Track: Tangiwai and Other New Zealand Railway Accidents*, Grantham House, Wellington, 1986

Fowler, Lynette, *Of Trains and Things*, Craig Printing, Invercargill, 1986

Grainger, J.M., *On and Off the Rails: A Railwayman's Story*, Whitcombe & Tombs, Christchurch, 1964

Hercock, Rex, *My Forty Footplate Years, 1943–1983: A New Zealand Enginedriver's Story*, New Zealand Railway & Locomotive Society, Wellington, 1987

——, *More Footplate Memories: Some More Recollections*, compiled by Don Rudd, New Zealand Railway & Locomotive Society, Wellington, c2005

Johnston, Albert B. & Robin M. Startup, *Mails By Rail in New Zealand: The Story of the Railway Travelling Post Offices of New Zealand*, Royal Philatelic Society of New Zealand, Wellington, 2001

## Select bibliography

Kerr, Rex, *Otaki Railway: A Station and Its People Since 1886*, Otaki Railway Station Community Trust, Otaki, 2001

Leitch, David B., *Railways of New Zealand*, Leonard Fullerton, Auckland / David & Charles, Newton Abbot (UK), 1972

Leitch, David & Bob Stott, *New Zealand Railways: The First 125 Years*, Heinemann Reed, Auckland, 1988

McClure, Margaret, *The Wonder Country: Making New Zealand Tourism*, Auckland University Press, Auckland, 2004

McQueen, Euan, *W.W. Stewart: 20th Century Railway Painter*, Grantham House, Wellington, 1998

——, *Rails in the Hinterland: New Zealand's Vanishing Railway Landscape*, Grantham House, Wellington, 2005

Mahoney, J.D., *Kings of the Iron Road: Steam Passenger Trains of New Zealand*, Dunmore Press, Palmerston North, 1982

——, *Down at the Station: A Study of the New Zealand Railway Station*, Dunmore Press, Palmerston North, 1987

Mahoney, Paul, *From the Station Platform: An Historical Account of Ormondville Station and District From a Railway Perspective*, Ormondville Rail Preservation Group, Wellington, 2000

Millar, Sean, *New Zealand Railway, Tramway and Bus Bibliography*, S. Millar, Auckland, 2000

Palmer, A.N. & W.W. Stewart, *Cavalcade of New Zealand Locomotives: An Historical Survey of the Railway Engine in New Zealand from 1863 to 1964*, rev. & enl. edn, A.H. & A.W. Reed, Wellington, 1965

Pierre, Bill, *The North Island Main Trunk: An Illustrated History*, A.H. & A.W. Reed, Wellington, 1981

Pierre, W.A., *Canterbury Provincial Railways*, New Zealand Railway & Locomotive Society, Wellington, 1964

Sinclair, Roy, *Journeying with Railways in New Zealand*, Random House, Auckland, 1997

Thompson, Hamish, *Paste Up: A Century of New Zealand Poster Art*, Godwit, Auckland, 2003

Troup, Gordon, *Footplate: The Victorian Engineman's New Zealand*, Reed, Wellington, 1978

Troup, Gordon (ed.), *Steel Roads of New Zealand: An Illustrated Survey*, A.H. & A.W. Reed, Wellington, 1973

Watson, James, *Links: A History of Transport and New Zealand Society*, GP Publications / Ministry of Transport, Wellington, 1996

## Trainland

White, Yuilleen, *Life Along the Steel Road: A Story of the Midland Railway*, Y. White, Renwick, 1998

Wright, Matthew, *Rails Across New Zealand: A History of Rail Travel*, Whitcoulls, Auckland, 2003

Yonge, John, *New Zealand Railway and Tramway Atlas*, 4th edn, Quail Map Co., Exeter, UK / Southern Press, Porirua, 1993

### *Theses and Research Essays*

Horner, John, 'Railway Art in New Zealand', Master of Fine Arts dissertation, Whitecliffe College of Arts and Design, Auckland, 2003

Verry, Angela M., '"I'm Going to See New Zealand Too!": The New Zealand Railways Publicity Branch and Family Holidays during the Interwar Period', BA (Hons) research essay (History), University of Otago, 2004

Waterson, Duncan, 'Railways and Politics, 1908–1928: A Study in the Politics of Development in a Twentieth Century Social Democracy', MA thesis (History), University of Auckland, 1959

# Index

*Numbers in bold indicate an illustration or table*

Accidents 34, 47, 75, 84, 132, 144, 159, 203. *See also* Tangiwai disaster
Advertising and publicity 14, 15, 48–9, 86, 98, 99, 101–2, **103**, 104, 105, 108–9, **111**, **112**, 113–17, **114**, **115**, **117**, **118**, **121**, 122, **123**, **125**, **127**, **128**, **129**, **132**, **133**, 168, **168**, **186**
Agricultural & Pastoral (A&P) Shows **68**, 68–9, 87, 108
Aickens **216**
Air transport 17, 107, 126, 134–5, 222
Alcohol 52, 92, 116, 133, 139, 156–60, 162, 167, 180, 184, 187
Amalgamated Society of Railway Servants 48
Angus, Rita 209, **210–11**
Anthony, Frank 81
Art 26–7, **34**, **36**, **96–7**, **191**, **197**, 200, 206–12, **208**, **210–11**, **213**
Arthur's Pass 43, 83, 87, 106, 110–11, 161–2
Ashburton 157, 172, 173, 183, 216, 219
Auckland 21, **21**, 23, 28, 30, 34–5, 36, 52, 70, 74, 84, 89, 102, 106, 126–7, 164, **169**, 174, 183, 190, 195, 197, 198, 212–14, **214**, 215, 219, 221
Australian railways 20, 25, **92–3**, 101, 108, 168

Balclutha 33, 88, 190
Ballance, John 45
Baloghy, George 212
Barraud, Charles **34**, 208
Bay of Islands 30, 98, **99**, 113, 198
Bethell, Ursula 33, 204
Blenheim 32, 91
Blue Streak 133, 184, **186**
Bluff 28, 30, 83, 91, 106, 159
Bookstalls, at stations **153**, 154–6, **155**, 173, 183, 199

Branch lines 13, 32, 38, 60, 65, 69, 120, 126, 142, 148, 194, 197, 205, 216
 closure of 26, 120, 190, 216–17
Brickell, Barry 212
British railways 10, 12, 17, 20, 28, 30, 34, 38, 62, 70, 101, 108, 130, 140, 144, 146, 184, 192, 199, 202, 206–7
Britomart transport centre 212, **214**
Brodgens' navvies 30, 32, 34
Bush tramways 41, **84–5**

Canadian railways 20, 108, 130, 184
Cape, Peter 171, 205
Carriages 39, 47, 99, 102, 112, 133, **136–7**, 138, 139–48, **141**, 143, 161, 165, 197. *See also* Classes; Dining cars; Ladies' cars; Sleeping cars; Smoking cars
Cass 55, 209, **210–11**
Christchurch 26, 32–3, 36, 57, 65, 67, 74, 84, 87, 90, 98, 106, 110, 116, **147**, 160, 161, 172, 174, 183, 216, 219
Christie, Agatha 192, 202
Cinema 72, 192, 202–3, 222
Circuses 68, 88, **88**
Classes, on passenger trains 76, 78, 89, 112, 138, 139–41, **141**, 144–6, 148, 201
Clinton 33, 173, 174, 183, 190
Coal 62, 63, 92, 94, 120, 129, 132, 144, 149, 184, 197, 218, 224
Coates, Gordon 15, 54, 60, 62, **63**, 94–5, 99, 100, 102, 109, 113, 116, 204
Commercial travellers 72
Construction of railways 13, 22, 25, 30–3, **31**, 35, 40–6, 48–52, **51**, **52**, 56, 98, 102, 123, 160
Conyers, William 34, 38
Cook Strait ferries 126, 156
Cowan, James 118

## Trainland

Crime  139, 156, 157, 161, 162, 192, 197, 199, 202, 206–7
Crockery  15, 171, 179, **181**, 181–3, **182**, 187
Cross Creek  55

Davies, Sonja  202, 217
Davis, Stanley  105, 116
Daylight Limited express  **112**, 112–13
Dean, Minnie  202, 206–7, **207**
Depression: (1880s) 40–1, 42, 84, 122
  (1930s) 15, 100, 107, 112, 120–2, 127, 196
Derrett, Rod  171, 181, 205
Dibble, Paul  212
Dining cars  93, 133, 146, 148–52, **150–1**, 169, 172, 184–7, **185**
Dining rooms  173, **174**, 174–5, 183, 198. *See also* Refreshment rooms
Dogs  63, **66**, 69, 166, 182
Donne, T.E.  104
Dunedin  **8–9**, 10, 32–3, 67, 73, 74, 86, 90, 109, 156, 157, 164, 175, **191**, 196, 216, **218**, 221, **225**

Education Department  78, 199
Electrification  16, 95, 124, **139**
Elizabeth II, Queen  107, **107**, 200
Enthusiasts, railway  17, 190, 191, 212, 218–21, 223–4
Excursion trains  15, 72, 82–7, **84–5**, **87**, 93, **94**, 102, 105, 109, 110–11, 127, 161–2

Fairburn, Rex  172
Farmers' Union  66, 108
Farming  13, 25, 32, 38, 61, 62, 65–9, **66**, 79–81, 109, 120, 127
Fay-Raven Commission (1924–5)  102
Feilding  154, 184
Ferrymead  26, 219
First World War  61, **92–3**, 92–4, **95**, 167, 172, 174
Food and drink  148–9, 169–73, 177, 178–9, **179**, 184, 187. *See also* Alcohol; Dining cars; Dining rooms; Refreshment rooms

Forestry  13, 25, 38, 40, 41, 43, 53, 54, 56, 60–1, 62, 63–5, 99
Fox, William  28, 29, 208–9, **208–9**
Foxton  40, 41, 42
Frame, Janet  67, 73, 142, 171, 190, 192–6, 202
Frankton Junction  54–5, 56, 99, 102, 112, **152–3**, 156, 159, 164, 166–8, **167**, 172, 174, 175, 179, 180, 182, 183
Freight tonnages  17, 56, 99, 100, 120, 125, 129, 190, 221

Gauges (track)  26, 28, 29, 32, 39
Gee, Maurice  197, 202
Gillespie, O.N.  192, 202, 203
Gisborne  55, 57, 123, 165
Glenbrook Vintage Railway  219, **223**
Godber, A.P.  211
*Goodbye Pork Pie*  202–3
'Goods with car'  67, 197
Gore  33, 34, **95**
Government Railways Board (1931–6)  122, 123
Grace, Patricia  197–8
Graffiti  139, 168–9, **169**
Grainger, J.M.  69, 160, 166
Greymouth  36, 57, 98, 107, 111, 124

Hall-Jones, William  47, 87
Hamilton  22, 70, 77, 184. *See also* Frankton Junction
Hanlon, Alfred  157, 207
Hastings  35, 125, 161
Helensville  24, **24–5**, 35, 41, 69, 75, 87, 172–3, 180, **180**, 183
Henderson, Helen  206
Henderson, Louise  **36**, 209
Hercock, Rex  88
Holiday traffic  73, 83, 84, 86, 104, 105, 113, 122, 126, 130, 135, 173, 200
Holmes, Robert  48
Horner, John  212, **213**
Horseracing  86–7, **89**, 89–90, 91, 93, 159, 180

# Index

Hotels **72**, 163, **164**, 177, 216
Housing **51**, 52, 54–5, **54–5**, 99, 163
Hunterville 41
Hursthouse, Charles 45
Hutt Valley 35, 36–7, 82, 90, 124, 125, 132, 161, 208, 212, 219, **219**
Hyde, Robin 82, 118, 138, 142, 144, 152, 156, 164, 187, 196, 204

Inangahua 43, **46**, 123, 217
Inchbonnie **195**
Indian railways 20, 28, 77, 108
Influenza pandemic (1918) 94
Invercargill 27, 30, 32–3, 34, 36, 70, 74, 83, 106

Kaitoke 35, 173, 198
Keller, Peter 50, 52, **52**
King Country 40, 45–6, 48–53, **50–1**, 56, 77, **84–5**, 159, 198
Kingston **12**, 32, 127, 133
Kingston Flyer 133, 203, 219
Kiwi Records 205

Labour government (1935–49) 13, 16, 54, 57, 74, 100, 123–4, 125, 129, 183
Ladies' cars 138, 146–7, 148, 152
Lawlor, Pat 117, 118, 119, 202
Lawson, Will 203–4
Le Cren, John 211
Lee, John A. 164–5
Liberal government (1891–1912) 13, 46–8, 50, 66, 72, 73–4, 78, 102
Lineham, Barry 178, 205
Literature 117, 119, 154, 191–205, **199**, 221
    'indecent' 154–6
    *See also* Poetry
Livestock 38, 63, 65, **66**, 68, 99, 122, 196, 202
Locomotives: diesel **132**, 133, **134**, **214**, 218
    electric 124, **124**, 129, **139**, 218
    *Lady Barkly* 27
    *Passchendaele* **109**
    *Pilgrim* 26, **26–7**
    steam 10–11, **11**, 17, 26, **26–7**, 27, 33, 35, 36–7, 39, **39**, 42, **63**, **87**, **95**, **96–7**, 99, 102, 104, **109**, 112, **112**, 133, **143**, **145**, **197**, 203, 207, **218**, 218–19, **219**, **223**, 224, **225**
Lovell-Smith, Rata 209
Lunatic asylums 84, 86, 161
Lyttelton 21, 25, 26, 41, 106, 159

Mackersey, Ian 202
Mackley, Garnet 123
McCahon, Colin 211
McQueen, Euan 216
McVilly, R.W. 62
Mail 62, 67, 70–1, 72, 165, 166. *See also* Railway Travelling Post Offices
Maniapoto, Rewi **44**, 45
Mansfield, Katherine 198
Maori 13, 25, 29–30, 32, 35, 40, 50, 52, 53, 57, 72, 75–7, **75**, **76**, 118, 159, 168, 200, 211, 212, 217
Marsh, Ngaio 202
Marton 45, 52, 55, 112, 164, 172, 174, **174**, 175, 179, 182
Maungaturoto 54, 183
Mercer 35, 75, 76, 172, 177, 180, 183
Midland line 43, 55, 57, 98, 110–11, 124, **134**, 135, 161
Midland Railway Company 43, 98
Mines and mining 13, 15, 25, 26, 57, 61, 63, 160
Mixed trains 67, 126, 142, 148, 165, 196, 202, 222
Model railways 192, 211, 224
Moorhouse, William 26
Morrieson, Ronald Hugh 196–7, 202
Morrinsville 77, 102
Morrison, Robin 212
Motor transport 15, 16–17, 24, **56**, 69, 74, 77, 94–5, 101–2, 105, 106, 108, 115, 120, 123, 125–6, 132, 200, 221, 222
Mount Maunganui 25, 65
Moutohora 55, 165
Mulgan, John 196

247

# Trainland

Museums 219, **219**, 224
Music 55, 83, 110, 152, 171, 192, 200, 205–6

Napier 30, 36, 40, 41, 56, 57, 106, 107, 113, 125, 149
Nathan, L.D. 76, 77
National Park **16**, 113, 187, 203
Native Land Court 72, 75, 76
Nelson 21, 23, 26, 36, 43, 84, 120, 202, 217
New Plymouth 21, 35, 36, 41, 42, 52, 70, 83, 106, 107, 124, 149
New Zealand Centennial Exhibition (1939–40) 129, **129**, 130–2
New Zealand International Exhibition (1906–7) 87, 109
New Zealand and South Seas Exhibition (1925–6) 109, 174–5
New Zealand Rail Ltd 135
New Zealand Railway and Locomotive Society 221
*New Zealand Railway Observer* 221
New Zealand Railways Corporation 126, 135, 215
*New Zealand Railways Magazine* 15, 113, 115–19, **116**, **118**, 123, **123**, 142, 156, 192, 193, 196, 202, 203–4, **204**
Newspapers 22, 72, 124, 154
Ngaio **54**, 55
Ngaruawahia 75, 77
Nicholson, Anne Marie 200–1
Night Limited express 60, 112–13, 132, 143–4, 195, 197, 199, 222
North Island main trunk line 10, 13, 41, 42, **44–5**, 48, **48–9**, 54, 56, **57**, 60, 70, 71, 98, 112–13, 118, 132, 133, 135, 140, 143–4, 145, 146, 149, 179, 196, 202, 214
    construction of 45–6, 48–53
    opening of 52–3, 56
Northerner 135, 148, 184
Nostalgia 10, 17, 139, 190–1, 216–19, 223–4

Oamaru 30, 67, 83, 86, 125, 172, 174–5, **175**, 183, 216

Ohakune 45, 50, 53, 55, 112, 173, **173**, 179, 180, 181, **182**, 183, 196
Oliver, Richard 39
Onehunga 21, 35, 52
Ontrack 215
Opawa **139**, 168
Opening ceremonies **23**, 26, 27, **33**, 33–5, 42, **44–5**, 45, **46**, 53, 83, 165, 209
Ormondville **55**, 87, 167, **220**
Otaki **75**
Otira 43, 110–11, 174, 177, 183, 196
Overlander 10, **16**, 17, 135, 187, 214
Oxford 66, 67, 69

Paekakariki 124, 149, **170–1**, 173, 180, 219
Paeroa 159, 183
Palmerston North 22, 41, 42, 45, 56, 81, 90, 112, 149, 164, 172, **176**, 178, 205
Parliament 20–2, 29, 38, 52, 65–6, 73, 122
Parliament Special (1908) 52–3, **53**, **73**
Passenger traffic 15, 16, 17, 56, 61, **61**, 73, 93–4, **94**, 99, 100–1, **101**, 109, 110, 111, 113, 120, 122, 125–6, 129, 130–2, 134–5, 190, 212–14, **215**
Pearson, Bill 196
Photography 211, 212
Picnic trains 15, 82, 83, 84, 86–7, **87**, 93, 102, 109
Picton 30, 32, 57, 123
Pillows 144, 182, 187
Poetry 33, 172, 192, 203–5
Police 34, 160, 162, 207
Port Chalmers 25, 32, 36, 65, 157
Private railways 42–3, 56, 98, 102, 126, 135, 215
Provincial railways 26–8, 35
    Canterbury 26, 32–3, 36
    Southland 27–8, 70
Public Works Department (PWD) 46, 50–3, 63, 123, 160

Rail Heritage Trust of NZ 221
Railcars 16, 95, 124, **124**, 126, 129, 133, 142, 148, 161, 184, **186**

# Index

Railway Broadcasting Studio **128**, 129
Railway Commissioners (1889–94) 46–7, 48
Railway Travelling Post Office (RTPO) 70–1, **70–1**, 145
Railway workers 12, **12**, 36–7, **37**, 47, 48, 54–5, 70–1, 72–3, 94, **95**, 99, 116, 120, 123–4, 130, 132, 149, 160, 179–80, 182, 193, 215, 224
    female 117–18, 130, 152, 179–80, **180**, **185**
    *See also* Housing
Railway workshops 12, 22, 36–7, **37**, 84, 92, 99, 102, 124, 130
    Addington **36**, 36–7, 65, 140, 160
    East Town 36
    Hillside 36, 37
    Lower Hutt 37, 102, 124
    Newmarket 36
    Otahuhu 37, 102, 107, 204
    Petone 36, 92, 211
Railways Department 15, 38, 40, 54–5, 60, 62, 73, 77, 82, 84, 90, 93, 95, 99, 102, 104, 108, 111, 113, 115, 120, 123, 125–6, 132, 149, 154–7, 159, 160, 162, 169, 172–3, 174, 177, 181, 184, 193, 199, 215
    Advertising Branch 105, 168
    Architectural Branch 54
    Commercial Branch 108
    Publicity Branch 15, 95, 113, 116, 122
    Railways Studios 105, 108, 113–16, 122
    Refreshment Branch 106, 172–3, 177, 182
    *See also* Railway workers; Railway workshops; Railways Road Services; Refreshment rooms
Railways Road Services 15, 70, 95, 102, **125**, 125–6
Rakaia 47, **47**, 65, 73, 84
Ranfurly Shield 90, **91**, 127
Ratana 77
Raurimu Spiral 48, **48–9**, 50, 52, 122, 196, 205
Reform government (1912–28) 13, 57, 60, 65, 66, 100
Refreshment rooms 15, **18–19**, 93, 110, 132, 152, 157, 167, 169–84, **170–1**, **173**, **176**, 194–5, 198, 205. *See also* Crockery; Dining rooms; Food and drink

Refrigerated meat industry 36, **64–5**, 65
Religion 72, 83, 84, 110, 154, 168
Richardson, Edward 84
Rimutaka Incline **34**, 35, 124, 199, 208
Rochfort, John 45
Ronayne, Thomas 82, 86, 146
Rotheram, T.F. 36
Rotorua 56, 76, 77, 94, 102–4, 106, 108, 113, **119**, 125, 149
Rous-Marten, Charles 27–8
Royal commissions on railways:
    (1880) 40, 42
    (1930) 122
    (1952) 175, 182, 216
Royal trains 94, **96–7**, 106–7, **107**, 165, 209

Safety 11–12, 39, 47, **47**, 106, 115, 144
Sargeson, Frank 77, 198
Scenic Daylight **132**, 133
School pupils 72, 78–82, **79**, **80**, 100, 173
Scott, R.J. 36
Second World War 16, 118, 129–32, 173, 175, 182–3, 196, 197–8
Seddon, Richard 13, 46, **46**, 78
Semple, Bob 123, 160
Sewell, Henry 20–1, 26, 60
Sex, on trains 160–1, 197
Shipping 11, 20–1, **21**, 24–5, 38, 40, 41, 42, 60, 101, 132, 144, 145, 149, 218–19, 222
Silver Fern 133, 184
Silver Star 133, **133**, 135, **158**, 184
Silver Stream Railway **197**, **217**, 219, **219**
Sleeping cars 112, 133, 143–4, **144**, 148, 195, 197
*Smash Palace* 202–3
Smoke nuisance 70, 141, 142, **143**, 144, 149, 218, **218**
Smoking cars 72, 91, 138, 147–8, 154
'Snow Specials' 87, 110–11, 160, 161–2
Somerset, H.C.D. 60, 66, 67
South Island main trunk line 33, 34, 38, 98, 118, 135, 146

## Trainland

Southerner 135, 184, **185**
Sports teams 72, 75, 89, 90–2, 156–9, **158**
Springfield 55, 184
Stagecoaches 24, 38, 101, 140
Stations **8–9**, 15, **18–19**, **23**, 29, 39, 47, **93**, 99, 102, **119**, 138, **139**, **162–3**, 162–9, **167**, **169**, **175**, 191, **210–11**, 212, **214**, 216, 221, 224
Stephenson, George & Robert 20, 34
Sterling, H.H. 81, 120, 122
Stewart, G.G. 50, 115, 117, 118–19, 202
Stewart, W.W. **26–7**, **96–7**, 209–11
Stott, Bob 165–6
Stout, Robert **44**, 45
Stratford 55, **58–9**, 69
Suburban traffic 16, 73–4, **74**, 95, 100, 124, 129, 142, 148, 161, **188–9**, 190, 212–16, **214**, 215, 221
Sullivan, Dan 123
Summit 55, 78
Sunday trains 83, **87**, 109, 110
Sydney, Grahame 212

Tablet system 47, **47**, 199
Taieri Gorge Railway 135, 221
Taihape **18–19**, 52, 55, 112, 162, 164, 174, 183, 184
Tangiwai disaster 107, 144–5, **146**, 200–1, 202
Taumarunui 40, 46, 48, 50, 53, **53**, 55, 112, 159, 164, 180, 183, 200, 205
'Taumarunui (on the Main Trunk Line)' 171, 205
Tauranga 57, 98, 113, 194
Tawhiao, King 40, 45, 75
Te Aroha 102
Te Awamutu 40
Te Kooti 25, 29, 45, 53, 75, 212
Te Kuiti 46, 55, 70
Teenage misbehaviour 111, 161–2, 167, 168–9
Telegraph 11, 99
Thames 37, 56, 90
Theatrical companies 72
Thomas the Tank Engine 192, 199, 222, **223**
Timaru 33, 34, 84, 90, 102, **107**, 113, 216, 219
Timber industry *see* Forestry

Toilets 139, 140, 141, 144, 161, 167, 168
Toll New Zealand 10, 37, 126, 187, 215, 221
Tourism 15–16, 95, 98–9, 102–5, 108–9, 110–11, 112, 113–115, 117, 122, 125, 126–9, 133–5, 177
Trams 24, 74, 105, 146
Transport licensing 122, 123
TranzAlpine 111, **134**, 135, 214
TranzCoastal 135
Tranz Metro **188–9**, 214
Tranz Rail 215
Troop trains **58–9**, 92, **130–1**, 132, 159, 161, 162, **166**, 179, 180, 182, 196, 197
Troup, George 10, 54, 55, 175, 221
Tunnels 25, 26, 29, 39, 48, 142, **143**, 160, 191, 197, 224
    Lyttelton 26, 159
    Otira 43, 110, 196
    Poro-o-tarao 46, 202
Turner, J.M.W. 206–7, 209
Tuwhare, Hone 172, 204–5

Uniforms 12, **12**, 149, **180**, **185**, **186**
Union Steam Ship Company 98, 104
United States railways 12, 20, 25, 28, 77, 101, 184, 192, **207**

Vandalism 116–17, 139, 156–7, **158**, 161–2, **168**, 168–9, **169**
Veolia Transport 215
Viaducts 48, 52, 116, 191, 224
Vice-regal cars 106, 107
Vogel, Sir Julius 20, 28–30, **29**, 32, 209
Volunteer Corps 35, 62, 72

Wahanui Huatare **44**, 45
Waihi 56, 159
Waiouru 162, 201
Waipukurau 165–6, 172, 183
Wanganui 23, 36, 42, 45, 106, 125, 154, 165, 177
Ward, Sir Joseph 53, **53**, 77, 104, 157
Wellington 21, 23, 30, 35, 42, 52–3, 54–5, 56, 70,

74, 82, 90, **92–3**, 102, 106, 107, 124, 126, 149, **162–3**, 164, 167, 174, 183, 190, 197, 203
Wellington and Manawatu Railway Company (WMR) 42, **43**, 53, 56, 70, 140, 148–9, 156, 203
Westport 36, **46**, 57, 123, 159
Whangarei 40, 57, 98
White, Robin 212
Woodville **164**, 172, 174, 182, 198
Woollaston, Toss 69
Workshops *see* Railway workshops